Contact

Contact

The Interaction of Closely Related Linguistic Varieties and the History of English

Robert McColl Millar

EDINBURGH
University Press

Edinburgh University Press is one of the leading university presses in the UK. We publish academic books and journals in our selected subject areas across the humanities and social sciences, combining cutting-edge scholarship with high editorial and production values to produce academic works of lasting importance. For more information visit our website: www.edinburghuniversitypress.com

© Robert McColl Millar, 2016

Edinburgh University Press Ltd
The Tun – Holyrood Road
12(2f) Jackson's Entry
Edinburgh EH8 8PJ

Typeset in 10.5/12 Janson by
Servis Filmsetting Ltd, Stockport, Cheshire

A CIP record for this book is available from the British Library

ISBN 978 1 4744 0908 7 (hardback)
ISBN 978 1 4744 0909 4 (webready PDF)
ISBN 978 1 4744 0910 0 (epub)

The right of Robert McColl Millar to be identified as the author of this work has been asserted in accordance with the Copyright, Designs and Patents Act 1988, and the Copyright and Related Rights Regulations 2003 (SI No. 2498).

Contents

Acknowledgements	vi
Glossary	vii
1 Some introductory thoughts	1
2 New dialect formation and near-dialect contact	16
3 New dialect formation and time depth	57
4 Linguistic contact and near-relative relationships	106
5 English in the 'transition period': the sources of contact-induced change	124
6 Conclusions	171
Notes	178
References	190
Index	206

Acknowledgements

The topics discussed in this book have concerned me since my late teens; over the last thirty years it has been my privilege discussing them in a range of fora, formal and informal, around the world. In recent years, many of these ideas have become focused when teaching advanced undergraduate and postgraduate courses; the input from my students has been invaluable.

Towards the end of the writing of *Contact*, I received very useful advice from Edgar Schneider and Anke de Looper which made my life a little easier. My dear colleagues here at Aberdeen worked a little bit more in the Spring of 2014 so that I could get relief from teaching. I am grateful to both groups and hope to return the favour one day.

Finally, a mention for my family. Sandra and Mairi are a source of endless fascination and rest for me. They both contribute immeasurably to my work and get very little in recompense. This book is dedicated to them.

Glossary

analytic Languages generally mark function through the position of phrases within a clause. Thus speakers of English primarily know which phrase in the clause represents the subject, direct object and so on, because of that phrase's position in the clause. The 'opposite' of an analytic language is a **synthetic** one. It should be noted that these are not absolute states: there is a continuum between an absolutely analytic language and an absolutely synthetic one. Tok Pisin is more analytic than is English, for instance.

case, grammatical A case system expresses functional relationships within the clause, normally marked through the use of inflectional morphology. Languages with a 'rich' case system often have a more flexible element order system than do those which have little or no case marking. Marking case through morphology is a powerful representation of **synthetic** tendencies.

convergence While most linguistic change is divergent, convergence, the coming together over time of previously discrete language varieties, is not uncommon. Historically, Modern Dutch may be descended not from one ancestor, but rather three, which have coalesced.

creole Most scholars believe that creoles are the descendants of **pidgins**. Creoles share many of their features with their pidgin ancestors, but are the native languages of some speakers. Their formation represents a radical breach from the **lexifier language**: essentially, creoles are independent languages, capable of the same nuances of expression as any 'natural' language. Because many creoles are spoken in colonial or post-colonial environments, a *post-creole continuum* often develops. In these circumstances, different forms of language develop; some of these are closer to the original creole, some to the lexifier language. It should be noted that stages along the continuum do not represent absolute states: native speakers regularly move along it, depending on social context.

creoloid It has been suggested that some language varieties – creoloids – have been formed by processes similar to, but not the same as, those which produce **creoles**. With creoles, it is believed that a radical breach with the lexifier language has taken place; this produces a separate language. No such breach is present with creoloids, which generally remain mutually intelligible with varieties of the lexifier languages for a considerable period after the change in state. They nevertheless exhibit many of the simplifying tendencies exhibited by creoles. Afrikaans is, perhaps, the most widely spoken creoloid.

divergence This happens when two or more language varieties become increasingly discrete from each other over time. Divergence is probably the mainstream form of language change. Thus Modern English and Modern High German share a common ancestor; for a while, the two varieties were dialects of the same language. Now little or no mutual comprehension is possible.

drift As proposed by Sapir, drift is the tendency by which a language (or, by extension, languages) develops across its linguistic system in essentially the same way, in essentially the same direction.

gender, grammatical Many languages employ a system something like a very large form of noun class, termed grammatical gender. In some languages grammatical gender appears to have some relationship with natural sex. This relationship is rarely straightforward; many other gender-bearing languages exhibit no such connection. Gender relationships can be realised through functional morphology and the use of definers.

lexifier language This is the prestigious standardised language of a (normally colonial or post-colonial) territory where a **pidgin** or **creole** (or both) is used. Its lexis is normally the central source of vocabulary for an incipient pidgin; it is also highly influential on the development of later creoles.

near-relative variety Most language varieties are related genetically (that is, by descent) to other language varieties. Naturally, most related varieties which are considered part of the same language – *dialects* – closely resemble each other. This means that mutual intelligibility is generally straightforward. Even when greater linguistic distance is involved, mutual comprehension is still possible, albeit with a little effort. On the other hand, languages are normally portrayed as being discrete entities, even in connection with their closer relatives. Of course, this is often the case: native speakers of Norwegian cannot understand German without learning that language, even though the two languages share many lexical, phonological and structural features. But occasionally, language varieties are considered discrete entities but nevertheless are sufficiently closely related to each other that some mutual recognition of similarity and at least some intelligibility are possible. What are the results of near-relative linguistic contact? How do these compare with other types of contact?

pidgin A pidgin is a radically simplified-use language created in situations where speakers of at least three languages have no language in common. Pidgins do not have native speakers; their nativised descendants are, according to most analyses, **creoles**.

synthetic Languages express function through form, such as through their use of **grammatical case**. Thus, in Polish, while there are mainstream element order patterns, most functional information is carried by inflections. It should be noted that there is a continuum between an absolutely **analytic** language and an absolutely synthetic one. Finnish is more synthetic than is Polish, for instance.

1 Some introductory thoughts

1.1 Introduction

Linguistic contact is universal. Working at a university with a diverse student and academic population means that I am in regular contact with speakers of other languages. The languages I have heard in the last two days have included Polish, Bulgarian, Romanian, Spanish, Arabic, Chinese and German, as well as more local language varieties. Most of the time, these everyday contacts have had no effect on my own linguistic behaviour beyond making me move closer to the Scottish Standard English end of my personal linguistic continuum than would be the case when interacting with native Scots or English speakers. But sometimes contact of this type has affected my linguistic behaviour considerably. More than twenty years ago, I lived in rural Norway. After I had learned the local language sufficiently, I found that I peppered my English with Norwegian words and phrases concerned with governmental and administrative structures, along with other cultural references. English equivalents existed; these were not exact enough, however, particularly in relation to their rules of behaviour, connection and outcome. There is no conceptual connection in any English-speaking country, for instance, which would produce the idea of a 'Church and Education Ministry'. Interestingly, I did this 'code switching' (if it can actually be termed such) even when speaking to other native English speakers (who, if they were long-term residents in Norway, did the same). I also noticed that I was beginning to pronounce some English words as if they were Norwegian, so that a word like *heart*, which I would naturally pronounce /hart/, began to have a final retroflex consonant.

Contacts of this type are not, of course, particularly profound. It is possible to learn and use a few words and phrases of another language without that language affecting the way you speak your native language naturally. That does not mean, however, that all language contacts are of such comparative unimportance. Michif, spoken on the western prairie borderlands between the United States and Canada, appears to be a genuine mixture of Cree, the local language, and French, the language of eighteenth- and nineteenth-century trappers. Simplifying somewhat, Michif has a Cree verb structure but is essentially French in its noun phrase structure (Thomason and Kaufman 1988: in particular 228–33). But since Cree marks noun grammatical gender on the verb, all nouns are associated with both a French and a Cree grammatical gender (both languages possess two genders, but assignment of a noun to a specific gender is based upon strikingly different precepts in each language in comparison with the other). A structure of this type demands profound levels of contact and probably a conscious desire to construct a new variety on the part of bilinguals, possibly as a form of identity construction for people who were neither wholly indigenous nor wholly European. While most contacts do not present such a complete transformation, Michif is not alone: other varieties with equally penetrating external influences upon their development, such as Copper Island Aleut, spoken on an island in Russia's Far East, exist (Thomason 1997a).

Most language contact phenomena fall between these two extremes. If we consider, for instance, the German influences upon Polish, it is apparent that a considerable amount of both prestigious and everyday lexis has been borrowed from the former into the latter. The structural influence of German upon Polish is practically non-existent, however (except in the Slavonic dialects of Silesia, perhaps, where greater and more intense forms of contact have been the norm: Przeździak 2015). Most contact, as we will see, fits into this intermediate 'slot'. Contact between languages can act, therefore, as a catalyst for powerful and deep-rooted change. But even when the results are not as penetrating as in noteworthy cases of this type, the input of language contact into language change is regularly apparent in language varieties spoken around the world. This chapter will act as a brief introduction to linguistic contact. It will also introduce the consideration of contact between closely related varieties and whether these related varieties are generally considered separate languages or dialects of the same language. These themes will be continued and deepened in later chapters of this book.

1.2 Theoretical models for the mechanics of linguistic contact

The study of the effects of language contact has a long and often distinguished history. It has acted as a corollary to the Neogrammarian (and later structuralist and formal) insistence on system-internal, rule-governed change as the primary means by which the historical evo-

SOME INTRODUCTORY THOUGHTS

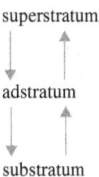

Fig. 1.1 A hierarchical model of linguistic contact.

lution of linguistic systems takes place. Instead, a dynamic model associated with external sources acting as a catalyst for change can be entertained. Although occasionally veering close to conspiracy theory in the hands of some of its less distinguished protagonists, contact linguistics has developed a set of theoretical rules (or, at the very least, expression of tendencies) in an attempt to analyse how contact takes place, the extent to which one language variety (or, indeed, more) has affected another and in what way. These follow a range of theoretical and methodological models.

One of the earliest and most fruitful of these analyses considers a three-part means of looking at language contact according to differentiated, largely vertical, power relationships. It can be illustrated as shown in Figure 1.1.

A *superstratal* relationship is one where a culturally, politically and economically dominant elite's language affects the language of a less powerful group. Thus Basque was flooded in Roman times with Latin loanwords (Trask 1997: 10–11), but the Basque lexical input into the modern Romance dialects of Iberia (such as Castilian Spanish) is very limited indeed, except where modern bilingualism was, or is, common. This represents a classic situation where unequal power relationships affect the nature of language contact phenomena. Roman (and, later, Castilian) power was too great for direct influence to spread from Basque and act upon the language(s) of the rulers. On the other hand, *substratal*-influenced changes do occur. Using the same contact scenario, it is possible to argue that the lack of /f/ in native Castilian words, with Latin /f/ > /h/ (the latter still found in some archaic dialects of Spanish, including that spoken by Sephardic Jews in, for instance, Turkey) > nothing, is due to Basque influence, since the last language has no historical /f/ phoneme. Thus pairs like *Hernan(do)* versus *Fernando* represent native and borrowed forms of the same name. The Basque connection is strengthened by the fact the many of the Gascon dialects of south-west France, where historically Basque (or its ancestor, Aquitanian) was spoken, also exhibit this change; the change's presence in some Alpine Romance varieties – where Basque influence is very unlikely – must be recognised, however (see Trask 1997: 427 for an attempted refutation of the substratal argument). The language of the submerged group – often the language of the majority – does not influence lexical use much (since that is likely to be enforced more by the centre). But the morphosyntax and phonology of the target Latin (in this case the ancestor of Spanish) would have been affected by the structures and constraints of the native language.

By the same token, it is intellectually plausible to make the claim that some of the peculiarities (in comparison with other European languages) of the modern Celtic languages, such as initial consonant mutation as a marker of morphosyntactic relationship and VSO element order, are due to contact with Afro-Asiatic (specifically Semitic) languages (Vennemann 2003). It is impossible to prove this, however. Documentary evidence as it happened for ancient substratal contact of this type is normally non-existent, in fact, given that the attention of commentators (who in pre-modern times were probably associated with the political, economic and social elite) tends to be on rather more prestigious matters. This means that they are particularly difficult to prove, even when we suspect that they might quite regularly be present. Superstratal influence is much more likely to be convincingly documented.

Superstratal influence can be found throughout the world, naturally. We need only consider the influence Spanish has had on the indigenous languages of Central and South America (for a discussion of the ramifications of these contacts, see the papers in Mufwene 2014) or the influence Arabic (particularly Qur'anic Arabic) has had on the various languages of the Muslim world to appreciate this. An apposite example of this type of influence can be found in the contact between Norman French and English in the centuries after the Norman Conquest of England in 1066–7. We will consider this contact further in Chapter 5.

Between these two extremes lie *adstratal* contacts, the influence felt between languages whose speakers possess essentially the same level of social, cultural and political power and prestige. Almost inevitably, rather fewer examples of this change present themselves than was the case with substratal or superstratal influence, largely because instances of two near-equal groupings living side by side with each other in peaceful coexistence for a sufficient period that long-term contact can take place are less than common historically. One population group has always tended to have more power of various sorts than has the other. Nevertheless, examples of this type do present themselves. In post-Roman Gaul, for instance, the relationship between the militarily dominant Franks and the Romano-Celtic population whom they ruled was not one of a genuinely superstratal versus substratal type. Instead, the relationships between the two groupings are best described as adstratal. While the military power of the Franks was considerable, their admiration for Roman tradition and lifestyle was perpetually present; they were often bilingual. By the same token, the Gallo-Roman elite appear to have been happy to take on aspects of Frankish culture – in particular, names – from an early period. No doubt they were more than aware of the centre towards which power, influence and capital of various sorts was now flowing. The Frankish influences upon the ancestor of modern French are visible, therefore, but they tend to be concentrated in particular semantic fields, such as the technology and practice of warfare and fortification, where the Franks' primary expertise and power base lay. A good example of this is Modern French *maréchal* 'supreme war leader', but originally 'leader of the cavalry', borrowed early on from Frankish. A further largely adstratal relationship – between speakers of Viking Norse and Old English in the north of England – will be discussed in depth in Chapter 5 of this book.

These gradations are, of course, painted with a broad brush. Just because one population is dominant over another in one part of a territory does not mean that the same relationship will exist elsewhere. At least since the high Middle Ages, the relationship of Scots and Gaelic in the Lowlands of Scotland has largely been one of dominance on the part of speakers of the former over speakers of the latter. Only a very limited amount of influence from Gaelic upon Scots – a small number of lexical borrowings, often found in Standard English as well – has persisted. In the north of Scotland, however, a rather different relationship obviously pertained, with Gaelic having a more profound influence on the local varieties. This difference is illustrated not merely by lexical use (although this is considerable) but additionally upon phonology and syntax (Millar 1996, 2009 and 2010a). This possibly explains the local /f/ pronunciation of <wh> (the equivalent to *what* is *fit*) and the use of *that* and *this* in plural contexts especially. Sociolinguistic influences can also be complex: although speakers of Viking Norse and Old English in the north of England lived in a state of fairly equal coexistence during the Viking period, the former may well have had a superstratal influence in governmental and legal contexts, as can be seen in the use from an early period of the ancestor of *law*, a point to which we will return in Chapter 5.

It appears, therefore, that the three-part analysis of contact according to social relationship possesses considerable virtues. But an essential problem with this type of analysis – no matter its many advantages – is that it treats most contacts in a 'one size fits all' way; there is little or no sense of how a range of factors – linguistic, certainly, but also historical, economic and social – interact differently in each instance of contact. For this reason, researchers have developed scales by which we can compare effects from one contact scenario to another. Other scales and comparative indices therefore need to be considered.

In recent years, the most striking schematisation of levels and effects of language contact has been that of Thomason (here reproduced from her 2001 book). Essentially, she envisages four stages of increasing influence from one language (or set of languages) upon another:

1. Casual contact (borrowers need not be fluent in the source language, and/or few bilinguals among borrowing-language speakers): only non-basic vocabulary borrowed.
   Lexicon Only content words – most often nouns, but also verbs, adjectives and adverbs.
   Structure None.

A good example of this level of contact can be found in the influence Yiddish has had upon the mainstream American English (and, by extension, on all other Englishes) of people who have no command of Yiddish (the vast majority). This has almost entirely involved lexical borrowing – such as *shtick* for 'piece, performance' – as well as the imitation (but not internalisation) of such 'Yinglish' structural features as (from the point of view of mainstream English) abnormal element orders, such as *an ulcer he has got*. No matter the extent to which this material has come into the mainstream, only speakers of Yiddish can understand that language at anything more than a basic level (Thomason and Kaufman 1988: 40, 177).

2. Slightly more intense contact (borrowers must be reasonably fluent bilinguals, but they are probably a minority among borrowing-language speakers): function words and slight structural borrowing.
   Lexicon Function words (e.g. conjunctions and adverbial particles like 'then') as well as content words; still non-basic vocabulary.
   Structure Only minor structural borrowings at this stage, with no introduction of features that would alter the types of structures found in the borrowing language. Phonological features such as new phonemes realized by new phones, but in loanwords only; syntactic features such as new functions or functional restrictions for previously existing syntactic structures, or increased usage of previously rare word orders.

SOME INTRODUCTORY THOUGHTS

The influence of French over English in the post-1066 period, discussed again in Chapter 5, could be said to fall into the upper end of this grouping. The effects of French upon English lexis are, of course, considerable; in many semantic fields they are all-pervasive. Yet the influence of French upon English phonology, prosody and structure, while tangible, is nowhere near as great. The influence of English upon the Yiddish of bilinguals also falls into this category. There is much lexical borrowing, in particular in relation to outgroup concepts and traditions, such as, for instance, the vocabulary of government (Thomason and Kaufman 1988: 40). Otherwise, influence is relatively minor and patchy. The same can be heard in the English of native speakers of Gaelic, although on this occasion it is phonology where the distinction with the English of other native speakers of the language is, at least initially, felt, probably because English has long been a standardised language, universal literacy (overwhelmingly in English) has considerable longevity in Scotland and functional bilingualism has been the norm in the Gaelic-speaking community for at least a century, so that there is a relatively rigid pattern into which Gaelic-influenced English is obliged to fit (for a discussion of these matters, see Shuken 1984).

3. More intense contact (more bilinguals, attitudes and other social factors favouring borrowing): basic as well as non-basic vocabulary borrowed; moderate structural borrowing.
    Lexicon More function words borrowed; basic vocabulary – the kinds of words that tend to be present in all languages – may also be borrowed at this stage, including such closed-class items as pronouns and low numerals, as well as nouns, verbs and adjectives; derivational affixes may be borrowed too (e.g. *-able/-ible*, which originally entered English on French loanwords and then spread from there to native English vocabulary).
    Structure More significant structural features are borrowed, though usually without resulting in major typological change in the borrowing language. In phonology, the phonetic realizations of native phonemes, the loss of some native phonemes not present in the source language, addition of new phonemes even in native vocabulary, prosodic features such as stress placement, loss or addition of syllable structure constraints (e.g. a bar against closed syllables), and morphophonemic rules (e.g. devoicing of word-final obstruents). In syntax, there are such features as word order (e.g. SVO beginning to replace SOV or vice versa) and the syntax of coordination and subordination (e.g. increasing or decreasing use of participial constructions instead of constructions

that employ conjunctions). In morphology, borrowed inflectional affixes and categories may be added to native words, especially if they fit well typologically with previously existing patterns.

In a sense, this level represents the crossing of a 'great divide' from what has come before. Here we must consider powerful and pervasive influence, often across a broad range of linguistic levels. Certain morphosyntactic and phonological features in the Indo-Aryan languages (a sub-family of Indo-European), for instance, have been traced by a range of scholars back to a profound substratal influence from the Dravidian languages (Thomason and Kaufman 1988: 15–16, 39–40, 43, 45), now found overwhelmingly in southern India and Sri Lanka, but historically, we conjecture, spoken further north in South Asia. On this occasion, there has been limited lexical influence upon the Indo-Aryan languages, but the profundity of the proposed exchange must nevertheless have been considerable. The influence which the SOV word order of the Cushitic languages of the Horn of Africa appears to have had over the originally VSO order of the Ethiopian Semitic languages also falls within this group (Thomason and Kaufman 1988: 18); the change itself is textually verifiable. Turkish has had such a profound effect upon Armenian morphology in particular as to alter its typological classification (although in other ways, such as phonology, Armenian has remained deeply Armenian) (Millar 2015: 296–7).

4. Intensive contact (very extensive bilingualism among borrowing-language speakers, social factors strongly favouring borrowing): continuing heavy lexical borrowing in all sections of the lexicon, heavy structural borrowing.
   Lexicon Heavy borrowing.
   Structure Anything goes, including structural borrowing that results in major typological changes in the borrowing language. In phonology, loss or addition of entire phonetic and/or phonological categories in native words and of all kinds of morphophonemic rules. In syntax, sweeping changes in such features as word order, relative clauses, negation, coordination, subordination, comparison and quantification. In morphology, typologically disruptive changes such as the replacement of flexional by agglutinative morphology or vice versa, the addition or loss of morphological categories that do not match in source and borrowing languages, and the wholesale loss or addition of agreement patterns.

Contacts of this sort are not as common as those previously discussed. This does not mean that they are unknown, however. Indeed, the cases of Michif and Copper Island Aleut, discussed briefly at the beginning of the chapter, demonstrate just such influence, even if they are unusual in their apparent association of influence of a particular language only with a particular syntactic and semantic role. The influence which Indo-European languages such as Yiddish, Polish, Russian and, later, English have had upon the developing Israeli Hebrew variety also may fall into this category (Weinreich 1953: 41–2; Thomason and Kaufman 1988: 41–2), although again the origin and development of that variety as a 'resurrected' language make analysis somewhat different from other contacts of this type. Asia Minor Greek, exhibiting an overwhelming influence from Turkish (but without a concomitant influence of Greek upon the Turkish of Asia Minor), is probably closer to the norm of this type of contact relationship (Dawkins 1916).

Thomason's grading model is undoubtedly both a major breakthrough and a great convenience for other scholars as a typology and rule of thumb when discussing specific contacts as well as contact in general. It needs to be recognised, however, that the model's concentration on *borrowing* at all levels leaves only a limited space for *interference*, in particular in relation to the formation in a language of features which are not present in either of the source languages. This is likely to be particularly the case where the two languages are close relatives, since issues of deep familial similarities in structure are in conflict with surface, small-scale but prevalent differences. These may involve considerable *simplification* (as we will see in Chapter 5, something of a loaded word) of inherited structure. As this book will demonstrate, interference of this type can be a profound and influential product of contact. The gradation employed by Thomason also does not take into consideration the 'grey area' between dialects and closely related languages in relation to contact, a point to which we will return.

1.3 The sociolinguistics of contact: a first consideration

Other reservations about Thomason's typology are also possible. In their 1988 work on contact, Thomason and Kaufman make the statement that 'The starting point for our theory is this: it is the sociolinguistic history of the speakers, and not the structure of their language, that is the primary determinant of the linguistic outcome of language contact' (Thomason and Kaufman 1988: 35).

To what extent is this the case? It is fair to say, for instance, that on some occasions where we would expect considerable evidence for contact phenomena between two speech communities, no such phenomena exist, primarily on sociolinguistic grounds. Sámi, for instance, has had little or no effect upon the northern Norwegian dialects, primarily because, until comparatively recently, members of the Sámi community were either ignored or actively discriminated against by Norwegian speakers and by the Norwegian state and its representatives (see Jernsletten 1997). On the other hand, while Thomason and Kaufman's statement does sound eminently and obviously feasible, it is necessary to recognise that one variable – nearness of relationship between language varieties – has not been included in their equation. How does closeness of relationship between two (or more) inputs affect the outcome? It is to this issue that this book is dedicated.

That does not mean to say, however, that Thomason and Kaufman's formula is incorrect. Sociolinguistic relationships in one form or another underlie all linguistic relations; they are particularly important for our understanding of language contact. But as this book will contend, close linguistic relationship makes for a much more nuanced (and sometimes unexpected) series of contact-induced outcomes. We also have to include into such an analysis a discussion of occasions of near-relative contact where the two (or more) varieties involved would normally be considered dialects of the same language.[1] We need, therefore to attempt to define what we mean by the terms *language* and *dialect*.

1.4 Language and dialect

This book deals with contact between what would generally be described as dialects of the same language, but we are also concerned with contexts where varieties considered to be different, but closely related, languages go through the same processes. Such a distinction begs a number of questions, however, primarily because it is difficult to define exactly what a *language* is in relation to what a *dialect* is.

In a perfect world it would be possible to define a *dialect* as being one of a range of linguistic varieties which are all mutually intelligible and are therefore dialects of the same *language*. Languages, on the other hand, would be varieties which are not mutually intelligible, even if they are close relatives. Following Heinz Kloss's (1967 and 1978) typology of varieties, the latter would be defined as being languages through *Abstand* 'distance'. Thus it would not matter if nothing had ever been written in Basque. Any contact with spoken forms of that variety, no matter the amount of Latin and Romance lexical borrowings into the language, would immediately alert speakers of the surrounding

Romance dialects to the fact that the linguistic distance between Basque and the other local varieties was absolute. More common is the experience of, say, a German speaker travelling from Germany to Poland on the train and finding herself, after crossing the Polish frontier, in a new language world where the dominant language, although distantly related to her own, is inherently opaque. If the same German speaker travelled across Germany's western frontier to the Netherlands, awareness of the close relationship between German and Dutch would be immediately present. Unless the German speaker came from a community near the border between the two countries, however, anything like full mutual intelligibility would not be possible. It can be said, therefore, that *Abstand* applies at least in terms of the contemporary varieties, even if we might suspect that, not that long ago, at least some understanding between the varieties had been possible. The problem of distinction is even more difficult than this, however. Someone from northern or central Germany visiting German-speaking Switzerland would have great – possibly insurmountable – problems in understanding people using the local dialect rather than Standard German. According to arguments based upon the principle of *Abstand*, Swiss German could well be treated as a language discrete from German. But, with the exception of a few activists, this argument is rarely made by speakers of these dialects. Something more than *Abstand* status must underlie how the difference between *language* and *dialect* is defined.

Max Weinreich is said to have observed that 'a language is a dialect with an army and a navy.' Modern Czech and Slovak could be analysed as examples of that issue. The two languages form part of a dialect continuum across a considerable part of Central Europe. Speakers from either end of this continuum would have difficulty understanding each other when using their native dialects (although some understanding might still be possible with some effort). Where the Czech Republic and Slovakia meet, essentially the same dialects are spoken on either side of the border, however. Indeed, if the state of Greater Moravia had not been overthrown by the Magyar invasions more than a thousand years ago, it is quite possible to imagine a culturally and linguistically homogenous territory across these regions. Instead, of course, the eastern parts of Greater Moravia were incorporated in the Kingdom of Hungary, while Bohemia and Moravia gravitated towards the largely German-speaking Holy Roman Empire. When Slovak nationalism began to develop in the course of the nineteenth century, activists were faced with the fact that their postulated 'national' variety was both very similar to, and heavily influenced by, Czech. Since the ideological equation of language with nation was particularly strong at the time, the decision was made to base the new national standard not on the language of the capital, Bratislava, but instead on the dialects of country districts somewhat to the east, since the capital's variety, situated on the border with the Czech lands, was more akin to Czech than many activists would have liked. Thus some distance was achieved. The planning process supplied more, in relation to the extent to which internationalisms (such as *telephone*) were embedded in the Slovak language, while Czech veered towards purism (see, for instance, Neustupný 1989). Kloss described languages of this type as having gone through *Ausbau* 'development'.

It should be noted that *Abstand* and *Ausbau* states are not mutually exclusive. Most languages have elements of both in the extent to which they are discrete from other languages. Thus Norwegian (in both of its standard forms) is considered separate from Swedish because of a number of linguistic differences and also through the conscious development and planning of the written varieties. It should be noted, however, that considerable mutual intelligibility is still possible between the two languages. If the medieval union between Denmark, Sweden and Norway had survived to become a unitary state in the Early Modern period, it is quite possible that we would now consider Swedish, Danish and Norwegian dialects of one *Scandinavian* language. Most famously, the Chinese dialects can be described as such only in *Ausbau* terms, since they all, at least presently, revolve around the norms and prestige of Classical Chinese and modern Mandarin. In *Abstand* terms they are as distinct from each other as are, for instance, French and Romanian. Levels of mutual intelligibility are generally very low. Many of the categories which define *language* are open to negotiation.

In relation to the contents of this book, a distinction has been made according to the regular scholarly assignment of *language* and *dialect*, largely following the arguments for classification underlying *Abstand*. Thus Chapters 2 and 3 deal with phenomena relating to contact between dialects of the same language, while Chapters 4 and 5 deal with contact between closely related but discrete languages. It is, however, a central part of the argument of this book that such a cleavage is problematical when it comes to closely related varieties. Indeed, as we will see, many of the same processes – *koineisation* in particular, perhaps – are at work on both dialects and closely related languages in contact situations. In relation to the use of *language* when considering the contact between English and Norse in the north of England in the early Middle Ages, for instance, common practice is to treat these as separate languages. How they were perceived by native speakers living through the contact is irrecoverable but may be at odds with modern scholarly interpretation.

Similar issues could be aired about the contact in the late nineteenth and early twentieth centuries which produced Cocoliche, the form of Spanish used by speakers of Italian dialects in Buenos Aires and Montevideo (Lipski 1994: 176–9). The ease with which people crossed what might have been considered by outsiders as the boundary between distinct and discrete languages, creating what could be analysed as a variety derived from both inputs, is noteworthy and of some importance to our understanding of change as induced by contact as a whole.

1.5 A brief excursus: mainstream analyses of linguistic divergence and development

This book deals in the main with what might be described, at least in historical linguistic terms, as abnormal forms of change. The mainstream view is that most linguistic change involves gradual change within languages across time (the speed with which these changes take place is a separate matter and will not be dealt with here). Over time, the changes – carried out differently in different varieties of a language – mean that these varieties are no longer mutually comprehensible; these varieties are now languages (in *Abstand* terms, as we discussed in the last section). Over time, these languages themselves develop dialectal variation which inevitably means that, over time, new and discrete languages develop. In theory this could go on indefinitely (a discussion of these issues can be found in Millar 2015: in particular, Chapter 7). With language families such as Indo-European, we can trace this kind of development across considerable periods, as the fairly conservative family tree of the language family demonstrates (Fig. 1.2).

While it is likely that most language change is of this divergent type, not all is. Convergence between different language varieties is not uncommon. On both occasions the influence of language contact is regularly to be felt. This book will be concerned with language contact but with a particular focus on those occasions where closely related language varieties come into contact. It will illustrate and analyse divergence and convergence phenomena in these varieties, paying particular attention to the occasions where convergence is particularly powerful.

1.6 The book

As we have seen, many of the authorities on linguistic contact do not discuss overtly or at length what happens when closely related varieties come into contact with each other, although a far larger literature exists on dialect formation through contact between dialects of the same

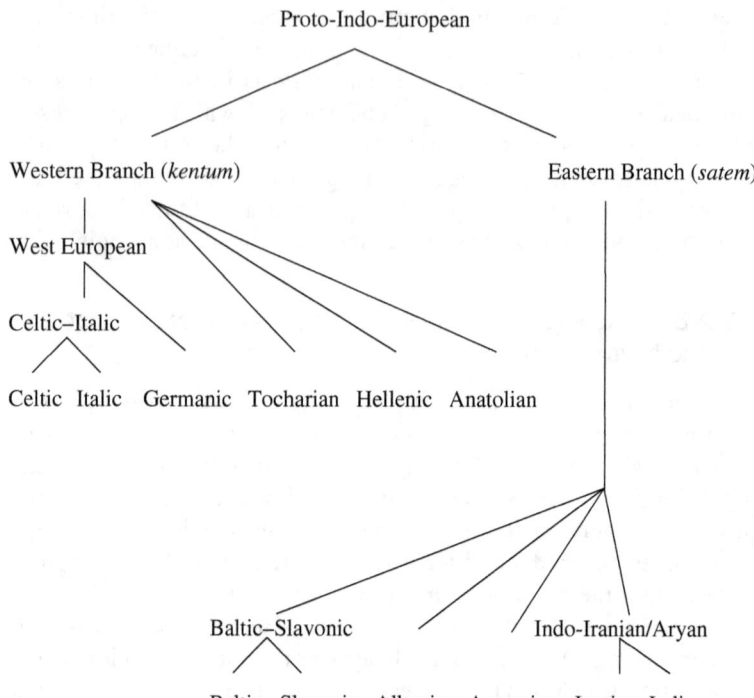

Fig. 1.2 A conventional Indo-European family tree (adapted from Barber 1993: 70-1).

language, largely formulated by sociolinguists. This book is designed to redress this imbalance, giving the reader the opportunity to read and consider a variety of different contact scenarios where the language varieties involved are close relatives. Are the results of contacts of this type different by their nature from where linguistically distant (or entirely different) varieties come into contact? As we have already seen, there are issues with the standard mainstream methodological and theoretical analyses of language contact where close-relative contact is involved. The rest of this book is designed as an attempt to fill this lacuna. In the first instance, it will consider the nature and results of dialect contact. The time depth of these relationships will be given particular emphasis, with two case studies – on the development of Insular Scots and the Germanic dialects of Ireland – analysed in Chapter 3. Then near-relative contact between discrete languages will be considered. Chapter 4 presents the arguments and evidence underlying these contacts. Chapter 5 is dedicated to an in-depth analysis of the morphosyntactic changes through which English passed in the period 900–1350, in particular in relation to near-relative contact. The book ends with a recapitulation of its main themes and a discussion of possible further research.

2 New dialect formation and near-dialect contact

2.1 Some introductory thoughts

The last five hundred years have witnessed an unprecedented global expansion of European languages, largely as a result of imperialism of one form or another. The official languages of all but four of the states of South and Central America are Spanish or Portuguese (although some states, at least constitutionally, *mention* indigenous languages); in North America, English and, in pockets, French, are dominant. In the Caribbean, French, Spanish, Portuguese, English and Dutch have all left traces of greater or lesser tenacity. In sub-Saharan Africa, a similar post-colonial linguistic ecology is dominant, even when, as is often the case, actual full command of the originally imported official languages is relatively limited among the population as a whole. In Asia, different patterns present themselves with, for instance, Spanish retreating in the Philippines and, somewhat more recently, Dutch in Indonesia and French in Indochina following essentially the same process. English has become omnipresent in many places. While native languages have held up fairly well among the inhabitants of most of the Pacific islands (albeit with different relationships between local varieties and the languages of the – former or contemporary – colonial power, as can be seen when comparing French Polynesia with, say, Tonga), European settlement colonies on their fringes, such as Australia and New Zealand, represent a situation where the language of the incomers has become dominant and, perhaps more vitally, ubiquitous. Native languages *do* survive in both countries; in the case of Māori, something of a resurgence has taken place in terms of use, speaker numbers and status since the end of the Second World War. With a few admirable exceptions, however, particularly with New Zealand, the language of imperialism is without doubt the primary language of choice or necessity in communications between speakers of aboriginal languages and speakers of the (former) imperialists' language. In other words, an unequal bilingualism exists where members of the colonising group are not normally in command of both languages, while the colonised are expected to be. So hegemonic do such linguistic relationships become that the colonising population and their descendants often do not even perceive this lack of equality.

In practically all of these situations, new varieties of the European language have come into being; sometimes these are strikingly different from the metropolitan 'norm'. A useful example of this phenomenon involves the Portuguese of Portugal in comparison with the Portuguese of Brazil, where genuine barriers to mutual intelligibility are present. In many cases, such as the Englishes of the (former and present) British Southern Hemisphere settler colonies, differences between the 'home' country variety and the local dialects are not as great, but are still present and appear, from what evidence we possess, to have developed over a matter of two or three generations at the beginning of large-scale settlement. What is important is that the linguistic connection between the varieties of the 'mother country' and their descendant colonial variety is rarely, if ever, straightforward. A central prop to this distinctiveness is the processes involved in two or more closely related linguistic varieties coming into contact with each other.

While we accept that all languages change, and that divergence is the most regular means by which this process is expressed, we still need to understand how these new varieties come into being. What processes are involved in their production? This question has long interested linguists (and, indeed, many non-specialists). It is only in the last thirty to forty years, however, that fully theorised and empirically reinforced research on the history of these varieties has begun to be produced. This chapter will deal with many of the issues that have been thrown up, as well as giving examples of contexts which exhibit unusual and unexpected phenomena.

2.2 Schneider (2007): a model of colonial language development[1]

In his 2007 book, Schneider proposes a schematic means by which we can observe and analyse the nativisation of an originally extrinsic language (one whose origin is elsewhere) within a newly settled society, considered from both a sociolinguistic and a linguistic viewpoint. He begins with the reasonable premise that in the early stages of the development of each colony of this kind there will be two essential types of inhabitants: settlers and indigenous. There are, of course, a few examples where few, if any, people other than the settlers were present in the early stages of colonisation (this tends to be particularly the case with island colonies, such as Saint Helena or La Réunion). Moreover, settlement or exploitation colonies (such as Newfoundland) will be more likely to have a relatively homogenous population than will a plantation-based economy, such as many of the sugar colonies in the Caribbean or, in a striking way, as we will discuss in Chapter 4 in particular, the Dutch colony at the Cape of Good Hope. On the latter occasions, the exploitation of slavery or coolie labour leads to a culturally and linguistically mixed, but socially stratified, society. Nevertheless, Schneider's model does genuinely appear to describe the central points of what happens linguistically in a new colony.

Schneider terms the first phase of settlement and nativisation *foundation*. The settler community are involved essentially in the 'pacification' of the territory, while the indigenous community become accustomed (no matter how reluctantly) to the new realities of occupation and the loss of both sovereignty and territory. The economic and social provision of the new settlement may not be entirely to the detriment of *all* indigenous people, however: at least some natives will become involved in the new trading possibilities produced by the presence of settlers.

At this time, the settlers primarily see themselves as being part of the original nation. We can see this, for instance, in the names given to nineteenth-century settlements in Australia and New Zealand, such as *Sydney*, *Melbourne* and *Auckland*, called after British statesmen of the time, or *Dunedin* and *Christchurch*, employed by exiles, albeit obliquely, in honour of places of distinction in their home countries. At the same time, indigenous people retain their sense of indigenous identity, not based on how the settlers define them (as an amorphous mass), but rather on the often striking differences (as perceived by natives) between discrete 'tribes' or 'nations', frequently identified and distinguished linguistically.

Sociolinguistically, settlers begin, inadvertently or not, to take part in cross-dialectal contact, a point to which we will return later in the chapter. While it would be too early to talk about a local variety of the settler language(s) coming into being, the first moves towards that state will begin at this point. Some indigenous people will also learn the settler language, thus developing a bilingualism based on trade and what could be either opportunity or compulsion (or, indeed, both). Linguistically, *koineisation*, the crystallisation of a new variety centred upon a convergence of the varieties upon which the koine is based, in relation to different forms of the settler language, will begin, a point to which we will return on a number of occasions in this chapter and later in this book. Some small-scale borrowing from indigenous languages is also possible, in particular in relation to the names of places and rivers. Thus in early colonial Virginia, the rulers of the home territory – England –

were honoured in the names of settlements like *Jamestown* as well as the *James River* (and, indeed, *Virginia* itself, named for Elizabeth Tudor). But native toponyms like *Chesapeake* (Bay) and the *Susquehanna* and *Potomac* rivers were also taken into English early on. In trade colonies, such as those founded by European merchants and traders along the west coast of Africa in the sixteenth and seventeenth centuries, pidginisation of the settler language (or, very occasionally, one of the native languages) began (we will return to this phenomenon in Chapter 4). Although most colonies were not initially set up as wholeheartedly plantation colonies (it takes some time for population levels to arrive at a point that plantations rather than farms can be supported), it is at this stage in the cycle of the development of plantations that similar forms of pidginisation take place, a matter which we will take up again in Chapter 4.

The next stage is defined as *exonormative stabilisation*. By this point the colony has stabilised and, when appropriate, been brought under central government control, rather than the enterprising individuals or companies of merchant adventurers (as with the British East India Company or its Dutch equivalent), whose activities marked the beginnings of a number of colonies, such as what was once Rhodesia. The settler language becomes the primary, if not sole, language of government, the law and education, each of which is likely to remain true to the models derived from the 'home country' even if some local 'colour' may be provided by the use of indigenous words, such as the American employment of *caucus* to mean a (political) party meeting or discussion, probably originally derived from an Algonquin language. Otherwise the language used will rarely, if ever, betray its colonial origins in official contexts. Settlers and their descendants will see themselves as 'British plus local', as having somewhat different lives from those lived by people who stayed on in the metropolis. These differences will not be interpreted as being fundamental to the construction of their identity, however. By the same token, at least some indigenous individuals will begin to feel themselves to be connected in some way to the imperial centre of the settlers, as the assumption of relationship and common outlook felt over the last hundred years and more between the royal families of a number of Pacific nations and the British ruling house seems to demonstrate.

Despite ongoing covert nativisation, at a sociolinguistic level, at this stage all settlers generally accept that the norm should be that of the metropolis, although there are greater levels of contact than was previously the case both between the settlers and the indigenous population, and between speakers of the different dialects (and languages) used by the settler population. Nevertheless, the received variety is still that of the metropolis. The colonial language(s) also spread in use into the elite of the indigenous population. Terms related to flora and fauna and, to some extent, indigenous culture will also be brought at this point into the settler language. Thus American English words like *raccoon* and *chipmunk*, for species which are not found in Europe, are derived from native sources. Even Falkland Islands English, which was established in practically a *tabula rasa* environment, retains some Spanish terms from a briefly settled Spanish-speaking population, such as *camp* 'area outside Port Stanley' (from Spanish *campo* 'field'), despite the position of British English as the sole variety in use officially.

As Schneider suggests, moreover, pidginisation, leading to creolisation, as we will discuss further in Chapter 4, would also be present in the evolving colony, in particular when trade (or, we might add, plantation-based exploitation) was at the centre of the territory's development. Thus the early European trading settlements along the coast of West Africa inevitably used pidgin varieties in order to communicate readily with the indigenous populations – not necessarily based upon their own languages, but regularly Portuguese, at least in the early days of European expansion in the sixteenth and seventeenth centuries.

The third stage Schneider envisages is *nativisation*. This stage is marked by 'weakening ties' with the metropolis. Local legislatures are likely to become, at the very least, autonomous in relation to the imperial parliament. Executive powers are also likely to be devolved, to a lesser or greater extent, to the colony. Full or near-independence is likely to follow, although the colony may remain in a cultural association, such as the Commonwealth of Nations, which at least begins by being dominated by the 'mother country'. Settlers by now generally think of themselves as coming from the territory in which they were born, although they are also likely to remember their association with the metropolis. Indigenous people may not share this final association, but they will begin to see themselves as being part of the same territorial complex as the settlers.

Sociolinguistically, Schneider argues, the nativisation phase involves *accommodation*, a movement (normally, but not always, unconscious or semi-conscious) towards the linguistic behaviour of another, often accompanied by a similar movement on the latter's part, due to regular and widespread contacts between the settlers and also between them and the indigenous population. The latter will move towards language shift, abandoning their native language in favour of local versions of the colonial language, albeit with 'indigenous' features (often seen as 'errors' by some of the settler populations) which are regularly carried on even after knowledge of the 'native' language has entirely dissipated (as demonstrated by some varieties – particularly urban – of Māori English in New Zealand: Holmes 1997). As part of these developments, tensions build among the settler population between radical nativists, who wish the local variety of the colonial language to reflect the local norms, and conservatives, who believe that only the metropolitan norm should be encouraged. From the latter point of view, in fact, local features should be actively corrected in the speech and particularly writing of local children. Evidence for the last is best found in the 'complaint tradition' of writing in to newspapers, but it is certainly a central feature of the local education ministry's advice and expectations (although these opinions are not necessarily held by everyone employed in these bodies). Most of the people who hold these conservative, metropolitan-centred views will not be immediately discernible linguistically from those who hold the opposing view; both are likely to be middle-class speakers of the local norm (something of the nature of these conflicts, as experienced in Australia, can be derived from Damousi 2010). Indeed, in my experience, Australian actors of a certain age used not to sound particularly Australian, except when playing comic characters; they were perhaps the last generation to be the product of a colonial rather than national education policy (possibly extended by the grip which London institutions like the Royal Academy of the Dramatic Arts would have had on 'colonial' acting, actors and concepts of linguistic propriety in drama), no matter when the official date of independence for Australia fell.

Linguistically, there will be heavy lexical borrowing at this stage from the indigenous language(s), in particular as its native speakers pass over to the colonial language. This cross-over may result in the transfer of larger-scale constructions (such as, possibly, American English *in this neck of the woods*, apparently calqued from a Native American source). As the new variety 'settles down', however, the nature of the inherited colonial language will shift, particularly because of, but not confined by, contacts between speakers of different varieties of the colonial language. This will be likely to include codes originally associated with particular social groups. New constructions which were previously unknown in the metropolitan variety of the settler language will come to the fore at this stage, even if there is some tension within the colony over whether they should be accepted. A striking example of this innovation is the use of *protest* + direct object (*protest the war*) in American English where British English (at least until very recently) would accept only an intransitive prepositional phrase construction with that verb (*protest against the war*). By this point at least, the local variety of the colonial language will have assumed a considerable number of identity associations, many of them highly positive.

In the fourth stage, which Schneider terms *endonormative standardisation*, not only the colony has become independent, but also considerable self-dependence is implied ('after "Event X"', when connections to the metropolis are demonstrated to be unhelpful). In the case of the United States of America this happened relatively early in the region's settlement history as a result of a series of insurrections related to the desire for self-determination. In the case of Australia it came relatively late with the awareness, after the fall of Singapore in 1942, that Britain (and, by extension, the British Empire) was incapable of protecting the country from attack by Japan. On both occasions, self-reliance, and a willingness to turn to local models in culture and eventually speech, were and are central to the new associations (in relation to these features, Australia may have been ahead of the United States). Inhabitants of the colony would no longer think of themselves as displaced citizens of the centre, instead seeing themselves as being tied to their native soil, as citizens of a new nation. Increasingly, the distinction between settlers and indigenous peoples will cease to be fully meaningful or, as is the case with the use of Māori *Pakeha* for New Zealanders of European origin, be reinterpreted in terms of the perception and language of the natives (if such a term can still be employed).

Sociolinguistically, the local norm of the metropolitan variety will be accepted as the primary form of that language within that territory. Although some conservative voices will continue to criticise the local norm, most speakers will have markedly positive views towards it. Generally, the standard written variety will remain essentially the same as that of the original centre, although developments in the nature of written American English and, to some extent, Australian English need to be borne in mind as counter-evidence. As part of this process, new dictionaries in particular, claiming to represent the local standard, will become increasingly authoritative. Grammatical description – and also prescription – is also likely to form part of this process. Often people speak and write about the homogeneity in speech across the territory, something reported for American English in the eighteenth century by some writers and still largely the case for Australian English today (although social variation will be likely to be present in any new colony from an early period).

In the final stage – *differentiation* – Schneider describes the beginnings of what might be described as 'normal' linguistic evolution: the development of social and geographical dialects within the former colony. Identity may become somewhat fractured, with smaller groups claiming the most loyalty from different speakers. If we consider Australia and New Zealand, settled from the late eighteenth century on (in the case of the former) or the early nineteenth century (for the latter), this process is really only now beginning to be felt in either country. Social and ethnic varieties do exist, but it is difficult to tell where someone comes from, from their speech alone (with the exception of many people from the New Zealand Southland, which has a different ethnolinguistic settler history from the rest of the country). If we look at American English, with two centuries more linguistic development behind it, something not dissimilar to, although perhaps not as diverse as, the linguistic variation found in the British Isles is present in those areas which have been settled longest (on the Eastern Seaboard). The further west you travel, the greater the problem you have in telling where someone comes from; by the Pacific coast it would be difficult to guess a person's native state. This is in line, of course, with European settlement history on the continent; in particular it relates to how long people of European origin have inhabited a particular place. Levels of literacy in Standard English at the time of early settlement might also have to be considered. Knowledge of this type will inevitably affect linguistic performance and, indeed, the breadth of an individual's personal linguistic continuum.

It is difficult to argue with most, if not all, of Schneider's model. It is clear and concise, and represents a progressive analysis and schematisation of what appears an often chaotic reality. What has to be recognised, however, is that, while Schneider touches upon the issue occasionally, his work does not provide much space for the actual linguistic and sociolinguistic processes by which new dialects come into being; instead the model is dominated by the sociohistorical input into the formation of new dialects. We will now turn to views on precisely these linguistic processes of dialect formation.

2.3 New dialect formation: models

As a starting point, let us imagine how we would approach the history and development of a well-known colonial variety of English – Australian English – *without* the considerable scholarship which now exists on the past and present state of the variety (a range of analyses of this subject are available; a particularly good survey is Peters 2008). If, like me, you come from the British Isles, the first impression you have on encountering Australian English is that it is very similar to, but not the same as, working-class varieties of the London region ('Cockney'; many North American speakers of English, not regularly exposed to either the vernacular English of the London area or Australian varieties, have considerable difficulty in distinguishing between them). For most people this 'almost but not quite' Cockney impression is formed from a series of comparisons. These include the nature of the vowel in words like *hate*, a relatively close diphthong in Received Pronunciation, but considerably more open in Cockney and Australian. The initial element of the diphthongal first vowel in *ride* is more back and normally closer to /ʌ/ in Cockney and Australian than it is in Received Pronunciation. Other features, such as the lack of full rhoticity in Australian English, appear also to suggest an identification with the dialects of the southeast of England. (Although it is now a feature found throughout almost all of England, we know that lack of rhoticity was rather more circumscribed until quite recently. In living memory, for instance, full rhoticity was commonplace in the south-west of England, rural Northumberland and central Lancashire; it is still found in pockets within these areas.)

There are, however, features which are *not* found in working-class London varieties, but are central to the nature of Australian English. These include the presence of /h/ in its historically 'correct' positions, something which is most certainly *not* normal in Cockney. The fronting and raising of /ɪ/ almost to the quality of /i/ in words like *bit* is practically unknown in southern England. In the latter varieties, the unstressed vowels in *running* and *Linda* are normally kept distinct from /ə/. In Australian English they have all fallen together in the latter position. On other occasions, London varieties appear to have gone through a change which is not present in Australian: for instance, the fronting of /θ/ and /ð/ to /f/ and /v/ respectively, a highly marked feature of contemporary Cockney (and, increasingly, other British urban varieties), is, at the very least, not a central feature of Australian English.

How can we explain these similarities and differences? To define Australian English as, essentially, a development of non-prestigious London English is very tempting, but as a position it could be accused of representing cherry-picking. There is also the issue that, in order to make this connection, we must assume that present-day Cockney is essentially the same as its ancestor of perhaps more than 200 years ago, when Australia was subjected to pioneer settlement from the British Isles. Given what is normally understood in relation to the considerable amount of linguistic variation and change which is present in every native speaker's repertoire and understanding, it would be most unlikely that the dialects of a major centre of population like London should somehow have remained in a condition of stasis for such a period. This is especially true in this context as there is considerable evidence to suggest that urban varieties are more likely than rural ones to change rapidly: urban environments have a tendency for encouraging intermeshing weak network ties and competing norms (see, for instance, Milroy 1980).[2]

We also have to take into consideration the historical record of the origins within the British Isles of immigrants to Australia and what proportions of overall settler numbers migrants from different regions represented. We also need to recognise an issue which at least used to be socially fraught in Australia – whether you were a voluntary free settler or an involuntary convict one. This final issue might not have been important to the development of Australian English, but the evidence would need to be sifted further (for a discussion of European settlement in Australia, see Barrie 1994).

It is impossible to do justice to such a complex issue in relatively few words. What must be recognised, however, is that, while we cannot pinpoint with accuracy the origins of all migrants to Australia in the first hundred years or so of the British colonies there, the south-east of England appears particularly well represented, with many migrants coming from London (although immigrants from rural origins in similar situations possibly outweigh these). Other parts of the British Isles – in particular, Ireland – also contributed a fair part of the settler population (although not to the extent that they formed a majority). Acceptance of a straightforward version of the 'Cockney origin' hypothesis therefore does not seem possible. Evidence for settler origins suggests greater depth and complexity.

We can now turn to a nearby English: that of New Zealand. For most people who have not had lengthy exposure to this variety, it can be difficult to distinguish New Zealand English from Australian English. Both varieties have the open 'Cockney' diphthongisation referred to above. Both also are non-rhotic (with the one exception in New Zealand of some varieties spoken in the Southland of the South Island; even here, however, rhoticity is retreating); both demonstrate coalescence of unstressed vowels at /ə/; both possess the non-Cockney features detailed above. But in other ways the two varieties are quite distinct from each other. New Zealand English, for instance, has gone through a series of sound changes (in particular with historically short vowels) not present at all in Australian English (indeed, these changes may explain why a minority of those who encounter New Zealand English speakers for the first time consider classifying their speech as being South African – another largely nineteenth-century established Southern Hemisphere English variety, albeit one which had considerable contact with Afrikaans in the early stages of its development). New Zealand English on occasion develops in diametrically opposite ways to Australian English. Thus while, as noted above, the latter has a markedly fronted (and somewhat higher) pronunciation for /ɪ/ than in Received Pronunciation, New Zealand English's equivalent is, to a considerable degree, centred and somewhat lower in the mouth than the Received Pronunciation equivalent, coming close to /ʌ/ (this makes New Zealanders sound – with this feature – rather like Scots; stressing this connection may be something of a red herring, however) (Gordon et al. 2004: Chapter 1).

Like with Australian English, an analysis of the origins of early settlers to New Zealand is problematical. What records we have are incomplete (although by no means fragmentary); there is also some evidence that how people's origins were defined in early censuses and less official surveys may not have been entirely accurate. Nevertheless, it is possible to say that immigrants from England made up somewhat more than half of the total number of migrants during the early settlement phase, while Scottish migrants represented rather more than a quarter of the total and Irish migrants rather less than that proportion. English migrants came from everywhere in that country, but there can be little doubt that people from south-eastern England (taken in its broadest sense to include both the 'Home Counties' and East Anglia) were demographically dominant, just as in England itself they made up a considerable proportion of the country's inhabitants (although perhaps not so much as was the case in New Zealand). From a linguistic point of view, we also have to bear in mind that not all Scottish migrants would have been speakers of Scots or Scottish Standard English (or, likely, both). A fair number of Gaelic speakers also came to New Zealand; conversely, some Irish settlers may have spoken Scots. On occasion, Scottish people may have made up a majority of the inhabitants of some early settlements. There would also have been some Irish and possibly Welsh speakers in the early colony, although not in the same numbers as there were Gaelic speakers. Nevertheless, English quickly became the dominant and soon the sole variety within the settler population (for a discussion of many of these matters, see the papers in Sinclair 1996).

Under normal circumstances we would now have to make extrapolations back from the present state of New Zealand English in tandem with our knowledge of what the present and past nature of the 'home' varieties was, as was essentially the case in our discussion of Australian English above. There might also be some literary evidence, often contradictory in nature and sometimes conventional in its usage. Complaint literature and the related criticisms of children's language by middle-class figures of authority, such as schoolteachers or school inspectors, are often more accurate than is the case with fictional representations, but tend to criticise usage at such a global level that it is difficult to say *exactly* what is being criticised – except modern life in comparison to the past, as conceived through the eyes of the metropolis and its middle classes. They also tend to mention linguistic issues which are held in common with disparaged dialects – such as Cockney – in the 'old country'. It must also be noted that, while some commentators were excellent natural phoneticians and phonologists, training (or expertise) in these subjects cannot always be assumed until a generation at least after settlement, when tertiary education (in particular, perhaps, teacher training) was beginning to be offered.

The study of the history of New Zealand English has one great advantage over the other nineteenth-century Englishes, however. Recordings exist for a considerable number of people who were members of the first native generation of New Zealanders of European origin (the *Pakeha*). That such a corpus exists is largely due to serendipity. In the period immediately following the Second World War, the New Zealand Broadcasting Service (Gordon et al. 2004: 3–4; Trudgill 2004: x–xi) came into possession of two vans, in which were lodged mobile recording machines. The plan was to travel around both of the main islands recording songs and musical performances from people who were less likely to be featured in the broadcast production of a radio system which inevitably favoured the output of the larger settlements. As an afterthought, almost, recordings were made of 'old timers', largely for archival purposes. As it turned out, the quality of the songs and music recorded proved disappointing and little, if any, material from the recording initiative was broadcast. The recordings remained in archives until they were 'rediscovered' in the late 1980s. On retrieval, the linguistic importance of the recordings as historical documents quickly became apparent.

That is not to say, of course, that the recordings are perfectly suited to historical linguistic analysis. They do not always possess the greatest sound quality; moreover, information on where and when a recording was made is occasionally missing, largely due to the treatment (or mistreatment) of the archive over the decades. Most importantly, the geographical spread of the recordings is patchy: some regions of New Zealand are well represented, while others are hardly touched. Nevertheless, the archive provides a unique witness which has engendered considerable scholarly debate.

Perhaps the most striking initial finding from the recordings is how unlike modern New Zealand English the accents of the first native generation of European descent actually were. The first assumption for this discrepancy is that the nature of the accents can be traced back to those of the parental generation rather than the developing society which surrounded the subjects in their early years. This is likely to have been the case with children who grew up – at least at times – on very remote farmsteads where everyday input (the only type that really matters) was confined to a small number of people who, as a family, extended or otherwise, generally came from the same region of the British Isles. This was not the case with most subjects, however. They lived in relatively open environments where contact with speakers with a great many different accents (and probably dialects) was commonplace; children from other families were regularly available as playmates. Under these circumstances, it is striking how *unlike* their parents' presumed linguistic background the informants often sound; on occasion they can even sound unlike any other English speakers, past, present and future (see, for instance, Trudgill 2004: 95–6). I will leave the in-depth discussion of these issues to the work produced by research on the recordings; what is very striking, however, is that even people who grew up at the same time in the same (relatively small) settlement, regularly playing together (and later socialising), do not sound even slightly similar. What can we make of these apparent discrepancies? How can we relate them to the later uniformity of most New Zealand speech? The following sections will present potential answers to this question. In order to do so, it is sensible to consider both the field and the work of individual scholars as being in a state of perpetual evolution (although this may not be the way individual scholars perceive their work).

2.3.1 Trudgill: the road to determinism

In a stream of research going back to the 1980s, Peter Trudgill has consistently attempted to explain what happens linguistically when people move to new places, whether as migrants moving into a territory only recently settled by people who speak their language or where a vibrant society with its own speech ways is already present, towards which migrants are expected (or aspire) to adjust and eventually to imitate.

This latter process is one which Trudgill has consistently considered and finalised to his own satisfaction quite early in his discussion of these matters (see, for instance, Trudgill 1986). Essentially, a form of relatively rough and ready accommodation, even convergence, is practised consciously or unconsciously (or often both) by immigrants who speak the same language, but in a different way from the locals (and, often, each other). Evidence of this type suggests that there is an in-built human desire to be accepted by the people with whom we live and that there are regular (essentially innate) ways in which speakers carry out these processes. In a sense, moving to places new to you where the same language is spoken is a relatively straightforward procedure; all the patterns to which you might accommodate are available to you and represent a mature system where variation tends to be geographical and social, rather than due to competing norms within the same groups. This is in marked contrast to those situations to which we will now turn where no, or few, previous norms exist. This will involve the discussion of how new varieties come into being.

In his early work on this topic (or set of topics), Trudgill (1986) produced a typology of how new varieties of a language developed, generally in new territories, based upon when and where a person was born and the level of contact which had taken place. Essentially, at this point in the development of his views, Trudgill envisaged new dialect formation happening through a process of three stages. In the first instance, some rudimentary levelling might take place between adult migrants in the new territory (or, indeed, on the long sea voyages which regularly preceded settlement). When possible, linguistic features which were believed to make comprehension difficult across the migrant group (or were perceived as such: the two processes do not necessarily amount to the same thing) were downplayed in favour of patterns which were readily comprehensible to nearly everyone else. This might involve borrowing other people's usage patterns, or it might demand a radical reworking of your native usage.

In the first native generation, the linguistic reality would involve, Trudgill theorises, extreme variability in terms of almost every aspect of native speakers' personal usage patterns. That much of this extreme variability actually masks ongoing levelling will be dealt with below. In subsequent generations, however, this extreme variability was replaced with a situation where focusing and levelling lead to a single variety for the territory being developed. What is remarkable about Trudgill's analysis is that its publication predates considerably the rediscovery of the 'Origins of New Zealand English' recordings discussed above.

In many senses, his more recent views on these matters have developed and deepened rather than altered this vision, as can be seen in his 2004 book, towards which we will now turn. In one matter – *determinism* – his newer views on the topic are rather more controversial, however.

2.3.2 Trudgill: determinism

In his 2004 book, *New-Dialect Formation: The Inevitability of Colonial Englishes*, Trudgill suggested five basic stages associated with the variation and change involved in the creation of a new variety of a language, a number of which form part of what he suggested in earlier work. In the first instance, he defines *mixing* as 'the coming together in a particular location of speakers of different dialects of the same language, or of readily mutually intelligible languages' (Trudgill 2004: 84). Thus a colony like New Zealand, in the early days of its foundation, would have contained speakers of many different dialects and accents. While some social attitudes towards language (and other matters) might have been imported from the 'mother country', no one variety was any more New Zealand in its nature or its associations than any other at this point. At the same time, however, a process of *levelling* (or, perhaps more accurately, a series of levellings in different places by different people) would inevitably have begun, a sorting process where, Trudgill (2004: 84) observes, 'the loss of demographically minority variants' occurs. Thus, since south-east English settlers achieved a bare majority within the new colony in its first fifty years, he would claim, we can therefore understand why non-rhoticity became the norm in New Zealand (although there are a number of issues with this argument – some of which Trudgill recognises – as a straightforward and transparent process of transfer, not least the actual proportion of rhotic to non-rhotic pronunciations in the rural south-east of England during the New Zealand settlement period). The same argument could be made for the apparently 'Cockney' nature of the New Zealand diphthongs discussed above.

He moves on from this to *unmarking*, which he defines as 'the tendency for unmarked forms to survive even if they are not majority forms' (Trudgill 2004: 85). A potential example of this phenomenon may be the survival of /h/ in New Zealand English. While it could be argued that something like a majority of settlers would have possessed this phoneme – the combination of Scottish, Irish, some northern English speakers and people from East Anglia (where /h/ only really began to be 'dropped' in the twentieth century; the process is not as yet complete; see Trudgill 1988) would have come close to 50 per cent, it is equally possible that the markedness of /h/ loss and the potential issues with comprehension which the lack of /h/ caused for /h/-full people might have discouraged its transfer into the developing colonial variety. The negative treatment /h/-loss received at the hands of middle-class authority figures might possibly have led to its lack of favour. Trudgill would argue, however – it is a difficult argument to refute readily – that this type of sociolinguistic interpretation ignores the fact that, despite almost 150 years of compulsory education in England, /h/ loss has continued to spread in working-class communities (although this interpretation itself ignores the efforts by middle-class speakers over the same period to maintain, or regain, prestige features like 'correct' /h/ use in their speech). Moreover, education in the first stages of white settlement in New Zealand was decidedly *ad hoc* or even non-existent outside the major settlements; lack of literacy was relatively common and contact with middle-class norm-upholding and norm-enforcing authority figures was low and sporadic. A related phenomenon, Trudgill claims, is *interdialect development*, the emergence 'of forms which were not actually present in any of the dialects contributing to the mixture, but which arise out of interactions between them' (Trudgill 2004: 86). The New Zealand short vowel system, while unlike any other system of English, may in fact represent a compromise between different systems brought into the colony during the early period of settlement, involving a unique vowel shift.

Finally, *reallocations* and *focusing* act as 'the process by means of which the new variety acquires norms and stability' (Trudgill 2004: 109). Focusing constitutes itself as the way in which the tendencies engendered by the application of levelling and unmarking become the norms of a whole community in New Zealand. With the exception of Southland, the mix of competing dialect features did not differ tremendously across the territory. Thus what happened at a relatively local level could also be perceived on a regional and national scale. Varieties formed in this way are strikingly different in their inception to the dialects which have developed over centuries of settlement. We will deal with *koineisation* in more depth in Chapter 4. Here, however, we will concentrate briefly on relatively small-scale examples of the phenomena based on dialect rather than language.

Convergence can be mapped and analysed within a language, with different dialect inputs being transformed into a new variety. This process could be defined as *koineisation*. A very striking example of this in relation to contact between dialects of the same language can be found in the development of local language norms in two towns – Odda and Tyssedal – specifically founded and developed in relation to industry in western Norway (in the following I am indebted to Kerswill's 2001 discussion of koineisation and his interpretation of Sandve's 1976 research). The two towns are situated a matter of kilometres apart on the same fjord, with relatively straightforward communication between the two centres. What is striking, however, is that, at least in the 1970s, the speech of natives from the two centres was strikingly different; moreover, neither of the towns' dialects is entirely in line with the local rural dialects. In a country like Norway, with its high mountains, deep valleys and, towards the west, fjords, these points matter. Simplifying somewhat, the dialects of eastern (particularly south-eastern) Norway are markedly different from those of western (particularly, perhaps, south-western) Norway. These differences can be phonological (so that, for instance, Western *au* is equivalent to Eastern *ø* (derived from Old Norse *au*) in words like *haust / høst* 'Autumn'), morphosyntactic (Western varieties tend to have a richer set of inflectional morphemes, in particular in relation to the noun phrase, perhaps, than do Eastern varieties) and also lexis. What is interesting about the dialects of Odda and Tyssedal is that they both show evidence of adopting *both* Western and Eastern forms, although at different levels, depending on the town.

On occasion, the dialects have both moved in the direction of Eastern forms, such as the use of *vi* rather than *me* for 'we'. At other times, Odda has tended towards Western norms, while Tyssedal has adopted Eastern; at yet other times, however, both or one of the new varieties assume(s) either a form which combines Western and Eastern features (thus apparently representing a convergence), such as Odda /vɛgaʁ/ 'walls', where Tyssedal has /vɛgəʁ/ (the Western form being /vɛɟjər/ and Eastern /vɛgər/), or a form which, while similar to the source dialect, is a new development, such as Odda /kɔmə/ (where Tyssedal has /kɔməʁ/ – the Western norm is /çeːmə/, the Eastern /kɔmər/). There are also occasions – such as with the use of /ʁ/ – where specifically local features, not universal in either West or East, are found.

In order to understand *why* such apparently anomalous material should be found, the origins of the early twentieth-century migrants to the newly established towns needs to be considered. What is striking about the information gathered for this purpose is that, no matter how similar in development and close in geographical space they are, the original settlers of the two communities apparently had very different geographical backgrounds. While the Odda metal works attracted an overwhelming majority of workers from the western parts of Norway, the equivalent in Tyssedal had almost as many workers from eastern Norway as from the west. This marked difference apparently explains why the present Tyssedal dialect analysed by Sandve has maintained many more Eastern features than has Odda. It also explains why both dialects show Western features – Tyssedal had a large number of settlers from that dialect area, even if they were not in the majority as in Odda. Moreover, the influence of the local dialects from the area around both towns, at the very least brought into schools by country children, must also have had some effect over the development of the first two urban generations' speech in the town. The simplified or interdialectal forms are particularly interesting, since they often appear to represent genuine attempts to square the circle between Western and Eastern patterns. This would be expected to be more the case with Tyssedal speech, given its apparently mixed origin. It is also occasionally true for Odda, however, despite the dominance of people of western origin for that town. It is likely none the less that the Eastern-oriented standard form of Norwegian, *Bokmål*, exerts considerable influence on places in the west which may suffer from something like *anomie* in comparison with the surrounding long-settled rural communities with established linguistic identity associations around them. Similar findings are also reported by Trudgill (1986: 95–9) for the new town of Høyanger, found in a comparable location and with a similar history. It is difficult to see in these apparent negotiations of usage how determinism, rather than a tendency towards majority influence, can be sustained.

Returning to Trudgill's views on the development of New Zealand English and other varieties, an eloquent case is made in his 2004 book for these stages and their interaction. Most linguists would not quarrel with the gradation he suggests (indeed, from an elevated enough viewpoint it seems eminently sensible). There are issues, however, with accepting everything which forms part of his model; experts in the field have not been slow to point these out. Indeed, Trudgill must be practically unique in being cited as sole author (Trudgill 2004) and joint author (in Gordon et al. 2004) of two books on essentially the same subject, published in the same year, the second of which actively disagrees with some of the conclusions of the former.

The primary problem for most specialists in the field is what Trudgill terms *inevitability* (but is often described as *determinism* by both Trudgill and his critics and detractors in relation to the formative processes of the new dialect). The issue is this: if we settle particular proportions of settlers from specific places, can we therefore say that these proportions inevitably dictate the specific nature of that variety?

If we return to some of the features discussed above, it does appear plausible that the fact that more than half of the settler population in New Zealand came from what are now non-rhotic areas in the British Isles might have strongly affected the lack of rhoticity in most varieties of New Zealand English. The same arguments could probably be made for Australian and South African English, along with the other less populous Southern Hemisphere varieties (although, as Sudbury 2001 points out, some speakers of Falkland Islands English, in particular from West Falkland, where settlements of any size are largely unknown, are at least partly rhotic). By the same token, as we have already noted, the presence of /h/ in Australian and New Zealand English can be seen as representing the 'victory' of either a bare majority's usage or of the unmarking process discussed above. A number of problems underlie the model's apparent success, however.

Trudgill adheres to the idea that identity, in particular group, regional or national identity, has little or no effect on the development of new dialects, a point he stresses in a brief article of 2008. His argument is difficult to gainsay – at least in part. How can a person take on linguistic features to express identity when the group of which he or she will eventually form a part – New Zealanders, for instance – does not as yet truly exist? The mixture involved in koineisation is therefore, in Trudgill's view, related wholly to accommodation, implicitly of an unconscious type. This complete disavowal of identity under these circumstances has been challenged by Tuten (2008), Schneider (2008) and Holmes and Kerswill (2008), among others (each with her or his own interpretation of identity and accommodation, which may not be mutually compatible).

In the first instance, the question of how to judge the effects of the constitution of the initial population upon the development of a local language variety bears with it the need to understand who actually makes up that population and when this period in a settlement's history ended (so that people who followed would feel the need to accommodate towards the founding group's speech ways). Trudgill takes a generally broad viewpoint of these issues. He may well be right in relation to New Zealand English. The broad range of dates between which the early *Pakeha* New Zealanders, recorded at the end of the Second World War and demonstrating the highly mixed phonologies described above, were born suggests a lengthy period of gestation for the variety. But we need to be careful not to allow our award of pioneer status to suit the model we are presenting. This kind of view does not lend itself to the fluctuations in numbers and origins of settlers found in the early decades of any new settlement. It is these niggling suspicions which compel us to turn to the competing theories on dialect origin. As we will see, however, there are also problems with blanket acceptance of these alternative views.

2.3.3 Mufwene: founder principle

In work published over the last twenty years and more (and in particular in his 2001 book), Salikoko Mufwene has argued persuasively and at length that, no matter the proportions of settlers at a later date, it is the language or dialect of the first significant population which wins out. This founder population need not necessarily be the absolute first settlers, who are often sidelined by later immigrants with more disposable capital. A good, although somewhat broad-brushed, example of this issue can be seen in the fact that, over the period 1600–1900, more German speakers entered what is now the United States of America than did English speakers. Pockets of German speech continue to this day, most notably perhaps among those descendants of Mennonite groups who have a tradition of maintaining a distance from the mainstream culture and its practices, such as the Amish. Until at least the First World War, considerable numbers of those living in the upper Midwest were of German descent or origin and spoke German on an everyday basis. Yet very few of these German speakers considered anything other than English to be the normal language of the United States (even if a minority entertained dreams of creating a German-using state, most found the idea at best unlikely; for a discussion of these matters, see Rippley 1984). English speakers had got there first and their language was, without any *de jure* status, the *de facto* language of government, education and intercommunal relations. Mufwene, carrying across ideas from evolutionary biology, would term this the *founder principle*.

Much closer to Mufwene's own research agenda is the history of African American Vernacular English. This has been a hot topic for well over forty years, partly because the debate has become ideologically driven on occasion, but primarily because any convincing answer to the puzzle of the variety's origin appears almost as distant now as it did in the 1970s (for a discussion, see the papers in Lanehart 2001).

Essentially, the problem is this. In the islands of the Caribbean where plantation economies based primarily on the exploitation of African slaves developed, genuine pidgins and creoles came into being with English or other languages (in particular, perhaps, French) as the lexifier, but with structures and phonologies very different from any variety of the lexifier language (we will return to the origins and development of pidgins and creoles in Chapter 4). In most of these territories (although not Haiti, where independence from the imperial power – France – came early and was essentially absolute), a *post-creole continuum* has now developed through mass education in the colonial language. This does not mean that the varieties were not originally discrete, however.

With African American Vernacular English, on the other hand, constructing such a straightforward model of relationship and development is impossible. Apparently creole features are present in the variety – some phonological material, such as the use of /t/ and /d/ (or /f/ and /v/) instead of more mainstream /θ/ and /ð/; a considerable amount of aspect marking not found in Standard English; the lack of number and person concord marking in the present indicative verb, and so on. But African American Vernacular English cannot really be described as a creole. In reality, it is essentially another mainstream dialect of

English, similar to, but not quite the same as, the varieties spoken by white southerners. Early findings might predict that this present state is a product of a long-running post-creole continuum, with earlier varieties being demonstrably more creole-like than the present variety. The problem is, however, that what evidence we have of earlier African American usage – recordings of ex-slaves' reminiscences in the 1930s, the form of language used in external settlements of black people of American origin in the Dominican Republic and Nova Scotia (for a discussion of these diaspora varieties, see Poplack and Tagliamonte 2001) whose ancestors left the United States before Emancipation, literary representations of black speech from the nineteenth century, and so on – do not seem to represent any more creole-like a form of language than what we find now in African American Vernacular English. Of course, the argument could be made that the people whose language was recorded and analysed in the ex-slaves' reminiscences and in the early external colonies might not be truly representative of the slave population as a whole. The colonists in the Dominican Republic were often educated. Some could be described as northern and middle-class (and therefore not representing the obvious originating population for African American Vernacular English). The former slaves recorded in the 1930s were already quite long-lived; it is perfectly possible that this longevity derived from their having had the less physically demanding roles associated with house slaves rather than those associated with field hands; house slaves would have had far more exposure to Standard English than field hands would have had. But these points still retain a central flaw: it is very difficult to argue from a lack of evidence.

Mufwene (2001) argued for a history of African American Vernacular English which recognises that the early history of black slavery in what is now the United States was strikingly different from the plantation society which was later dominant (and which arguably produced the United States' only true English creole, Gullah, spoken now on islands off the Atlantic coasts of South Carolina and Georgia, and historically in coastal rice and indigo plantations; see Montgomery 1994 for a range of discussions of Gullah language and culture). In the seventeenth century, the pioneer period for early English colonies like Virginia, most African slaves lived in close proximity to – perhaps in the same building as – their owners and families. They were also regularly in direct contact (and, no doubt, conflict) with white indentured servants – essentially temporary slaves who paid for their passage by working for a set number of years afterwards in payment to their 'benefactors' (see Galenson 1984 for a discussion of this process). These servants at least would have very likely spoken an English which demonstrated social and geographical origins different from those of the Standard. Most, if not all, Africans would have come to the colonies with a very limited amount of English, if any at all. But the English they learned was that of native speakers with whom they communicated regularly, Mufwene suggests, in stark contrast to the considerably lower level of native speaker English input with which slaves on Caribbean plantations came into contact. The dialect(s) Africans and their immediate descendants developed in North America would have been very similar to the evolving white varieties of the colonies, but with a slightly different 'mix', caused by their identities as Africans, slaves and, very likely, non-native speakers, particularly in the first generations of settlement.

During the eighteenth century, this *homestead phase* of American slavery was replaced by one where much larger plantations became, if not the norm, at least central to the economy of the southern region. This naturally meant that the regular, personal and often intimate contact between whites and blacks which had characterised earlier colonial life was replaced with the industrial use of gangs of slaves whose contact with white native speakers of English must have been limited. Those who came directly from Africa would again have needed to learn English rapidly, often as adults. But those who had been part of the homestead phase, and spoke the black local variety of English, would, Mufwene suggests, have played the part of educators (particularly in relation to behaviour and the use of language) to the newer slaves. Their language would have been the founder variety for the new social situation. No doubt speech varieties something like pidgins in their earliest stages would have existed in the plantations; these would not have won out against the native African American variety both because the homestead phase slaves were of considerable importance and standing in the community, and because everyone – newly arrived slaves and old hands – would have seen the advantage of using an English dialect. Thus, departing somewhat from Mufwene's interpretation, a number of founder populations can be envisaged, some more important than others. The initial pioneer population must have had an effect on those that followed. In the case of African slaves, however, their indentured servant contemporaries were probably involved more in the creation of the new African American varieties of English than was the case with white varieties. Moreover, the variety of English used and formed by Africans in the homestead phase was the model for the English learned by plantation slaves. Of course, as Mufwene makes plain, these last two stages would also have had African linguistic elements embedded in them, even if this represents something of a minority element in the variety's make-up. This multiplicity of source material will be fruitful for a range of analyses later in the book.

This line of argument is, of course, very attractive and presents an opportune means of explaining some particularly difficult issues in the record, but general scholarly consensus would suggest that it is not always applicable: put plainly, it cannot explain all the issues which appear to have been thrown up in our account of new dialect formation. If we take New Zealand English as an example again, it rapidly becomes apparent that the founder principle can explain, for instance, why the apparently non-standard South-Eastern English phonological features, probably interpretable as representing the speech of the fundamental founder population for the colony, dominated. It cannot explain, however, why features not associated with that part of the English-speaking world should also be present in the evolving (and, indeed, evolved) language variety. It is much more likely that it is the 'colonial mix' of early stages in the variety's development which should act as the foundation of the later dialect (something, to be fair, which Mufwene posits for African American Vernacular English in his model for the early development of that variety). In a sense, this view is not, in fact, that far away from Trudgill's model (something Mufwene recognises in an article of 2008), with the proviso that it does not demand an unquestioning acceptance of proportions of settler origins in explaining how a new variety comes into being, since there is a likelihood that power or prestige could have encouraged the preference of one variant over another, something not really possible in Trudgill's postulated process (although it would be deeply foolhardy to discount population input proportions entirely: they are likely to be central to any development of this type. The question is focused rather on the extent to which we can apply such an interpretation mechanistically). What can be said, however, is that the *founder principle* is an attractive means of viewing new dialect formation. It does not provide all the answers we might wish for, however.

2.3.4 'Swamping'

An apparently opposing viewpoint has also been postulated to explain how new varieties of a language develop: *swamping*. In a number of colonial situations – South Africa being a particularly interesting case (Lass 1987, 1990, 1995, 2004) – the apparent 'old country' origin of the local variety of English cannot be analysed as deriving in a straightforward way from the early settlement history of the colony. Thus modern South African English appears to derive largely from a typically Southern Hemisphere blend of South-Eastern English dominance along with other features, which seems to demand the input of variants from other varieties. Indeed, South African English may be more 'Cockney' than other such varieties, since /h/ use is variable. This analysis does not, of course, enter into a discussion of the influence Afrikaans has had on this variety – or the nature of the sound which replaced /h/ in these varieties (Lass 2004: 379). There is some evidence which suggests, however, that this South-Eastern English predominance does not represent well the history of the first English-speaking immigrants of the 1820s, when the Cape and its surrounding districts had newly been brought under British control. (English speakers would have been regular visitors to the Cape during the period of Dutch rule; they would have been unlikely to have made a lasting impression on the linguistic history of the region, however.) The settlers of the 1850s in KwaZulu–Natal may be more representative of the later speech patterns of South African English (for a discussion of this settlement history, see Lanham and Macdonald 1979).[3] Practically all evidence for any local variety of English predating this central event has been expunged from the present dialect. Thus the nature of an initial variety is *swamped*. While Trudgill (2004) is dismissive of a complete acceptance of this proposal, it has to be said that, applying Ockham's razor, swamping's appropriateness in explaining why a variety might have developed in a particular direction at least sounds very likely. Indeed, Gordon et al. (2004) look kindly on the theory's applicability to the development of New Zealand English, seeing that variety's founding moment as being in the second half of the nineteenth century, when south-east English settlement was not just in the majority in the colony, but actually overwhelming in most places. They make a case that this change in dominance is reflected in the 'Origins of New Zealand English' recordings corpus, with those born in the late nineteenth century realising a rather less (geographically) diverse set of variants, most of which point directly and unequivocally to south-eastern England. This suggests that Trudgill's analysis of all early speakers without employing a more nuanced time division might be flawed. In Trudgill's defence, however, this South-East English swamping interpretation does not explain why features apparently derived from other dialects, such as /h/ retention, should be present in modern New Zealand English.

The processes apparently underlying the *founder principle* and *swamping* may not really be contrary to each other. Mufwene does not claim that it is the absolutely first settler group which assumes the role of producing the dominant colonial variety. Questions of economic and social power, along with numbers of speakers, are central means by which a founder group comes into being; this is not particularly different from the features associated with swamping, although it needs to be noted that the levels to which identity was interpreted, in relation to founder and weight of numbers input in each model, render the difference between the two theoretical positions more marked.

2.3.5 Discussion

In this section we have considered various means of explaining how new varieties come into being. As we have seen, all are useful in explaining this type of development; none can be said to be entirely successful, however. In the next section we will consider a number of new variety scenarios which apparently test – to a lesser or greater extent – the models presented. These include those situations where a new dialect is formed in a region with a small, often geographically dispersed, population. These contexts will be contrasted with the development of urban varieties. Finally, comparison will be made to the development of new written varieties under similar circumstances.

2.4 Case studies of new dialect formation

2.4.1 New dialect formation and low population

2.4.1.1 Tristan da Cunha English

A particularly interesting example of a *tabula rasa* context with a highly limited population can be found with the English of Tristan da Cunha, an archipelago (of which only one island is inhabited) in the South Atlantic which is arguably the most isolated settlement on earth. Its English variety has been ably discussed and analysed by Schreier (2003; examples from Tristan da Cunha English given below derive from this source).

Tristan da Cunha English is in most ways a mainstream Southern Hemisphere English, different from, but of the same type as, the Englishes of New Zealand, Australia and South Africa. There are, however, some features in Tristan da Cunha English which are either unusual or entirely unknown in these other varieties. Verb–subject concord, for instance, is rarely equivalent to that of the standard; instead, a number of features, deriving from both southern and northern British English, are at work in the system, suggesting an oral transfer of features which has rarely been dominated by standardised literate practice. Some features, such as completive *done*, normally more closely associated with the black and white vernaculars of the southern United States, are relatively common, as in the example

> Is S. *done* finish diggin? 'Has S. completely finished digging?'

Arguably the most striking morphosyntactic feature, however, is delineating *usta went* 'used to go' (and other past tense/past participle) constructions. In habitual situations, the mainstream *used to go* is common:

> Sometimes we *used to go* round together, all round the beaches *we used to go.*

With other contexts, however, an unusual feature can be produced:

> I *useta went* Nightingale with my father when I was a boy.
> We never had no good schooling ... all we *usta done* was sums an' a bit of reading.

It should be noted that it is not the actual formation which is unusual or even aberrant; 'past infinitives' are to be found in a range of languages, including Latin. It is the fact that it is to be found in a fairly mainstream variety of *English* which is noteworthy. Since its origin cannot be traced to the varieties from England which appear to act as Tristan da Cunha English's primary source, we need, therefore, to consider the history of the Tristan da Cunha variety.

Unlike many of the other varieties described in this book, this is in many ways a relatively straightforward matter, since the number of people who have ever spoken Tristan da Cunha English is highly circumscribed; moreover, the time depth since the foundation of the settlement is relatively brief, meaning that there cannot be a great deal of doubt over which evidence should be considered central to the colony's development.

In essence, it can be said that, while colonists came from a wide range of places both within and outside the English-speaking world, two founder populations stand out: speakers of non-standard forms of southern British English (whose users began arriving towards the beginning of the nineteenth century) and speakers – mainly female – from St Helena, brought in 1827 as wives for earlier settlers. As we have seen, of course, most features of Tristan da Cunha English are mainstream, demonstrating an essential connection to southern British English.

The presence of St Helenian natives is of some importance, however, since St Helena stands out among Southern Hemisphere British colonies in having a history of slavery. In his work on the origins of the dialect of that island, Schreier (2008) traces the origin of the slaves both to West and southern Africa and, in particular, Madagascar. Although present-day St Helenian English is *not* a creole, Schreier presents the persuasive argument that the creole-like features of the variety represent a merger, probably in the nineteenth century, in the main between the Southern British vernacular of the free population and the creole of the non-free inhabitants, something supported by the fact that, unusually for a slave colony, all native St Helenians are now of 'mixed race'.

The women who came to Tristan da Cunha from St Helena in 1827 were likely at least to have spoken a creole-influenced variety of English, therefore, and possibly a full-blown creole (particularly since there is a good chance that those who volunteered to jump into the unknown by migrating to Tristan da Cunha were unlikely to have been among the most economically empowered in St Helena). Indeed, as Schreier (2008) points out, many of the more unexpected features of Tristan da Cunha English – including the past infinitive – are shared with St Helena, even if features of this type are much more common in the latter variety.

As has already been noted, it is dangerous to make too much out of such a small native population in relation to analysing Tristan da Cunha's linguistic history from the viewpoint of models we have discussed above. Nevertheless, it could be argued that while Trudgill's ideas do not fully suit such a small population, they have some bearing on them. Can we say, for instance, that the influence from the dialect(s) of the female St Helenian settlers ever truly constituted a majority input into the colony's language, however? It would be fairly straightforward (although not necessarily capable of achieving full proof) to apply either the founder principle or ideas connected to swamping to the material. It is likely that, as we have come to expect, each theoretical perspective carries with it many elements applicable to the other, to the extent that they might be seen as mirror images.

2.4.1.2 An apparent anomaly? Falkland Islands English

It is worth comparing Tristan da Cunha English with another low-population variety, Falkland Islands English. Following Sudbury (2001 and 2004), the English of the Falkland Islands, an archipelago in the South Atlantic, is very difficult to categorise. It sounds a little like other rather more populous Southern Hemisphere Englishes – such as South African or Australian, or perhaps even particularly New Zealand, English – but in other ways it lies much closer to mainstream southern English varieties related to Received Pronunciation. Is this unusually mainstream development merely due to its being the 'newest' English variety (dating, really, from the middle of the nineteenth century at the earliest), or is it because the variety is spoken, with the exception of the only town, Port Stanley, in relatively isolated areas inhabited by only a few people on occasion? Or is there some other reason for this relative lack of identifiably 'Falkland' features, with the exception of a small number of Spanish phrases learned on the islands in the late nineteenth century, when 'gaucho' shepherds from the South American mainland were present in parts of the islands? These issues are made even more difficult to analyse by the fact that we have a less than full sense of where the initial settlers came from, exacerbated by there being evidence throughout the colonies' early history (and to an extent up to the present) of immigrants moving on after their initial tenure was complete. What Sudbury (2001 and 2004) points out, however, is that the most common background for early settlers who stayed on for any period was, in the first instance, from both the Scottish Highlands and, with rather fewer people, the south-western counties of England (especially Devon and Somerset), making this settlement considerably easier to analyse than that of Tristan da Cunha, despite the rather greater number of inhabitants. But the native dialects of these two areas appear to have had little or no impact upon the present variety, with the possible exception of patchily attested full rhoticity (which could derive from either south-west England or Scotland – or both) among some older speakers and the pronunciation of *with* as /wɪθ/, this being essentially confined elsewhere to Scotland.

In relation to the founder principle, Sudbury (2004: 405) notes that

> [a]lthough Mufwene's hypothesis may hold in large-scale dialect contact situations, where the size of later groups of newcomers will be far outnumbered by the established population, it may be less applicable in the Falkland situation. The smallness of the population and its relative instability, with such a high turnover of people, suggests that the dialect features brought by new arrivals may possibly have a greater effect on the developing koiné than in other koinéisation situations. This means that the origin of later settlers is also important when considering the dialect input of F[alkland] I[slands] E[nglish] features.

Thus the founder principle needs to be abandoned in the face of a weak and fairly diffuse form of swamping. Did the founding Scottish population largely speak Gaelic as their first language? In the nineteenth century this would have been perfectly possible. In that case, was the dominant English variety largely learnt – or at least fleshed out – in the Falklands? That does not explain, however, why something like the South-Eastern English of England should have become the primary focus for the developing variety, however. This sounds like a swamping event, but there is no evidence that such a population surge from south-east England ever happened (although it may be that education, formal and informal, could have had a similar, albeit less intense, effect in a period where largely prescribed, externally motivated learning became the norm). For very similar reasons, Trudgill's views are also problematical.

We may be considering the variety too early in its trajectory. Falkland Island English is not fully stabilised, with considerable regional variation, due to different settler backgrounds, exacerbated by the small population and geographical remoteness and expanse. Moreover, returning to our discussion of Schneider's typology, Falkland Islanders have not yet cut the 'umbilical cord' with the 'mother country'. Under normal circumstances, another generation might have led to a fully developed local allegiance encapsulated by a discrete new variety. The events of 1982, which produced an altered local demographic and linguistic ecology, including the arrival of a great many temporary outsiders to the islands, along with increasingly effective mass communication, may mean that these developments will either be halted or be channelled in ways not predictable if the development had been largely without external influence.

2.4.1.3 Newfoundland English

Similar points can be made about Newfoundland English, but with considerably greater time depth. Unlike Falkland Islands English, however, the vernacular varieties feeding into Newfoundland English are, as Clarke (2004) ably demonstrates, actually sundered from each other both by place – since they are situated on a large but sparsely populated island – and by cultural and religious adherence. There is a strong impression that, at least until recently, there was highly limited contact, only when necessary, perhaps, between the two communities, who derive largely from the south-east of Ireland and the south-west of England respectively. There is a good chance, in fact, that the immigrant populations were already quite linguistically homogenous because of these common origins when they arrived on the island and that this homogeneity has been emphasised, focused even, in the specific communities over a considerable period. What has not happened, of course, is the focusing of the Newfoundland variety as a whole, thus making an application of either Trudgill's or Mufwene's ideas somewhat problematical. In recent years, however, the connection with Canada (since the former Crown Colony's accession to the Canadian Confederation in 1949) and the growth of the mass media have meant that more generally North American features are now available and increasingly used on the island. The extent to which this could be perceived as a swamping event is at present difficult to say.

2.4.1.4 Discussion

Thus it could be argued that, while elements of the main theories of dialect formation discussed above do work in circumstances of low population or geographical spread (or, indeed, both), the lack of development of large-scale population centres, along with the low populations and their geographic dispersal, tends to make the existing models patchy in their usefulness – other theoretical and methodological models may exist. In the next set of examples we will consider another potentially problematical context: the development of urban dialects.

2.4.2 Urban new dialect formation

2.4.2.1 Glaswegian Scots[4]

The Glaswegian dialect of Scots has rarely been overtly prestigious in the modern age. It has been considered as 'ugly' or 'corrupt' by a wide range of commentators, whether espousing views rooted in the prescriptive embrace of (Scottish) Standard English or the portrayal of the 'purity' of rural varieties. Such views are, of course, not unknown in relation to urban dialects in the modern age. In part as a consequence of these views, two sources for the difference between Glaswegian Scots and the rural dialects which surround the city have been proposed: speakers of Irish English (and Irish) and Scottish Gaelic (or the Highland English which lived beside Gaelic and in many places replaced it) figure strongly among the immigrant population over the last 250 years. To what extent is this double (if not treble) origin observable in the present dialect? Can we make the claim that a range of identity constructions underlies it?

Glasgow's proximity to the Atlantic Ocean and the presence of coal and iron in considerable quantities in its hinterland were central to the city's exponential growth in the period after 1750. Glasgow became central to the tobacco trade with Virginia (taken in its broadest sense) and was, at the very least, at the edge of the slave trade, with cotton goods being manufactured at an industrial level in the city's suburbs and satellite towns from the early nineteenth century on. Exploitation of local coal and iron encouraged this industrialisation and the developments which fuelled it, such as a workable steam engine – initiated in the area – and a range of other new technologies and products. Both represent the strengths of these changes and contributed to their goal. The city became famous in particular for its steam locomotives and, perhaps pre-eminently, its shipbuilding. By the middle of the nineteenth century its inhabitants had taken to describing the settlement as 'the second city of the Empire', although this position was swiftly lost to Birmingham, Manchester and a small number of 'colonial' towns. By the Second World War, Glasgow was in considerable decline, with only limited shipbuilding being carried out down to the present day. Although unemployment is markedly lower than it was in the 1980s, it is still considerable and appears chronic.

Since the beginning of the industrial age, Glasgow has always been a city of social contrasts, with a small moneyed class being strikingly outnumbered by a large working class, until relatively recently often housed in crowded and insanitary conditions. Among the unskilled poor, often in the majority, existence was largely of a hand to mouth type. Casualisation also regularly hit more skilled occupations – in particular, perhaps, shipbuilding and the various cloth trades – with a cycle of work followed by 'idleness' recurring, depending on the global economy. Uncertainty bred fellow feeling across the working people, although this solidarity was threatened by fault lines within Scottish and Irish society: in particular, the division between Protestant and Catholic inhabitants. Despite all the problems, however, Glasgow continued to suck in immigrants until at least the Second World War, when changes in work patterns and a desire for slum clearance led to an 'overspill' of Glaswegians into surrounding towns.

It is a commonly held belief that these 'new' Glaswegians came largely from Highland or Irish (both Protestant and Catholic) backgrounds. But although these immigrant groups have had a considerable impact upon the city's sense(s) of identity and origin, what evidence we have of immigrant origin tells a very different story, with most incomers coming from the counties surrounding Glasgow – Lanarkshire, Renfrewshire, Dunbartonshire and, at a small remove, Ayrshire and Stirlingshire. If, as seems correct, that is the case, why would people – often well-informed people – espouse the Irish and Highland hypothesis?

Glaswegian dialect shares much with the more rural dialects surrounding the city, phonologically, morphosyntactically and lexically. There are, however, features which outsiders recognise as specifically Glasgow and not 'of the soil' (although, originally, specifically Glaswegian features are not unknown now in the surrounding counties, where Glaswegian influence, often of a covertly prestigious nature, is considerable). Specifically Glaswegian features include some lexical items, such as *know* (pronounced /nɔ/) being used exclusively in place of mainstream Scots *ken*; some morphosyntactic features, such as *int it* instead of *is it no* for *isn't it* (although the Scots form is also heard in Glasgow); and phonological, as with <are> and <air> words like *hair* or *care* being pronounced /ɛr/ rather than more mainstream /er/ (so that, mockingly, non-Glaswegians would say that a Glaswegian had

had *a rerr terr at the ferr in Err* 'a rare tear [a very good time] at the fair in Ayr'), or the ongoing loss of /x/, not only in Scots words like *nicht* 'night', but also in place names, so that the first syllable of *Sauchiehall* has /k/ rather than the historical /x/. Some pragmatic features also express difference, such as the clause final use of *so*, as in *That wis the end o that, so*. Many, if not all, of these developments have been attributed to an Irish provenance.

But such an analysis ignores the large number of features held in common by Glasgow speakers and speakers of the surrounding dialects. Glaswegian dialect is a Scots dialect; it is not a traditional dialect, however (just as Manchester dialect betrays its origins in the dialects of southern and central Lancashire, but does not have the traditional lexical richness of its source dialects even as they stand today). It may be that the views of some scholars – and others – are based in the very human trait of accentuating differences even when they are much outweighed by similarities – rather like the ways in which users of British English notice the spellings which mark off American English from their native variety rather more than the overwhelming number of spellings which do not.

We can say, therefore, that, working from Trudgill's theoretical position, Glasgow's dialect has developed largely through the movement into the city of immigrants from relatively close by. From my own experience as a speaker of a fairly traditional West Central dialect, I can say that I am regularly taken for a Glaswegian not only in other places but also in Glasgow itself. The links are tangible. While we cannot break this influence down county by county, this dominance does partly explain the fundamental nature of the Glaswegian dialect. It does not explain everything, however. Trudgill's ideas on dialect formation appear to hold up to scrutiny to some extent, although they do not fully explain why the 'Irish' features survived in the dialect, particularly since they must have appeared highly marked to most citizens of Glasgow at the time.

With reference to the *founder principle*, this predominance of West Central features in the local dialect is unsurprising. Both native Glaswegians and also the first immigrants from the surrounding territories were the founding population for the working-class (and, indeed, middle-class) dialects in the city. By the time speakers of Irish English and of Gaelic came to the city, this variety was already largely in place. But this explanation does not tell us why and how the external features cited above managed to come into the city's dialects, no matter the ethnocultural origin of individual speakers.

Could Irish English influence in particular be seen as representing something like a *swamping* event, at least for some sub-varieties of Glaswegian Scots? Both Catholic and Protestant Irish in-migration was common from the middle of the nineteenth century on (although in different parts of the city, generally; often neighbourhoods became dominated by the new arrivals). In their communities these new inhabitants may have been present in sufficient numbers to affect the development of the local dialect. The speakers of these swamped dialects might themselves have spread these innovative features into the language use of other dialects (where speakers of the Irish English dialects may also have been present, albeit in smaller numbers) by means of the products of dense social networks being spread from one working-class community to another through the medium of loose social network ties. We could argue that this spread represented a marker – covert and possibly overt – of a new Glaswegian identity which would eventually affect all speakers. It is salutary, however, to note that we have little or no documentary evidence for such a development actually taking place in what was one of the most 'modern' cities on earth some 150 years ago.

2.4.2.2 Milton Keynes and 'Estuary English'

Similar (although lesser) processes are at work in the formation of a range of dialects spoken around the world. In the most straightforward sense, new varieties appear to have been initiated and developed through new settlement. In England, for instance, the 'new city' of Milton Keynes came into being from the mid- to late 1960s on in a region of the southernmost south Midlands of that country. The site had not previously been heavily settled. Most, but not all, of the settlers came from London and its extended suburban regions; a fair social mix of lower middle- and working-class people formed its core. Some people from the Milton Keynes area also took part in the settlement. As Kerswill and Williams (2000) have demonstrated, the distinctive Milton Keynes variety which has come into being over the last few decades is, predictably, largely a South-Eastern variety with little trace of the original dialects of the region. What is striking, however, is that the new variety, while resembling the source varieties, middle- *and* working-class, brought into the region at the time, is not identical to *any* of them. It could be argued that the convergent variety created is in some ways a marker of a new Milton Keynes identity, although the process by which such identity symbols come into being, whether the usage pre-dated the identity connection, is difficult to plot. In a sense, therefore, Trudgill's ideas on dialect formation appear vindicated. That identity might have constituted a part of this formation at the very least problematises Trudgill's position, however. The founder principle (and swamping) work here, but only partly.

A similar, but rather more nebulous, series of developments appears to have brought into being the variety often termed 'Estuary English' (see Przedlacka 2002 for a discussion of the phenomenon). Analysed by some scholars as the successor to Received Pronunciation as the prestige variety of the English of England, 'Estuary English' has proved difficult to pin down, in particular in relation to what sound sets are associated with it and, perhaps, most strikingly, with reference to the new urban varieties coming into being in inner city and ethnic enclave forms of English in London (see, for instance, Cheshire et al. 2011). What can be said, however, is that something a little like 'classless Cockney' does seem evidenced in the speech of many people from southeastern England, including politicians such as John Major, the former British Prime Minister, and celebrities like Mick Jagger. While difficult to tie down, the variety is striking in its convergence of Received Pronunciation and Cockney vowels while at the same time maintaining the 'correct' use of /h/ and /θ/. What is particularly interesting about these developments is that they are also related to teaching practice and external models of acceptability. It could be claimed that a spur to the development of Estuary English was the desire for 'classlessness' which flowed through cultural life in London in the 1960s, along with a delight in 'slumming it' during the same period among the younger products of 'the Establishment'.

2.4.3 Written new dialect formation: Scottish Standard English

Is it possible to take this discussion beyond the nature of language varieties dominated by the spoken form and include the formation of new written dialects? In order to judge this, we will consider Scottish Standard English, a variety which came into being in the late eighteenth and early nineteenth centuries.

In Scotland, the standardisation process was of a more complicated type than was the case in England. By the mid-1500s, the native Germanic vernacular, Scots, was moving towards endonormic standardisation, becoming the primary language of administration and authority in the country. But even before the Union of the Crowns in 1603, Scots was being gradually displaced by Standard English in all written spheres. In the seventeenth century, this changeover to an exonormic standard became ever more noticeable. Even before the Union of the Parliaments of 1707, written Scots had become something of a rarity, in particular in writing intended for a public audience. Indeed, in this standardisation, as Devitt (1989) and Meurman-Solin (1993 and elsewhere) have shown, the close relationship between the two varieties meant that a piece-by-piece move from Scots to English was possible, rather than a sudden imposition of an external standard. Nevertheless, Scots remained the spoken norm for all but the highest nobility of non-Gaelic Scotland well into the eighteenth century. That should be the end of the story of Scots, but the opposite is the case.

Scottish Standard English is full of words and constructions which are not to be found in any other variety of English. Some of these are culturally specific, such as *Hogmanay*, the Scottish New Year festival; others are not, such as *ashett*, a large (serving) plate. Often Scottish people use these words and phrases without recognising them as Scots. On the other hand, there are a number of occasions where people are very aware that a specifically Scottish usage is being employed, such as *kenspeckle* 'well known' or *dreich* 'dreary, drab, endlessly and crushingly repeated'. People may use these Scotticisms without actually speaking Scots on any occasion. Moreover, there are some Scotticisms, such as *outwith* 'outside of, beyond' and *furth of* 'beyond, outside of', which are not Scots *per se*, instead being used only in Scottish Standard English contexts. Simplifying somewhat, Aitken (1992) suggested that within Scottish Standard English there are two types of Scotticism: *covert*, when speakers do not know that the word or phrase they are using is Scots rather than English, and *overt*, where the Scottishness of the word or phrase is the very point of using it; specific emotional responses in the listener related to group identity are being triggered. Dossena (2005; see in particular pp. 24–6) provides a more detailed, but not of itself inherently different, taxonomy of the process (Jones 1993 and 1995 provide information on and discussion of the 'Anglicisation' of pronunciation during the period).

It is, of course, not unusual for elements of dialect vocabulary to be used in otherwise standard speech, whether consciously or unconsciously. This goes much further, however. Scottish Standard English is a separate entity: one that would not exist without its non-English material. The only variety which comes anywhere near this level of divergence is Irish Standard English, where a considerable number of Irish words in particular can be heard, as well as read, along with some grammatical features, such as the *after* 'anterior tense' marker. Yet unconscious though their use often is, lexical Hibernicisms in Irish Standard English are almost all culture-specific. This is not the case with its Scottish equivalent.

This survival – indeed, successful deployment – of Scotticisms in modern Scottish Standard English is particularly surprising, given that, as has been well covered by a number of scholars, most notably Dossena (2005), there was a powerful campaign in Scotland in the mid-1700s to extirpate Scotticisms from writing and speech, which attracted a great deal of attention from the (upper) middle classes. In general, published language attitudes of this period tend to be negative towards Scots, as the following examples demonstrate:

> The people of north Britain seem, in general, to be almost at as great a loss for proper accent and just pronunciation as foreigners. And it would be surprising to find them writing English in the same manner, and some of them to as great perfection as any native of England, and yet pronouncing after a different, and for the most part unintelligible manner, did we not know, that they never had any proper guide or direction for that purpose. (Buchanan 1757; cited in Jones 1997a: 269)

> The language spoken in this parish is the broad Buchan dialect of the English, with many Scots idioms, and stands much in need of reformation, which it is to be hoped will soon happen, from the frequent resort of polite people to the town in the summer. (Peterhead, Aberdeenshire, Original Statistical Account, 1790s; Sinclair 1978: XV, 417)

Given that most of the people making these statements are opinion-makers at a local or national level (Millar 2003), it is surprising that there are any Scottish features at all in their apparent creation, Scottish Standard English. Why is this not the case?

In the first instance, the survival of the Scottish church settlement and, more importantly, Scots Law, after the Union of 1707, meant that at least some Scots vocabulary – *propone, procurator fiscal, kirk session* – continued (and continues) to be used by people whose social background was (and is) divorced from Scots. Moreover, many Scots speakers would have continued to use Scots turns of phrase (such as *sore head* for *sair heid* 'headache') – often Anglicised phonologically – because they considered them English or did not know any other way of saying something. Many people from this background – a literate lower middle class – would have had less contact with the purist anti-Scotticism mobilisation of the upper middle classes of Edinburgh in particular, although they were obviously exposed to Standard English through their reading.

Thirdly, at the time when many lower middle-class people (themselves a relatively new mass social grouping) were passing from Scots to English in considerable numbers, probably in the early nineteenth century, there would have been insufficient models available derived directly from the Standard English of England, unlike what was the case, perhaps, for the upper middle classes of the preceding generations. Inevitably, Scots features entered the Standard English of many elements within this group, whose life and work had linguistic effects upon those with whom they had contact – schoolteachers in particular but also religious ministers – and were then replicated by those they influenced. Probably in relation to this, the large-scale population movements away from points of linguistic origin, necessitated by the agricultural and industrial revolutions, made the newly fully literate working class more open to acceptance and replication of varieties other than their own.

Finally, and most importantly, the vernacular revival of the eighteenth century, itself riding the wave of forms of nationalism (or at least particularism), gained force. Largely associated with poetry, it also connected itself to the idea – later to be played up in the saccharine *kailyard* literature of the late nineteenth century – of Scots being the language of the heart and of honesty. We can see this shift in the ways that pro-English views, prevalent in the 1790s (Millar 2003), were largely replaced by a regret for the passing of the 'old ways' by the 1830s (Millar 2004). Of course, it was (and is) possible to love literature in Scots (and its language) but dislike the same language in its non-literary setting, a phenomenon which McClure (1985: 2) has termed the *Pinkerton syndrome*. Nevertheless, most people exposed to the literature will have some positive views about the spoken variety; the nature of much literary output and the way in which it was associated with the written word meant that the words employed often had prestige to users, as we see in the following comment, made by an English admirer of Scots (Häcker 2006):

> Dunbar and Dunkeld, Douglas in *Virgilian* strains, and later poets, Ramsay, Ferguson, and Burns, awake from your graves, you have already immortalised the Scotch dialect in raptured melody! Lend me your golden target and well pointed spear, that I may victoriously pursue to the extremity of south Britain, reproachful Ignorance and Scorn still lurking there: let impartial Candor seize the usurped throne. (Adams 1799; cited in Dossena 2005: 87)

All of this is well known and uncontroversial. But the standard explanation consists largely of the description of factors, rather than of an analysis of how these factors interacted with each other. It also generally concentrates upon the written nature of Scottish Standard English. In the following narrative its spoken nature is given emphasis, however, in an attempt to gain new insight into the process.

2.4.3.1 Contact, identity and the standard

From at least the late seventeenth century on, almost all literate people in non-Gaelic Scotland could write a form of Standard English – which could be termed *Scottish Written English* – although they continued to speak Scots. Naturally there would have been occasions when Scots features would 'bubble up' in the written mix, but, as time went on, this would have become increasingly uncommon, particularly given the move towards 'linguistic appropriateness' in print in the middle of the eighteenth century. Since part of the same process was the 'amelioration' of Scottish middle-class speech, Scottish Written English would undoubtedly have had considerable influence upon spoken norms. From a very early period, a situation might be envisaged where literate Scots speakers were able to produce a – probably rather stilted – form of spoken Standard English in formal contexts. Even during this most Anglicised period, there would have been some Scots words in use in written English in Scotland – primarily those associated with the language of the Law and the Church, where often there was no equivalent English form and where 'guild loyalty' would encourage the perpetuation of words and phrases even when they were no longer necessary.

Somewhat later in the century, the vernacular revival took hold and Scottish national symbols – including its languages – began to be aired regularly in print and elsewhere – both in poetry and in the dialogue of novels. Given the fame of Burns and Scott, it would be very unlikely that many literate Scots had not read and understood literary Scots. Many of the overt Scotticisms would have come into Scottish Standard English through this process, as prized symbols of difference and solidarity (and, on occasion, a jocular expression of identity). But the covert Scotticisms in Scottish Standard English probably derive from a different source.

In the late eighteenth and early nineteenth centuries, the expanding urban lower middle classes began to abandon their native Scots in favour of English; nevertheless, those who made this leap originally would have been, in the first place, surrounded by Scots speakers, both among the older members of their family and also, if they worked in commerce, among the people with whom they traded. Scots words, which might have been much more obviously so in other contexts, would have been far less noteworthy. Therefore, their Standard English would have been full of covert Scotticisms – constructions which most Scots today think of as Standard English – until they meet someone not from Scotland.

There are a number of ways in which dialect formation theory can be employed to elucidate this set of contacts. It is helpful, for instance, to consider founder effect. It could be argued that two basic effects are at work here, both directed towards Standard English. One founder source is limited in its acceptance of Scottish linguistic material, while the other carries a considerable amount of unconscious Scottish lexis and constructions. The final result of the standardisation process is caused by mixing, levelling and unmarking processes (to use Trudgill's 2004 terms) between the two; the *interdialect* which develops is, particularly in the written form, skewed towards mainstream Standard English.

We might also want to follow Schneider (2007) and consider Scottish Standard English as a post-colonial English (something he would not himself do). In his description, Schneider envisages a time when colonial settlers begin to move towards indigenous forms as a marker of their new identities – a process he terms 'nativisation'. Scotland has not had an exogenous settler class since the high Middle Ages, so the settlers must, on this occasion, be seen as those who, for whatever personal or professional reason, chose to take on the Standard English of England as their norm and goal. The indigenous grouping could be analysed as continuing native Scots speakers. Scottish Standard English came about, therefore, when the English-speaking elite move towards the indigenous variety became manifest, at around the same time that members of the indigenous group moved towards Standard English. As a result, a new, heavily Scottish, English came into being. It should be noted, of course, that, unlike almost all of Schneider's examples, English and Scots are close relatives and the jump from one to the other is relatively straightforward.

A schematisation of these developments can be found in Figure 2.1.

2.4.4 Conclusion

We can see, therefore, that many of the features postulated in the theoretical positions discussed above do appear to hold true to a considerable extent. But it is very difficult in urban contexts to break down how the social, economic, cultural and historical origins of the speakers of the varieties which formed the new dialect interacted in order to create this dialect. Which group (or, indeed, groups), for instance, had the upper hand in the formation? To some extent this is mirrored in discussing the formation of (at least to begin with) purely written varieties. The variants involved – and the ways in which contemporaries interpreted them – are rarely clear and may not even be recoverable. With varieties formed in places with low populations with considerable dispersal, the main issues relate to the extent to which focusing has taken place. The models discussed in this chapter do apply to a degree, but can only be applied with great caution.

NEW DIALECT FORMATION AND NEAR-DIALECT CONTACT

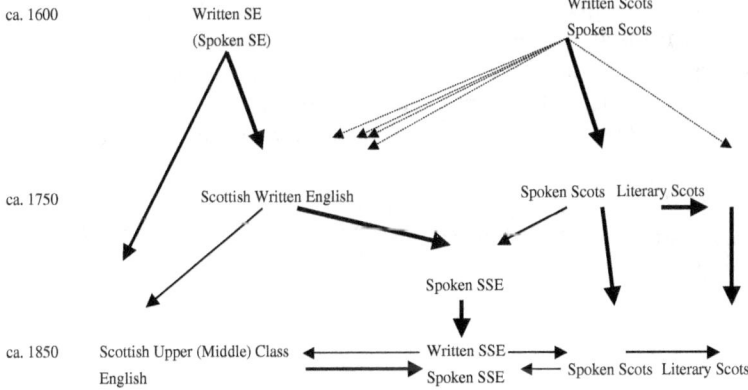

Fig. 2.1 The development of Scottish Standard English. *SE* = (English) Standard English; *SSE* = Scottish Standard English. The thinner the line, the less the influence felt. Broken lines demonstrate particularly weak influence.

The formation of new varieties of a language does appear to follow set patterns, based in particular upon the original inputs derived from the linguistic backgrounds of early settlers. A number of scholars – most notably Trudgill – are convinced that it would be possible to predict the outcome of this mix from the proportion of different origins in the initial settlement. Others are unconvinced by this argument, in particular in relation to a 'mindless' application of proportions, without reference to personal and group identities and the shifting linguistic attitudes found in all societies. Nevertheless, analyses of this type are useful in making us think about both origins and evolutionary change.

Equally useful, but also suspect, are the concepts of *founder effect* and *swamping*. The primary issue with these explanations is that they are very effective in some contexts, but do not seem to have much effect elsewhere (as Trudgill (2004: 164) says, the former 'works unless it doesn't'). The fact that the two apparently antagonistic views are actually sometimes similar and may well work together under certain circumstances needs to be borne in mind. Whatever their full applicability, both are useful metaphors for how some parts of a population can affect the development of a new variety even when they are not in the majority.

In the next chapter we will consider the history and development of two less well-covered varieties – the Scots dialects of Orkney and Shetland. Study of these varieties will lead us to a deeper understanding of how contact between dialects of the same language and contact between closely related but discrete languages interact with each other across considerable time periods – a major theme of this book. We will also consider the development of the Scots and English varieties of Ireland. On both occasions, greater time depth in the formation of new varieties will be considered than has been the case in this chapter. To what extent does this time depth add to our understanding of the theoretical models introduced and analysed in what we have covered before?

3 New dialect formation and time depth

3.1 Introduction: time depth

Most discussions of new dialect formation are confined to cases with evidence of primary foundation from the last two to three centuries. The decision taken by many scholars to restrict analysis to relatively recent phenomena of this type has often been reached on sound methodological grounds. Evidence from comparatively recent times is likely to be available in ways which are much more trustworthy and provide greater depth in contrastive information than those varieties whose development has involved considerably more time. Methodologies of this sort do have one significant weakness, however. They ignore the development of varieties whose historical depth is considerable, but which we can claim went through something like new dialect formation at a relatively distant point (or points) in the past.[1]

In this chapter, therefore, we will concern ourselves with two rather different examples of new dialect (or dialects) development with considerable time depth: the origins and growth of the Scots dialects of Orkney and Shetland and of the English (and Scots) dialects of Ireland. The narratives involved are more complex than those associated with later events or processes of this type: the time depth is greater; the evidence is more open to interpretation; the history of a given region and its population may be more susceptible to ideological pressures, past and present. Nevertheless, the risks involved are worth taking. These contact situations are particularly interesting because they are concerned with contact with another language (rather than solely with other dialects), thus bringing our thoughts to bear on some of the themes of later sections of this book. Especially noteworthy, perhaps, is the contact between the near relatives Scots and Norn in the Northern Isles and its effects upon the development of the Scots dialects of those islands. In apparent contrast, the contact between Scots and English in Ireland focuses our attention on what happens when the speakers of closely related varieties, which are on the edge of comprehension, find themselves in a region of new settlement where relations with the indigenous majority are problematical on linguistic and cultural grounds.

3.2 The origins of Shetland and Orkney Scots

3.2.1 The geography and history of Shetland and Orkney

The Shetland Isles lie some 150 km north of the Scottish mainland and around double that away from the Faroe Islands and Norway. The climate is typical of the North Atlantic. Sub-zero temperatures are not unknown in the winter, but generally the islands are subject to relatively mild, damp and windy weather. The omnipresent wind, along with the large sheep population, means that there is practically no native woodland. The archipelago consists of the Mainland and some hundred or so other islands (Map 3.1), of which fewer than fifteen are permanently occupied. There are presently around 22,000 inhabitants (not including seasonal oil workers), some 8,000 of whom live in the only sizeable town, Lerwick. Ferries from Aberdeen (via Orkney) and (in the summer, at least until very recently) Bergen and Torshavn dock at that port.

The Shetland Mainland physically dominates the rest of the archipelago. Even the larger islands, such as Yell or Unst, are small in comparison. The Mainland is made up of a series of relatively elevated plateaux, cut into by *voes*, long sea lochs. Some of the islands – Foula and Fair Isle in particular, but also to a lesser extent Whalsay and Out Skerries – are situated at a considerable distance from the other islands and, until the advent of modern transport, could be cut off for weeks at a time. Until recently, communication was easier by sea than by road, even between different communities on the Mainland. It should be noted, moreover, that local notions of place and identity, as well as quirks of history, may make the speech of places which are readily accessible to each other highly distinctive.

The islands are not particularly fertile. This means that, coupled with the proximity to the sea which almost all Shetland settlements have, the way of life for most inhabitants, well into living memory, was a combination of subsistence farming and fishing. The rather cold water surrounding the islands was historically rich in fish; for centuries, harvesting this bounty involved seasonal visits by fishing fleets from elsewhere around the North Sea and even the countries around the Baltic Sea.

The combination of these features has contributed greatly to considerable dialectal variation across a relatively insignificant space. But the

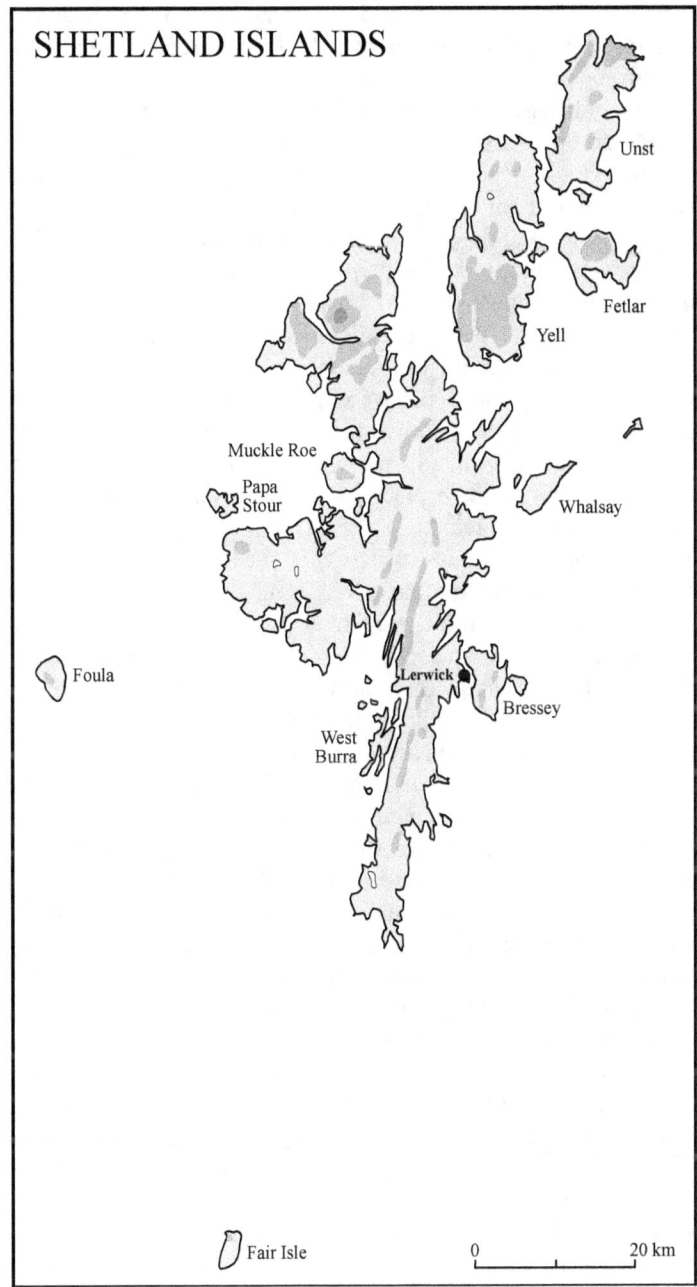

Map 3.1 Shetland.

geographical distance from other Scots-speaking areas has encouraged an overriding similarity between the Shetland varieties which is combined with separation from external varieties.[2]

The first language spoken in Shetland for which we have much evidence is Norn, brought by Scandinavian settlers from around the seventh century on. This language, as Barnes (1998) points out, formed part of a West Norse dialect continuum which stretched from Norway through Shetland, Orkney, Caithness (and probably the Scottish Western Isles), the Faeroes, Iceland and Greenland. Shetland, although not always administratively connected to Orkney in the Middle Ages, followed the southern archipelago in gradual movement towards Scottish trading and eventually governmental hegemony during the period. Indeed, by the time that both island chains were mortgaged to the Scottish crown by the King of Denmark–Norway in 1468–9, considerable Scottish cultural influence was already present (although the official transfer of the islands did not take place until the seventeenth century, the Scottish authorities treated the islands as an integral part of the Scottish state from 1468–9); Orkney in particular had become quite heavily Scotticised even before the handover, from the ruling family down. In the following centuries, considerable numbers of Scottish settlers also moved to both archipelagos, from a range of locales in Lowland Scotland, no doubt bringing their native Scots dialects with them. More discussion of their origins will be given in 3.2.3. Some, at least, of the settlers would also have been literate in Standard English.

Throughout the Early Modern period, Shetland was a centre of the international whaling and fishing industries, with particular connections to Holland. It was this boom period which stimulated the foundation of Lerwick by the excellent natural harbour of Bressay Sound. But the near tax-exempt economy of the islands was ended in the early eighteenth century by tighter controls from the British state (particularly over the excise on salt), leading to a steady but never complete decline of the trade.

During this same period, native rights of inheritance and land tenure under a common *Udal Law* were in retreat in the face of Scots Law. Many people who had been landholders – *Udallers* – became tenants of often absentee landlords. The *improvement* movement of the eighteenth and early nineteenth centuries also led to the curtailment of the previous peasant lifestyle of the majority of Shetlanders, with preference being given to new 'scientific' crofting and fishing methods. Marginal farming was replaced by the rearing of sheep. In fact, nineteenth-century Shetland saw a series of enforced population movements as traumatic as, but less well known than, the Scottish Highland Clearances of the same era.

The new opportunities presented in Lerwick and the increasing incorporation of the islands within the British governmental orbit led to continuing immigration from Scotland in particular. This immigration never came near to equalling the emigration caused by the Clearances and the general perception of the greater opportunities available in Scotland and beyond, however. During this period, Shetlanders continued to take an active part in both fishing and whaling, both in-shore and in the *haaf* (deep-sea) fisheries. In the course of the twentieth century these declined, to be replaced from the 1960s on by primary and ancillary employment related to the exploitation of the northern North Sea oilfields; large-scale immigration took place during this period. Other immigrants were attracted by the 'simpler' lifestyle they perceived in the islands. It is only since the 1950s, in fact, that the inhabitants could be described as economically 'comfortable', perhaps even affluent. But it is with the period of boom and decline from the sixteenth to mid-nineteenth centuries, and the unique dialect created then, that this discussion is particularly concerned.

Many similar points can be made about the Orkney Isles (Map 3.2), although, unlike Shetland, the southern parts of the Orkney archipelago are very close to the Scottish mainland, meaning that the sense of separation from the mainstream of Scottish life may be less than in Shetland. Physically, Orkney appears 'softer' than Shetland, primarily because the dominant geology of the southern archipelago is based upon sedimentary rather than metamorphic or igneous rock, as is the case with the northern. This geological distinction has meant that it has been possible to work only as a farmer on the good agricultural land to be found throughout Orkney, although a combination of farming and fishing was, until quite recently, the norm for many inhabitants. It should also be noted that, unlike Shetland, the western Mainland of Orkney includes a number of parishes which do not face primarily on to the sea and have developed away from the close ties most people from the Northern Isles historically had with seaborne occupations. By the same token, Orkney possesses, in Scapa Flow, lying in between the southern coast of the Mainland and the southern islands of the archipelago, one of the best natural harbours in northern Europe, strategically important since at least Viking times. As with Shetland, native woodland is very rare (although locals have had more success in recent history in importing and cultivating tree species from Scotland and beyond than have their Shetland equivalents). Situated at the northern end of an isthmus which connects Scapa Flow and the northern waters of the archipelago, the city of Kirkwall (population somewhat above 6,000 in 2011; these figures do not include some of the city's suburbs; the islands as a whole had a

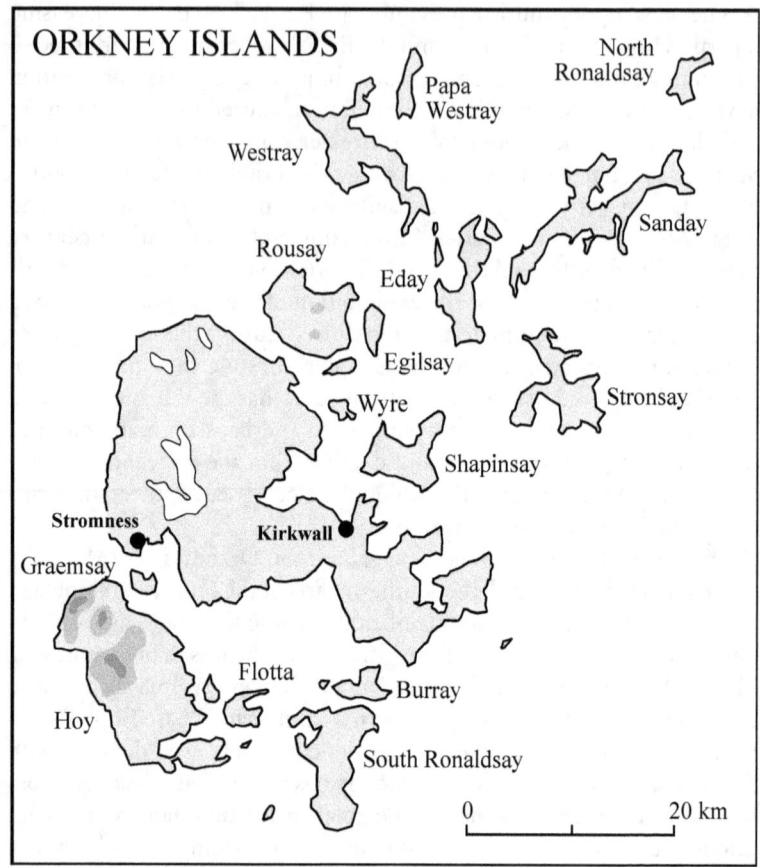

Map 3.2 Orkney.

little over 21,000 inhabitants in 2011) is the main urban settlement on the islands. It is also where ferries from Aberdeen and Shetland, as well as many of the local ferries, dock (along with cruise ships, particularly in the summer). The other urban centre is Stromness (population just above 1,600 in 2011), at the south-western end of the western Mainland. It receives ferries from Scrabster on the north coast of the Scottish mainland and some ferries from the southern islands of the archipelago. Until recently, ferries from Aberdeen and Shetland called at this port. Historically, the town was particularly connected to the whaling trade and, by extension, with the trapping trade in Canada and elsewhere. It was also often the final provisioning port for ships heading north for Arctic exploration and exploitation.

As with Shetland, the different islands are often culturally discrete from each other. Some islands – such as Hoy, Westray and Shapinsay – are particularly distinctive in relation to the Mainland, largely because of their size. Others, such as North Ronaldsay, are far enough removed from the Mainland to have developed autonomously in a variety of different ways, cultural, economic and linguistic. Until relatively recently, most inhabitants stayed close to their island or parish roots, although out-migration has been commonplace since the Early Modern period.

Orkney shares much historically with Shetland, although often differing at particular points, most of which, in the medieval and Early Modern periods, are connected with the fact that Orkney was a governmental (and ecclesiastical) centre while Shetland was not. At various times, the rulers of Orkney have had close ties to, or even ruled, both the north and west coasts of Scotland. Orkney was also connected to the Irish Sea world and beyond. Evidence points to Orkney's having a highly developed culture from at least the Neolithic period, evolving over time into the Pictish civilisations which flourished in the early Christian period, leading to the construction of the monumental *brochs*, apparently defensive fortifications, found throughout the islands. This culture was largely replaced, we believe, by Scandinavian settlement from the seventh century on, although these new arrivals may have represented an over-class rather than there being radical changes in population. Nevertheless, Scandinavian dialects eventually replaced Pictish. How long this took is impossible to say, but the lack of Pictish lexical items in what Orkney Norn we have (and, by extension, in the modern Scots dialects of the islands) is probably indicative (although see Lindqvist (2015) for an alternative analysis).

As we have seen, the Scotticisation of Orkney began well before 1469–70. When direct (or near-direct) rule was imposed under the Stewart earls in the sixteenth century, these changes grew apace. They were particularly remarkable in the period following the Scottish Reformation (which began in earnest in the 1550s, with Protestantism becoming the established form of Christianity in Scotland in the following decade), where ministers from Scotland were generally preferred throughout the islands and were undoubtedly, at least in part, agents of earl and king. This change was more marked in Orkney than in Shetland, perhaps.

Given the attractions of the islands to other settlers, it is not surprising that incomers from across Scotland came to Orkney from the Early Modern period on. The east coast of the country may have been particularly well represented (especially the north-east: there has been considerable coming and going between Orkney and that region for centuries, in particular between the agricultural communities); close ties have also been maintained with nearby Caithness, however. By the eighteenth century, therefore, it could be argued that a relatively mixed population inhabited the islands, although social distinctions probably counted for more than ethnic or cultural origin.

3.2.2 Insular dialects and the other Scots varieties: potential connections (Map 3.3)

What, then, are the central features of these insular dialects? Can we get any sense of their origins in the dialects of the Scottish mainland? To what extent are the usage patterns of the two archipelagos distinct from each other? In this section we will consider these issues. At times, each of the archipelagos will be treated separately for ease of comparison. Whenever possible, however, Orkney and Shetland usage will be discussed together.

The Shetland dialect, northernmost of the Scots dialects, is something of a conundrum. Although it is obviously a Northern variety, indeed so Northern that, for speakers of a Central dialect like me, a considerable amount of adjustment needs to be made before full comprehension of dense dialect is possible, at the same time there are elements of the dialect which do not seem Northern at all. It is not uncommon, in fact, to be faced by a feature – whether lexical, structural or phonological – which Scots speakers from the Scottish mainland would associate with more southerly locations and not with much closer mainland dialects. Thus, although the Northern form *een* 'one' is present in Shetland dialect, so also is the form *wan*, normally associated with West Central, South-Western and Ulster dialects of Scots. Is this purely due to chance, or can we see patterns of contact and influence? Are there ways in which we can explain these patterns and how they interrelate? Similar points can be made about Orcadian dialect, although, with a number of provisos, that variety probably represents a more mainstream tradition than Shetland Scots.

Evidence for the following non-exhaustive discussion of some of these apparently contradictory features has been derived from a range of sources. Lexical material has come primarily from the corpora of either the *Scottish National Dictionary* (Grant and Murison 1929–76) or the *Linguistic Atlas of Scotland* (Mather and Speitel 1985), read, wherever possible, in conjunction with local dictionaries (such as Graham 1993 and Lamb 1988) and word lists. Lexical items cited may not be found in all parts of the Northern Isles; they may no longer be used, although they certainly have been within the last hundred years. Naturally, the

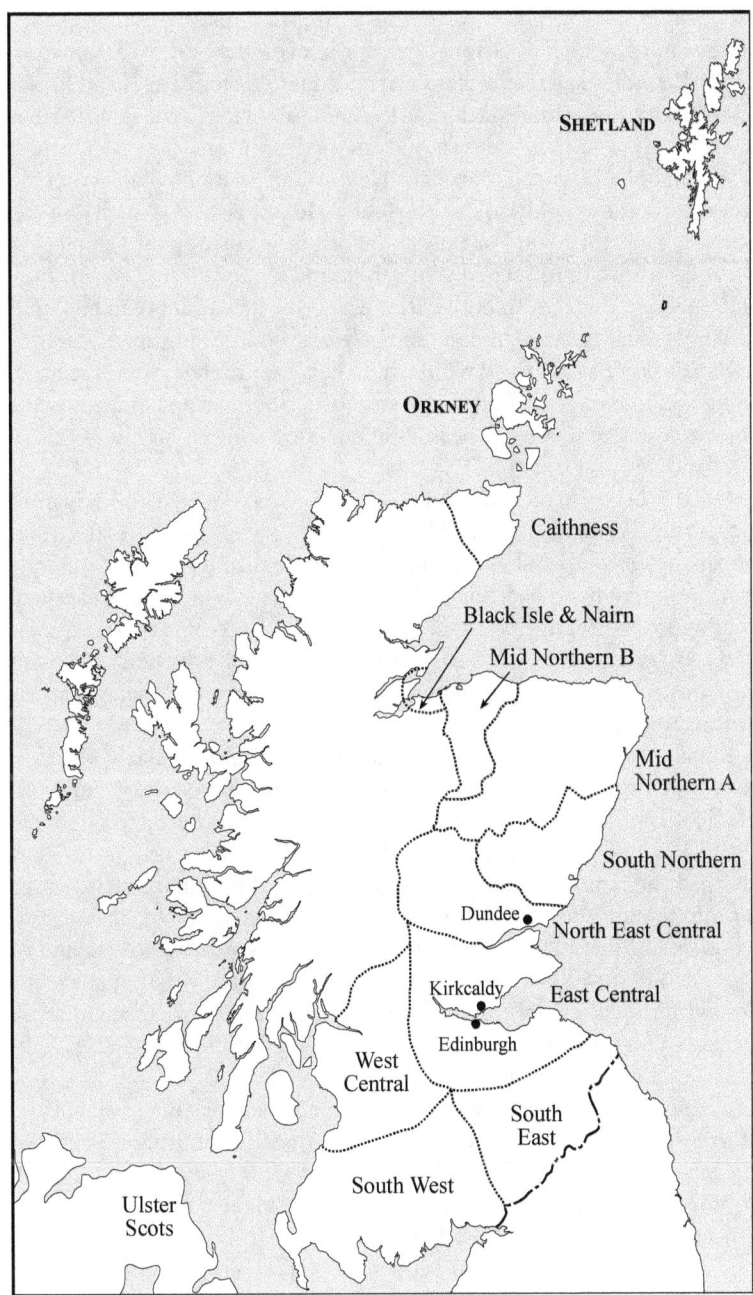

Map 3.3 Dialects of Scots.

usual caveats about 'ghost' words and misrepresentations of provenance and meaning, which occasionally occur in even the best of dictionaries, apply. Phonological material is derived from Johnston (1997) and Millar (2007); structural from Macafee (1992 and following) and, again, Millar (2007).

As might be expected, the central features of Shetland dialect include elements common only to the Northern Isles. Lexis items, such as *andoo* 'row a boat against wind or tide so that it keeps position for fishing' and *piltick* 'a coalfish in its second year', are found in records for both Orkney and Shetland dialects; in both varieties, /y/ or its variants can be found in words such as *mune* 'moon' and *scheul* 'school'. Additionally, words such as *thought* and *brought* regularly have a diphthongal pronunciation along the lines of /əu/. In terms of structure, Shetland and Orkney Scots possess a discrete second person singular or familiar pronoun (*du* in Shetland; *thoo* in Orkney).

On the other hand, Orcadian dialects do not evince the apparent merger in Shetland dialect of /θ/ and /t/ as well as /ð/ and /d/ in words such as *thing* and *brother* (although place-name evidence suggests that they may have had this feature in the past); nor is the archetypal Shetland *be*-perfective construction along the lines of *A'm dön dis wark for twinty year* 'I have done this job for twenty years' prevalent, although this construction used to be common in the southern archipelago, and is still heard occasionally.

Equally predictably, the dialects of Shetland (and regularly Orkney) have much in common with those of Caithness, the nearest county on the Scottish mainland, which also shares their Norn heritage (Thorsen 1954). Varieties of both Insular and Caithness dialects use *ill-best* 'best of a bad lot', among other lexical features; all three dialects also share *old*-diphthongisation, *cold* being /kəul/. On the other hand, the characteristic Caithnesian merger of /tʃ/ and /ʃ/ in words like *cheese*, and of /f/ and /ʍ/ in words like *faar* 'where', does not occur (with one exception with the latter) in Shetland dialect. They are not realised at all in Orkney. Voicing of voiceless plosives in final position, so archetypically Caithnesian, is unknown in either archipelago.

There are also many elements common to all (or almost all) of the Northern and Insular dialects of Scots, but not to Central or Southern dialects. In terms of lexis, words, such as *riach* 'greyish-white, drab, brindled' (strikingly, this is a borrowing from Gaelic and can therefore almost certainly be considered an importation from the Scottish mainland into the Northern Isles) and *rebig* 'rebuild', are found in varieties dotted across the region. In phonological terms, however, there are many features generally considered 'Northern' by outsiders, whose distribution, on closer inspection, is demonstrated to be rather more complex. None the less, there is a general tendency towards conservatism in relation to the application of the Scottish Vowel Length Rule and other Central Belt innovations. One feature which Shetland does not share with most of the other Northern dialects, but does with the North-East dialects, is the raising of Scots /e/ to /i/ before /n/ in words like *stane* 'stone' and *ane* 'one', a point to which we will return. Orkney dialects tend to keep closer to the mainstream Scots pronunciation on these occasions, although there is some variation in this.

In all of the dialects of the region, *this* and *that* (in their various local pronunciations) are used with plural nouns, a feature which, again, may well be of Gaelic, and therefore logically of mainland, origin. *No* is used throughout the area as negativiser, in constructions such as Shetland *A'll no dö dat* 'I won't do that', with the exception of the North-East, where it is *nae*. *No* is also normal in southern and central Scotland, however.

Up until this point, we have been largely employed in marking out a dialect continuum from Shetland into northern Scotland and beyond. This normal and predictable layout begins to be distorted, however, by the numerous concordances which exist between the dialects of the North-East of Scotland and those of the Northern Isles, but not with the intervening Northern dialects. There are many lexical items common to varieties of both dialects not found outside these regions, such as the use of the words *cair* 'mix together' (probably of Scandinavian origin and therefore likely to have been transferred from the Northern Isles to the North-East) and *eister* (of wind) 'shift towards the east'. Many of the phonological features uniting the two regions have already been covered; two might be repeated. In the first place, unlike the other Northern dialects, as we have seen, in Shetland the reflex of Scots /e/ is raised before /n/: Scots *stane* 'stone' is /stin/. Most unusually, moreover, while the archetypal North-East merger of /f/ and /ʍ/ does not happen regularly, on one occasion – *foo* 'how' – it does. Varieties of both dialects also evince palatalisation of initial velar plosives. Yet despite these similarities, Shetland Scots also shares features, as we have seen, with other Northern dialects which are not found in the North-East.

Orkney usage also appears to fit into patterns found across the north of Scotland, whether with Shetland, as with *swats*, referring to, as the *Concise Scots Dictionary* puts it, 'the liquor resulting from the steeping of oatmeal husks in the making of sowans' or without the northern archipelago, as with *stound*, referring to a bout of depression. There are also occasions when Orkney dialects and specifically North-East Scots appear to share lexis and idioms. Often this connection is shared with Shetland, as with *rag*, referring to a wet mist or drizzle, or *gebbie*, a horn spoon; regularly, it is only Orkney which appears to interact with the North-East, as with *mill-lavers*, the beams to which horses driving a threshing mill were connected, or *scrat*, the shallow first furrow made in commencing a rig in historical types of cultivation. There are also occasions where the same lexis is employed by Orkney and North and East Central Scotland, as with *scutter*, the 'doing of work awkwardly or dirtily', as well as of Orkney, the North and other non-contiguous regions of Scotland including a number, such as *ill-set*, meaning 'evilly disposed', which are found in the South-West of Scotland.

Another striking element in the make-up of Shetland dialect is the considerable number of correspondences the dialect has with the dialects of East Central Scotland – Angus, Fife and Lothian (along with, more marginally, lowland Perthshire and Kinross). These are largely lexical, including *en-wye* 'progress', *be forby oneself* 'be beside oneself, out of one's wits' and *nochtifie* 'disparage'. It may also be appropriate to note that front rounded vowels in words such as *mune* 'moon' are also found in some rural Angus dialects, although other reasons could readily be put forward for this concordance. With the exception of northern Angus, however, all of these dialects traditionally employ discrete plural forms for *this* and *that*, although, like all Central and Southern dialects, the negativiser is, as in Shetland and Orkney, *no* rather than *nae*.

In addition to this, there are also occasions where varieties of Shetland dialects, North-East Scots and the East Central dialects have elements in common. These are practically solely marked in lexis, with words such as *drockle* 'drench, soak', *pack* 'the state of being packed or crowded together, a crush, a squeeze' and *quirk* 'a riddle, catch question, arithmetical problem' providing evidence. Phonological and particularly structural features are not prominent in this connection.

Beyond these North Sea connections, Shetland dialect also shares many lexical items with other Scots dialects. These include *clamp* 'a stout, heavy shoe, clog', found, according to the *Scottish National Dictionary*, only in Shetland and Stirlingshire (in central Scotland), and *leap*, of the face, 'flush with blushing or with a skin rash', found only in Shetland and Roxburghshire (in the Scottish Borders). A striking concentration of these concordances can be found between Shetland and the dialects of West Central and South-West Scotland and with their offshoots in Ulster. Lexical overlaps include *key* 'fasten with a key, lock', *prickle* 'a prickling or stinging sensation' and, most strikingly, *wan* 'one' as an alternative to the Western and Southern dialect form *yin* or Shetland *een*.

Similar patterns can also be found with Orkney dialect. This includes *the nicht afore the morning*, referring to the day before a major event in the calendar, found in Orkney and the south of Scotland or *sookan*, a one-ply straw rope used for binding and thatching in the fields, found in Orkney, Dunbartonshire (in west central Scotland) and Bute (an island in the Firth of Clyde). Interestingly, this appears to be a Gaelic borrowing.

Does this evidence imply dialect mixture – as first exposure appears to suggest – or can other explanations be put forward? In order to gauge this, we need to consider whether the Northern Isles situation reflects the forces identified in the discussion of theories of new dialect formation found in the preceding chapters. We also need to ascertain whether analogous conditions were present in the late medieval and, in particular, Early Modern Northern Isles.

3.2.3 The nature of Insular Scots dialects reanalysed in relation to new dialect models

3.2.3.1 A null hypothesis: Insular Scots as relict dialects?

It is, of course, possible that all the features which in combination make the Insular dialects unique are the result of Orkney and Shetland being relict areas for Scots. This is at least partly the case with certain features – such as, probably, the survival of the second person singular pronouns and some lexis (often only found in other largely non-urbanised parts of Scotland). As I discussed in Millar (1999), originally widespread words and phrases have gradually retreated in use in response to innovation and urbanised koineisation in population centres. I would baulk at this as the sole explanation for the patterns involved, however. It certainly could explain why some features are shared only by Shetland, Orkney and possibly Caithness: the usages have 'retreated' into these traditional (and, in relation to Scotland as a whole, marginal) areas. But it is difficult to see how a connection between, say, Shetland and Midlothian (the county in which Edinburgh is situated) could be so interpreted, or what to make of the particular prominence which the more southerly parts of the east coast of Scotland appear to have in relation to the origin of Insular dialect lexis. Before we accept this null hypothesis, it is worth considering other sources for the present nature of the dialect: the influence of other Scots dialects and of Norn.

3.2.3.2 The Northern Isles as a Scots tabula rasa

As we saw in the last chapter, in many of the 'new dialects' surveyed in recent years, a *tabula rasa* situation existed at the time of the first settlement of speakers of the colonising language. Obviously, this is most purely the case with settlements such as the Falkland Islands (as studied by Sudbury 2001) and Tristan da Cunha (as studied by Schreier 2003), where no – or very few – humans had previously lived for any period. New Zealand (Trudgill 2004 and Gordon et al. 2004) and French-speaking Canada (Mougeon and Beniak 1994), perhaps the best-surveyed modern colonial settlements linguistically, had considerable native populations before the coming of English or French. None the less, scholars are generally agreed that the aboriginal languages had little more than token lexical influence upon the colonising language: in effect, again, a *tabula rasa*. As we will see, this is nothing like the case with the Northern Isles. It might nevertheless be worth our while considering the mainland roots of the Scots dialects of Shetland and Orkney as if it were.

What do we know about the origins of Scots-speaking settlers in the Northern Isles? The most ready answer is 'not enough'. Unlike the various colonial settlements of the nineteenth, and perhaps even eighteenth, centuries, there is little detailed documentation. The evidence is also often open to interpretation, as Donaldson (1983) demonstrates for Shetland. Nevertheless, we can make some assumptions. As we have seen, even before the Earldom of Orkney (including Shetland) was mortgaged by Denmark–Norway to Scotland in 1468–9, Scots speakers were already making their presence felt. Given that the last autonomous ruling house of Orkney was from Caithness, it would be very surprising if there had not been a considerable number of people of Caithness origin in the Earl's retinue. While some may have been Gaelic-speaking, there are likely also to have been Norn or Scots speakers (or, most likely, both). Over time, Scots speakers would have become more numerous. But increasing centralisation, particularly after the handover, would have implied that speakers of Lothian dialects – especially that of Edinburgh – were also present in the new Stewart Earl's court. Given that the centre of power was in that archipelago, it is very likely that most of these migrants would have been based in Orkney. With the Protestant Reformation, however, suitably educated ministers, who had at least been educated in one of the ancient universities, would have been expected to tend to congregations throughout Orkney and Shetland (although few of the more isolated islands of Shetland had residential ministers; indeed, some made do with a visit from a missionary or minister once or twice a year well into the nineteenth century). Many of these clerical incomers would have spoken a form of metropolitan – in other words, Edinburgh-based – Scots, no matter their place of birth.

Trade was also a primary focus for the incomers; on this occasion, in fact, Shetland may have been rather more attractive to potential migrants than Orkney, given that it was, until the end of the seventeenth century, at the heart of a major fisheries and whaling enterprise, associated in particular with the Dutch, but also with many Baltic and Scandinavian territories. Evidence suggests that, throughout this period, particular interest was taken in this business by merchants from Fife and Angus (in the East Central area) – from Dundee and Kirkcaldy especially. But while these groups certainly dominated, people from throughout Lowland Scotland and beyond were attracted by these opportunities. It is, of course, likely that the variety of East Central Scots which was most influential in relation to the natives of the islands was not the dialect of the merchant venturers themselves, but rather that of their followers, in a process similar to that suggested by Mufwene (2001) for the development of African American Vernacular English in relation to the dialects of indentured servants, as discussed in the previous chapter.

Throughout this period, however, a primary connection was maintained between Shetland, Orkney, Caithness and the other Northern Scots-speaking areas. This was particularly the case with the northeast, with many islanders settling (temporarily or permanently) in that region, and many people from the north-east coming to the archipelagos. Indeed, there is a neighbourhood in Lerwick – *Scottie toon* – whose name commemorates such a movement in the late nineteenth and early twentieth centuries. The developing fishing business in the nineteenth century – in particular the herring fishery – encouraged and extended these links. The people of Shetland in particular became involved in an annual trade which stretched from Great Yarmouth (in southern England) all the way round the Northern Isles to the northern coast of Ireland.

So, even before the present, largely oil-based immigration, Shetland and Orkney exhibited considerable diversity in terms of the origin of its settlers. Can we find any linguistic evidence for these movements?

The answer is, of course, 'yes'. There are elements of Shetland dialect which certainly appear North-Eastern – the raising of /e/ to /i/ before /n/, as in *steen*, equivalent to Central Scots *stane* 'stone' being a striking example. There is also considerable sharing of lexical usage between the two, although some of this at least seems to be directed from Shetland to the North-East, rather than the other way round. With Orkney dialect this connection does not appear to be as secure phonologically, although, as we have seen, there are undoubted connections between Orkney and the North-East lexically. But some features which are archetypically North-Eastern (although also Caithness), such as /ʍ/ becoming /f/, are not represented in the Insular dialects except for, as we have already noted, *foo* 'how' in Shetland. Other North-East features, such as negativiser *nae*, are not represented at all. Instead, Shetland and Orkney Scots is in line with the other Northern dialects in using *no* (a feature also shared with the dialects of central and southern Scotland and Ulster). This 'general Northern' connection is also favoured in lexis. It might be suggested, in fact, that the 'invisible hand' (Keller 1994) behind the development of the Shetland and Orkney dialects carried out a balancing act between marked and unmarked forms in the creation of the dialect, with North-East usages not found elsewhere in the North generally being avoided (although not wholly). Even the lack of /f/ for <wh> (with one exception) suggests the choice of an unmarked form, in the terminology employed by Trudgill (2004), with reference to all Scots dialects, with the exception of those spoken in the change's Northern heartland. I would be very surprised if a more in-depth survey of historical and contemporary lexical use (if that were possible) did not exhibit many of the reallocation strategies proposed by Trudgill and Schneider in relation to general Northern and specifically North-Eastern lexical features in Shetland in particular but also Orkney.

Given the settlement history, we might also expect traces of Angus, Fife and Lothian dialect influence to be discernible in Insular Scots. To some extent this is true. There is some lexical concordance between the areas. The retention of /y/ in the Northern Isles and rural Angus could also be taken as evidence of this connection (although there is every chance that this pronunciation was much more widespread in Scotland at the time of the first settlement; there is an alternative explanation for its retention in the islands as well). The use of variants of /ʍ/ rather than /f/ variants in Shetland and Orkney may also have been reinforced by the influence of the dialects of East Central Scotland. The evidence is distinctly muted, however. It could even be suggested that it has gradually been overlaid by Northern features from closer sources, as a 'natural' dialect continuum based on geographical proximity established itself.

An interesting, largely lexical, pattern brings together Angus (and, to a lesser extent, Fife) with both the North-East and Shetland in particular (although traces are also to be found in the Orkney dialects). While, again, fishing connections may explain elements of this pattern, it is tempting to see parts of it as rather older and therefore representing an earlier phase of colonisation.

There is also lexical evidence, of course, for connections with the Scottish Borders (and not just the fishing communities), West Central Scotland, the South-West and Ulster. While many of these are doubtless as a result of retreat and some due to the nineteenth- and twentieth-century herring fishery, they may well contain some evidence for settlement patterns also. As Knooihuizen (2009) points out for Shetland, these external influences may not have been spread across the islands in a homogenous way. Some areas may have been more influenced by the language of one group than by others. We will return to this issue in the following sections.

Interesting though it is, however, this analysis gives us only a partial and rather surface explanation for the origins of the insular varieties. Historical evidence might suggest which extra-territorial elements came first. It does not explain all the unique features of Shetland and Orkney Scots.

3.2.3.3 Norn: an alternative founder source?

The Northern Isles were not, of course, a *tabula rasa* for 'colonial' Scots – not even in the ways in which New Zealand was a *tabula rasa* for 'colonial' English. The archipelagos were inhabited by speakers of a language – Norn – which was a close (although not mutually intelligible) relative of Scots. Moreover, most modern inhabitants of the Northern Isles are at least partly descended – genetically and culturally – from these Norn speakers, again in contrast to the situation in many eighteenth- and nineteenth-century English language colonies in relation to aboriginal languages (and thus not in line with the situations proposed by Schneider, discussed in Chapter 2). What would be the effects of this contact in the colonial 'mix'? Would the numerical prevalence of speakers of Norn give it influence within the new Scots dialect which was forming?

It is commonplace to make observations of the following type in attributing Norn influence in the present make-up to the modern Scots dialects of the Northern Isles (a good example of argumentation derived from such conclusions can be found in Heddle 2010):

1. The undoubted presence of many Norse lexical borrowings, some unique to one archipelago, many shared between the Insular Scots dialects and a few with Caithness (in other words, the areas where Scots and Norse came into direct contact with each other from at least the high Middle Ages on).
2. The presence of a discrete second person singular pronoun, realised as *thoo* in Orkney and *du* in Shetland, compared to Modern Norwegian *du* and Old Norse *þu*.
3. The presence of a rounded front vowel in a set of words which includes the equivalent of English *moon*. Rounded front vowels are found in most North Germanic languages (although not all, as the

vowel system of Modern Icelandic demonstrates – Faeroese does have front rounded vowels, however) in words like Norwegian *bøker* 'books' or Danish *by* 'settlement, town'.
4. The use of /t/ and /d/ for /θ/ and /ð/ in words like *thing* and *father*, presently realised only in Shetland dialect (and there generally only initially and medially). Marwick (1929 [1995]) points out, however, a similar pronunciation was probably present in earlier Orcadian Scots varieties, demonstrated through place names and borrowings.
5. The *be* perfective construction, as in *A'm dune this job twinty year*, found in both archipelagos, but probably now considerably more common in Shetland.
6. The supposed survival of grammatical gender in the use of *he* or *she* in relation to inanimate objects, times of day, and weather or abstract concepts.
7. The Orcadian 'singing tone', generally interpreted as representing similar basic prosodic patterns to those found in many Norwegian and Swedish varieties.

The first point is very much the case: the Insular Scots dialects have a large amount of Norn words in their central vocabulary. They also, of course, share much of their lexis with other traditional Scots dialects, but that does not take away from the fact that the Shetland, Orkney and, to an extent, Caithness varieties are unique among Scots varieties in being Norse primary contact dialects. The use of /t/ and /d/ for /θ/ and /ð/ is also undoubtedly a Norn influence, although it must be recognised that the feature has now been lost in Orcadian dialect and that therefore an explanation needs to be sought for the process of replacement by more mainstream pronunciations. Less can be made of the use of *thoo* or *du*, however. While it is striking that similar forms can be found in the North Germanic languages, it is important to note that the oblique form, *thee* (or *dee*), represents the expected West Germanic form, not the North Germanic equivalent. Moreover, Scots *thoo* has been retreating northward over the last two centuries. It was found in pockets of central Scotland in the early nineteenth century; memories of its use at least can be found in Black Isle communities such as Cromarty to the north of Inverness. In that sense, therefore, Orcadian *thoo* and Shetland *du* could be argued to demonstrate the dialects' nature as a particularly traditional – perhaps even relict – Scots dialect. Of course, it is certainly possible that the presence of a Norn equivalent in the islands during the bilingual period has encouraged the form's retention.

The retention of a rounded front vowel in both Orcadian and Shetland dialect (with a few exceptions, such as that of Stronsay in

Orkney: Millar 2007: 28–9) is indeed striking in a Scots context. It is also true that most – although not all – North Germanic varieties have just such vowels, normally in a pair of different heights. There are, however, a number of issues with seeing their presence as a straightforward carry-over from Norn. Firstly, and most importantly, the Insular Scots rounded front vowels are not found in the positions where such a pronunciation is realised in, say, Norwegian *ny*, which is *new* in both archipelagos. This is not just a matter of a few words which do not behave as might be expected; it is systemic. With a small number of exceptions, which can be explained internally, the words which have a rounded front vowel in Orkney and Shetland dialects do not have one in North Germanic. Thus Orcadian *mune* /myn/ 'moon' is equivalent to Norwegian *måne* /moːnə/. Moreover, Marwick (1929 [1995]: 32–3) suggests that Old Norse /y(ː)/ (although not necessarily Old Norse /ø(ː)/) was unrounded in Orkney Norn at a date considerably before the final switchover to Scots in at least the southern archipelago. Finally, as we have seen, at least one mainland Scottish dialect – that of rural northern Angus (Millar 2007: 27–8, 131) – also has a rounded front vowel in exactly the same positions as in the dialects of the Northern Isles. Evidence suggests that in words like *mune* and *scheul* 'school', which now generally have front unrounded vowels in most Scots dialects, a front rounded vowel was normal throughout the Scots-speaking area 500 years ago. Thus it appears likely that this seemingly Norn feature is another example of the Northern Isles dialects' being more traditional in their patterns than most other Scots varieties. In a sense this proves the Insular dialects' ultra-Scottishness, rather than separateness.

The *be*-perfective construction can be compared with similar structures in the North Germanic languages (or, for that matter, in several of the West Germanic). Pavlenko (1997) took a different analytical view, seeing the construction as representing *interference* phenomena in the shift from Norn to Scots. This is an attractive explanation, although some of the evidence he employs is, at best, dubious. But it must also be recognised, as Yerastov (2010) points out, that the construction, while by no means common in present-day English, is found in a range of dialects, including that of the Lumbee people of the Appalachian mountains. Rather less attractive is the supposed survival of grammatical gender in the use of *he* or *she* with nouns ostensibly following the Norn pattern. It is not impossible that such a cross-over actually took place, although the length of time since the last native speaker of Norn spoke the language (of which more below) makes the survival of such a limited pattern rather unlikely. Moreover, it ignores what a grammatical gender pattern actually represents and what its purpose is (for a discussion of this matter, see Corbett 1991). Simplifying somewhat, it seems that grammatical gender classes normally have no intrinsic connection to natural sex. This is particularly the case with the Indo-European languages. In those languages which have grammatical gender, each class could instead be interpreted as a means of corralling smaller-scale units at a level above that of noun class. In any event, the Northern Isles system may be an extension of the common habit among some speakers of English of attributing (normally female) sex to inanimate objects like cars or boats (although this analysis does not explain why Orkney speakers prefer using *she*, while Shetlanders prefer *he*: see Ljosland (2013) for further discussion).

Finally, there is the Orcadian 'singing tone', arguably the most distinctive feature of Orkney speech. This pattern, where the highest 'note' is reached on the syllable *after* the main stress in the word or phrase, is certainly very striking. It also sounds similar to patterns found in eastern Norway (although not, at least now, in the South-Western dialects normally considered to be the primary sources for settlement in the Northern Isles: Jakobsen 1932: xxxi–xxxvi; see Heddle 2010 for further discussion). Van Leyden (2004), on the other hand, associated tone with the direct influence of Gaelic (which has a similar tonal pattern) upon Orkney speech. At least until recent times, it is unlikely that there has ever been a period when some Gaelic speakers did *not* live in Orkney; historically, Orkney has also had ties with the northern Scottish mainland and with the Western Isles, including periods where the Earldom exercised some authority over these regions. The contact with both Scots and Gaelic-speaking Caithness must also be borne in mind. But the idea that a sufficient number of Gaelic speakers was present in the islands to affect the prosodic structure of the local dialect would seem very unlikely, at least as a primary explanation for the phenomenon. A feature which van Leyden does not mention is the rather similar patterns to be found in the rural dialects of central Fife, in east central Scotland. None of these explanations can truly be central to the construction of an explanation for this unique feature, however (although, as we have seen, East Central Scotland probably acted as a central source for Scots-speaking immigrants to the islands). It is possible that more than one source lies behind the feature, its centrality to Orcadian language being reinforced in this way.

What can be said, therefore, is that, beyond lexical borrowing, the effects of the earlier North Germanic dialects on the modern West Germanic dialects of Orkney and Shetland seem to a considerable extent intangible, or at least unquantifiable. That does not mean, however, that the death of Norn on the islands did not encourage the development and use of features which make the local dialect different from any dialect on the Scottish mainland. It is to this death that we will now turn, taking Shetland and Orkney in succession.

The process and actual date of death for Shetland Norn is something of a vexed question. The mainstream view espoused by Barnes (1998), that the language was essentially moribund by the middle of the eighteenth century, seems most reasonable. But what happened afterwards is unexpected. One of the surprising things about Jakob Jakobsen's fieldwork on Shetland in the late nineteenth century was that a considerable number of people could remember a significant amount of Norn – not just words and phrases, but whole sentences and even some rhymes. Well into the twentieth century, fishermen from the islands continued to use an argot on board ship to avoid taboo concepts like 'pig' or 'minister'. This trade-specific usage was dependent to a large extent upon some understanding of Norn (Fenton 1968–9 and 1978; Knooihuizen 2006 and 2007). Again, this represents not just a few words but, at the very least, many phrases. In her fieldwork in the late twentieth century, Melchers (1980) found a considerable number of people who could tell her accurately which words they used were Norn and which not. A 200-year survival after 'death' at that level is worthy of comment, surely?

But how much do we actually know about what happens when two close relatives come into contact? This is something of a vexed question, as we will see in Chapters 4 and 5. Nevertheless, we can assume that the long-term and intimate social contact between Norn speakers and Scots speakers in the Northern Isles, while unlikely to have been equal, was none the less sufficiently so for large-scale bilingualism to be present, particularly perhaps for the Norn speakers. Unlike the close-contact situations already mentioned, the influence that growing literacy in Standard English (and Standard English alone) would have had on the development of the Scots dialects of the Northern Isles must also be recognised.

Although there was obviously a perceived need to move over to the dominant language in the course of the eighteenth century, largely due to political and economic changes, local identity must have been tied to the old language (note that the last major piece of Norn to be recorded from either archipelago, the *Hildina* ballad, was recited on Foula by a man, William Henry, who did not understand what he was saying, only comprehending the subject matter of the poem). As discussed by Sasse (1992), these 'final flings' of a language represent just such an identity device. Sasse identifies the survival of elements of a lost language in group-centred ideas and activities, running the gamut from ritual use to in-group jokes. He also identifies the presence of elements of the abandoned language (A) in the target language, largely derived from a combination of what Sasse terms T_A, the variety of the target language affected by the structure of A as combined in the mouths of bilinguals. I have argued elsewhere that this Norn element, kept self-consciously going in the speech community, may have had tangible effects: it acted as a 'feedback loop' reproducing elements of the old language after its death (although, as the years passed, the signal would become increasingly faint and eventually incomprehensible) (Millar 2007 and 2012). The apparently gradual but inexorable loss of Norn lexis in Shetland dialect reported by Graham (1993) may also represent this feature.

How can we evidence this transition and apparent partial survival? What can be said is that, at the beginning of the eighteenth century, a descendant of Old Norse was still spoken in parts of Shetland, as the following version of the 'Lord's Prayer' demonstrates:

> Fy vor or er i Chimeri. Halaght vara nam dit. La Konungdum din cumma. La vill din vera guerde i vrildin sindaeri chimeri. Gav vus dagh u dagloght brau. Forgive sindorwara sin vi forgiva gem ao sinda gainst wus. Lia wus ikè o vera tempa, but delivra wus fro adlu idlu. For do i ir Kongungdum, u puri, u glori, Amen.

As a matter of comparison, here is the same prayer in an Old Norse translation (this version will be discussed further in Chapter 5):

> Faþer vár es ert í himenríki, verði nafn þitt hæilagt. Til kome ríke þitt, værði vili þin sva a iarðu sem í himnum. Gef oss í dag brauð vort dagligt ok fyr gefþu oss synþer órar, sem vér fyr gefom þeim er viþ oss hafa misgert. Leiðd oss eigi í freistni, heldr leys þv oss frá öllu illu.

This late example of Norn exhibits many of the traits we would expect from a (West) North Germanic language (although these are somewhat obscured by the fact that whoever transcribed the prayer appears not to have had a knowledge at least of how the morphological structure of the language worked). This evidence includes the presence of enclitic definers, such as *i vrildin* 'in the world' and the remnants of what appear to be dative plural endings, as with *fro adlu idlu* 'from all ills'. But even more striking is the fact that a number of words – *delivra, puri, glori* – are undoubtedly of Scots or English origin, even if they have been realised with North Germanic inflectional morphology. While it would not have been impossible for Norn to have continued with a large amount of external lexis (after all, English became saturated with French lexis following the Norman Conquest and still managed to continue as a discrete language with a large number of speakers), the power relationships between different languages in the Shetland mix did imperil the autochthonous variety as the economic relationships of the islands changed.

But although Norn had probably died out by the middle of the eighteenth century in Shetland (bearing in mind the unusual Foula survival into the late eighteenth century), something unusual was to happen to the language in the next century: people remembered considerable amounts of the dead language – and not just lexis.

When he visited Shetland to carry out fieldwork in the last decades of the nineteenth century, the great Faeroese scholar Jakob Jakobsen was surprised to find that people in a range of places around the islands were able to produce not only words but also phrases in the apparently dead language. A striking example of this, recorded on Foula, is:

> *Jarta, bodena komena ro'ntəna Komba* 'My heart, the boat has come round "de Kaim"' (Nynorsk: Hjarta, båten er komen rundt om Komba)

A number of scholars (most notably Rendboe 1984 and 1987, who provided the Nynorsk transliteration) have made the claim that this verse actually represents the survival of the Norn language as a whole into at least the mid-nineteenth century. Because of other evidence, however, and the fact that the rhythm of the phrase appears to matter more than the grammatical purpose of the multiple /nə/ endings, I would suggest that, instead of survival, we have evidence here for impressive memory and transfer across a range of generations.

Something similar can be seen with the following two versions of one riddle, both recorded, interestingly, in north Yell:

Version 1:	Version 2:
Flɔkəra flūra *fedderless*,	*White fool fedderless*,
ut kɔm modərə häŋa*less*,	ut kɔm modərə hä'ŋta*less*,
häŋæ beŋæ gōra*less*o	tsa gōa bɛnder*less*
	and plucked awa white fool fedderless

> (Very rough attempt at translation: 'White bird (bird flying) without feathers; out came a handless man, who could also walk without legs, and plucked the white bird without feathers')

These verses are almost macaronic, with no one clause being entirely Scots (in italics; I here follow Jakobsen's practice) or entirely Norn, and most – not all – of the Norn lexis having immediately available cognates in Scots – *ut* 'out', Scots *oot*, being a particularly good example of this. It would be relatively straightforward for someone to carry this type of verse in her head without understanding exactly what every word meant; even so, the second version appears to demonstrate an ongoing slippage towards Scots, with words and phrases being reinterpreted to suit the new linguistic reality. Very little Norn inflectional morphology survives in either version.

With this in mind, let us consider another piece of verse transcribed by Jakobsen (on this occasion <" "> implies that the piece of vocabulary is of Scots rather than Norn origin; strangely, Jakobsen does not include *ca'* 'call' among the former set):

> De vaar e (vera) gooa tee,
> "when" sona min "guid to" Kaadanes:
> haayn kaayn ca' *russa* "mare,"
> haayn kaayn ca' *bigg* "bere"
> haayn kaayn ca' *eld* "fire"
> haayn kaayn ca' *klovandi* "taings".

> 'That was a good time, when my son went to Caithness: he can call *russa* "mare", he can call *bigg* "bere" [a form of barley], he can call *eld* "fire", he can call *klovandi* "taings" [tongs]' [my translation].

At first glance this appears to celebrate the triumph of Scots over Norn, presumably during the period when this process was taking place. But, after consideration, it becomes apparent that the change evoked is a matter of lexical substitution – the actual lives of the people affected have not changed, just the words. In modern Shetland dialect the word *skyimpin* refers to the mocking of someone for their pretentiousness, for their desire to appear different from their fellow Shetlanders. There is a considerable likelihood that this is what is happening here.

We can relate these points to William Henry and his recitation of the *Hildina* ballad in late eighteenth-century Foula to the Reverend George Low (of whom, more below). Henry was a native Scots speaker, but the language towards which he aligned himself was Norn. This cannot have been a unique association. As the examples of nineteenth-century Norn demonstrate, there can be little doubt that, at the very least, interest in the moribund language was present among many local people. This memorialisation (and memorisation) really only halted in the early twentieth century, when the Norn input had become so encumbered by almost two centuries of the 'static' of not being fully understood that it could no longer be processed by either listener or speaker. As I have suggested, evidence like this implies something like a 'feedback loop' embedded in the Scots language as it was acquired by speakers who were abandoning Norn. Underlying it must be a sense of personal and group identity.

In Orkney, Norn was last recorded (and therefore, we assume, still spoken) in the late seventeenth century. A version of the 'Lord's Prayer' also survives for these islands, published in the first instance in Wallace (1700), here as reproduced in Barnes (1998: 48). It presents a particularly effective means of ascertaining the level of contact influence and interference in Norn's last stages:

> Favor i chimrie. Helleur ir i nam thite, gilla cosdum thite cumma, veya thine mota vara gort o yurn sinna gort i chimrie, ga vus da on da dalight brow vora. Firgive vus sinna vora sin vee Firgive sindara mutha vus, lyv vus ye i tumtation, min delivera vus fro olt ilt, Amen [Or:] On sa meteth vera.

As both Marwick's (1929 [1995]: 29) and Barnes's (1998: 48–9) analyses demonstrate, there can be little doubt that, as with its Shetland equivalent, this is representative of a North Germanic, rather than West Germanic, dialect. Non-exhaustively, we could demonstrate this with practically every word: grammatical case and gender appear still to be present, as in the expression of the typically Norse enclitic definite particle, as with *yurn* 'the earth' (Modern Norwegian *jorden*) or *olt illt* 'every evil', where <t> gives inflectional marking for an unexpressed neuter noun. But there are also a number of words which, as with the example of Shetland Norn, are undoubtedly not Norn, such as *tumtation* or *delivera*, derived via Scots and Standard English. Interestingly, these words are, to a degree, abstract or at least conceptual. From such a small amount of evidence it is naturally dangerous to derive radical conclusions. But it could be suggested that, just as was the case for philosophical, theological and generally abstract Anglo-Saxon words in the Middle English period, often replaced by French or Latin equivalents, these French- and Latin-derived Scots words may regularly have been used by only a rather circumscribed (and normally literate) elite who were in the vanguard of language shift. In both cultural settings, these elites either opted for a new language or ceased to be elite. In a sense, in fact, while the idea put forward by Marwick and his contemporaries that there was a gradual, and to an extent, semi-conscious shift from Norn to Scots is not supported by the evidence (or, indeed, our knowledge of how language shift takes place), there does seem to be evidence of a gradual movement of T vocabulary into A, perhaps particularly in these heightened contexts. Whether this was conscious or semi-conscious may have depended on the speaker and the context, of course. But we can be fairly certain that, by the first decades of the eighteenth century, only older people on the outer, especially northern, islands of the archipelago and particularly in the central parishes of the Mainland would have continued to speak Norn as their everyday language.

The Reverend George Low (whose importance to our understanding of what happened to Shetland Norn through his transcription of the *Hildina* ballad is considerable) was also the Church of Scotland minister for the United Parishes of Birsay and Harray, the former on the northwest coast of the Orkney Mainland, the latter inland. In his parish contribution to the Original *Statistical Account of Scotland*, compiled in the last decade of the eighteenth century, he states that 'The ancient Norse language long prevailed in Harray, more so than any part of the country, but is now worn out: the names of places are all undoubtedly Norwegian' (Sinclair 1978: Orkney, Birsay and Harray, 21), probably providing the last explicit reference to the everyday use of Norn in Orkney; it is unfortunate that the date for these last speakers is not given, although Low's personal knowledge of the phenomenon suggests the relatively recent past.

How did the process of language shift proceed in Orkney? What were its linguistic outcomes? As we noted above, social and political change in the islands led to increasing numbers of Scots speakers coming to Orkney and, perhaps more importantly, steadily growing overt prestige for Scots (and written Standard English, underlying it). Inevitably, all of these features would have encouraged the transfer – first by the land-holding classes, then the urban middle classes, then the working people of the towns and, finally, the peasantry – from monolingualism in Norn to bilingualism in Scots and Norn to, finally, monolingualism in Scots, with literacy, where this existed, in Standard English. The more distant speakers were from the relatively cosmopolitan life of Kirkwall and Stromness, the later this cross-over would probably have taken place. Do we see evidence for this? The answer is 'yes, probably'. Most of the final examples of, or evidence for, Orkney Norn come from the landward parishes of the west Mainland, which, despite their geographical proximity to the two main trading centres, were considered culturally and technologically undeveloped (or just 'different') well into the modern era. The people of the landward west Mainland were also famous for their independence of behaviour. In 1674, for instance, the militia had to be sent in to protect tax gatherers. This group, according to *Peace's Orkney Almanac and County Directory* for 1925, considered Harray to be 'a place where devils dwelt' (Thomson 2001: 314). It is not surprising, therefore, that Norn is likely to have survived longest here.

We can therefore state that, as predicted by our interpretation of Sasse's model, the shift from Norn to Scots in Orkney was largely instigated by social pressures; Norn became associated with the past (and eventually a peasant past which many Orcadians appeared happy to jettison), while Scots – and eventually (Scottish) Standard English – came to be associated with the future. As links with Norway loosened throughout the Early Modern period, Norn inevitably became seen by many as an illiterate language of past times. Nevertheless, it must also, at some level, have been seen as a local identity symbol, possibly because of the ambivalent feelings about past and present already suggested for Shetland.

What about the 'residue knowledge' which, as we saw above, Sasse discusses at this stage? In the introduction to his *Orkney Norn*, Marwick discusses occasions where local people were able to recite Norn poetry well into the eighteenth century. How can we square this with our assumption that the language was moribund something like a generation before these records were made? Again we must assume that the passing language had strong (albeit covert) positive identity associations.

Although perhaps not as striking as that discussed above for Shetland, there is some evidence in Orkney for the survival of Norn turns of phrase and even verse into the late nineteenth century at least, albeit with considerable Scots interference. At first glance, the most striking of these is a verse Marwick took down from a William Sinclair, a fisherman from Sanday, here given in Marwick's own transliteration (Marwick 1929 [1995]: 27–8), although he also produced a slightly different version, derived from the informant more recently than his original fieldwork. From the very beginning of Marwick's analysis, however, we know that, disappointingly, Sinclair had learned the verse from a Fair Isle fisherman, thus placing it outside (albeit only just) the Orkney dialect area. Marwick does not say whether Sinclair could analyse the verse, but the fact that Marwick himself only partly understood the material *after* his learned analysis suggests that Sinclair's comprehension was at best unclear. Nevertheless he still bothered learning the verse, which suggests that it had a particular resonance for him individually and as an Orcadian. Such an activity is cognate, albeit of a lesser sort, to the feat of William Henry of Foula in Shetland, as discussed above.

An equally interesting apparent survival can be found in Marwick's dictionary proper, in the discussion of *tara got* (which he considers to be descended from Old Norse *þat er gort* 'that is done'). It is worth giving in full:

> **tara got** (tarə gɔt): an old phrase signifying 'That is done', or 'that's finished'. I have heard this phrase in two connexions:
> 1. (from Rousay). An old man, now dead, told me of a witch who used

to live in Wasbister, Rousay. One day she was down at Saviskaill doing churning for the family. She went on plunging up and down until the milk began to foam out over the mouth of the kirn. Then, giving over, she exclaimed: '*Tara got!* that's done ! Seviskeel's boat's casten awa' (i.e. lost) on the Riff o' Saequoy'. And so it was, according to the tale.

2. (from Birsay) In this case, the story tells how an old woman, who lived alone with her son, resented it very much when the son brought home a wife to join them. The young couple did not pull well, in consequence, and one day when the pair were passing along the cliffs at Venniebaa, near Coasta Head, the husband pushed his wife over. When he went home he is reported to have said to his mother (or vice versa, it is uncertain which) – '*Tara gott*, that's done'. The tale goes on to narrate how he was arrested and condemned to death for murder. While he lay in Kirkwall tollbooth, however, awaiting execution, his mother smuggled in to him a cake full of powdered glass, by which agency he escaped the ignominy of hanging.

In the introduction to his *Orkney Norn*, Marwick says that he had picked the examples up while carrying out fieldwork on separate occasions (Marwick 1929 [1995]: 29), although it might be important that Birsay, while on the Mainland, is physically not far from Rousay, perhaps suggesting a regional survival. At the end of the entry, Marwick observes that 'In both stories it is highly noteworthy that the phrase is immediately translated as soon as spoken.' No doubt there was a time when people used *tara got* although the actual meaning had begun to become opaque; this must have encouraged the use of a translation with the original phrase. Under these circumstances, it is impossible to tell whether the next stage – not knowing that there was a semantic correspondence between the Norn and Scots phrases – had been reached. The performative nature of the phrase, both in its original 'magical' use and in its position as a climax to a story, is noteworthy. Obviously, to some people (probably in the late nineteenth century, when the narrators were themselves elderly – it is unfortunate that Marwick does not say *when* he heard something, only *where*), the effort needed to remember linguistically opaque phrases (and even longer examples) was considered worthwhile. Personal or group identity is likely to underlie this. Nevertheless, both of these Orkney survivals use Scots inflectional morphology; the Norn material is primarily lexical.

In Early Modern Orkney, therefore, as with Shetland, we can postulate two contrary processes at work upon the language use of the great mass of inhabitants. The stronger was the perceived need to cross over to the more prestigious and useful Scots or (in writing and increasingly in speech) English; the lesser was the desire to preserve difference by the continued use of the communities' greatest cultural marker: their language. Norn, it could be argued, became contained in a set of domains associated with the performance of the culture, such as the recitation of ballads and the use of riddles and children's songs. As the distance between this stylised set of uses and the time of the death of the last native speakers increased, inevitably these fragments would have become more garbled. It would take a long time before they were abandoned completely, however.

On each of these occasions the fact that Scots and Norn are close relatives, with similar lexis, structure and phonology, would have facilitated the survival of many features more easily both in everyday language and in these marked domains than would varieties only distantly related, if at all, despite the lack of mutual intelligibility.

As with Shetland, a feedback loop probably developed in seventeenth- and eighteenth-century Orkney where an apparently 'dead' language, preserved to a limited extent for highly defined purposes, continued to feed into the language which had replaced it in everyday use, long after we would have expected it to, thus perpetuating certain features: in particular, lexis. Over time, of course, this loop would begin to fail, to become corrupted, so that Norn features in Orcadian (and, indeed, Shetland) Scots would be less likely to be reinforced and maintained. The documentary narrative for these phenomena seems to demonstrate that the effects of this feedback loop were stronger in Shetland than Orkney. This may well have been the case, but other reasons could be put forward for the relative abundance of Shetland evidence, not least the date when Jakobsen collected his data in comparison with the date of Marwick's research.

But although evidence of this type for both Orkney and Shetland makes some of the processes involved in the creation of Insular Scots less opaque, they are achieved primarily by our backtracking from contemporary evidence. We still cannot fully see how a new native speaker Scots variety was produced in the islands, how these new varieties combined with non-native speaker Scots to form a T_A, and what effects Norn had on both sets of developments. Evidence from Shetland appears to suggest that this is possible.

3.2.4 Historical representations of and commentary on Shetland dialect

Since varieties of Scots have existed in Shetland from at least the seventeenth century, and the modern varieties are so striking to the ear of other Scots speakers, it might be expected that we would possess a considerable number of examples of the dialect from a relatively early period. But this is not the case, sadly: what little evidence there is is open to considerable (and divergent) interpretation.

Documents produced in Shetland during the fifteenth to seventeenth centuries (Ballantyne and Smith 1994 and 1999) show, when written in Scots, no evidence of local features. The plural of *this* is always Central Scots *thir* (until English *these* becomes prevalent); there is no evidence for the merger of /t/ and /θ/, and so on. The vocabulary used is resolutely legalese, with a few references to the local, normally Norse, common law terminology of the islands. After this period, Standard English becomes practically the sole language variety used in official writing. We must therefore turn to the comments made by both locals and visitors for any primary evidence for the way people spoke at a particular time.

In 1633, the Orcadian laird Robert Menteith observed that:

> The inhabitants of the South Parish [in Dunrossness] are (for the most part) strangers from *Scotland* and *Orkney* whose Language, Habite, Manners and Dispositions are almost the same with the *Scottish*, only here they are much more sagacious and subtile, and withall false and deceitfull, proud above measure, stubborn if softly, but flexible if roughly handled, not unfitly compared by a certain Gentleman to the Thistle, which if you grip not hard, will prick you.
>
> They are generally great Drinkers, and withall Venereous and Quarrelsome, their Language is the same with the Scottish, yet all Natives can speak the *Gothick* or Norvegian Tongue: they are generally very sharp, and very docile: by reason of their Commerce with the *Hollander*, they promptly speak Low-Dutch. In this Parish are many Gentlemen, who are either Sinclairs or Stewarts, the Offspring of several Earls of *Orkney*, or *Bruces* from *Scotland*, who are (except some Kings-Land and some *Udal-Land* possessed by some of the *Udallers*) Proprietaries of all *Dunrossness*.
>
> The inhabitants of the North Parish are, very few excepted, Natives of the place, yet of the same habit, Manners and Disposition with the other, excepting that here they are very sober, less venereous and Quarrelsome, and withall richer. Here are many *Udallers*, Proprietaries of the Land manned by them, these are Men of substance: all the Inhabitants of this Parish can speak the *Gothick* – or *Norvegian* – Language, and seldom speak other among themselves, yet all of them speak the *Scots* tongue, more promptly, and more properly, than generally they do in Scotland. (Menteith 1711 [1845]: 48–9; emphasis and punctuation as in original)

Focusing on Fair Isle, Menteith mentions that '[t]he Inhabitants of this Isle, are (for the most part) from *Zetland*, whose Language, Habit, Manners and Dispositions are almost the same as with theirs' (Menteith 1711 [1845]: 52; emphasis and punctuation as in original). It is, of course, impossible to tell whether the language referred to is Norn or Scots.

Later in the century (1665), an English Naval Commander, Edward Montagu, visited Shetland in order to harass Dutch shipping. His comments in his diary are also open to interpretation:

> The principal town is Scala Vo [Scalloway], of about 100 poor houses and one pretty stone house of the King's where the Governor resides. Lerwick also in this Sound hath about 80 very poor houses, but the cottages most miserable, as bad as the dens of beasts, I believe. The people very civil and well taught, by reason of their ministers, and much commerce with foreigners in the fishing season. They be all of Scotch extraction and speak English not in a very broad dialect but such as we pleasantly understand, and also they speak the language of Norway and Jutland and Holland, with whom they converse in the fishing. (Flinn 1989: 25)

In both of these seventeenth-century discussions, therefore, the local 'English' dialect is described as being more like Standard English than was the case in mainland Scotland, a point to which we will return on a number of occasions in this section.

There is little testimony for Shetland dialect for the first three-quarters of the eighteenth century. In his description of large parts of Orkney (where he was based) and almost all of Shetland, which he visited in 1774, the Reverend George Low makes a number of comments about language use. Although most famous for his discussion and exemplification of Norn on the isle of Foula and in Coningsburgh, Low also has some interesting things to say about other language varieties used in Shetland. With reference to the people living round Lerwick, he states:

> The country folks are very smart in their bargains with the Dutch; they are now paid in money for everything, no such thing as formerly trucking one commodity for another; almost all of them speak as much Dutch, Danish, and Norwegian as serves the purpose of buying and selling, nay some of them speak these languages, especially the low Dutch, fluently. (Low 1879: 67–8)

Low is also one of the few writers in this period who attempts to give a representation of contemporary Shetland dialects, noting on Foula:

> Here the Pronunciation differs a good deal from the rest of Schetland, both in the tone and manner, and pronouncing particular words. To a man they misplace the aspirate, affixing it where it should not be, and

leaving it out where it should, *e.g.*, one of the most sagacious of the natives was teaching his son to read the Bible, and to know the numbers of the Psalms; he told the boy the Vorty'th and Zaxt Z'am, XLVI, was a Hex, a Hell, a Hu, and a Hi. (Low 1879: 104–5)

This representation, to which we will return, is absolutely unlike any Shetland dialect found now or in the recent past (although see Lindqvist 2015: 9–10) for examples of apparent /h/ loss in Norn).

Also in the late eighteenth century we find a number of comments about language use in the Original *Statistical Account of Scotland*. Most of these use a few 'typical' phrases, often representing local flora and fauna, such as 'The wild land fowls are plovers, pigeons, curlews (commonly called whaap), snipes, ... tirricks, (such is the vulgar name) ... ' (Sinclair 1978: Unst, 503), or local customs and work methods, such as 'The fishermen direct their course in sailing by observations on the land, called *meeths*' (Sinclair 1978: Unst, 505). But one comment, that for the parish of Delting on the Mainland, states that 'The language is the same as in the Continent of Scotland. The inhabitants, however, have less of a provincial brogue than many parts of North Britain' (Sinclair 1978: Delting, 424). Again, the lack of density of the dialect is emphasised.

From late July to early September 1814, Walter Scott, the celebrated poet and coming novelist, took a cruise with the Northern Lighthouse Commissioners from Edinburgh, around the Northern Isles, through the Western Isles to the Firth of Clyde, via the north coast of Ireland, ostensibly to collect material for his work in progress, the poem *The Lord of the Isles*. He spent two weeks in Shetland, Orkney and Fair Isle; he appears to have been particularly taken with Shetland, whose situation and state at the time were no doubt attractive to fashionable Romantic sentiments. In the course of 1821, Scott wrote *The Pirate*, a novel set in the seventeenth century, largely in the southernmost parts of the Mainland of Shetland. As well as using his own experience, Scott also carried out a considerable amount of research on the history and environment of the islands (Scott 1822 [2001]: 393–5).

There is no doubt that Scott had a good ear for language and, in particular, for Scottish dialect (Tulloch 1980). It is disappointing, therefore, that his Shetland characters' dialects appear to be rather nondescript Scots, particularly in comparison with the incoming Scots-speaking characters. For instance, in the following passage, Tronda Dronsdaughter, a native Shetlander, is having a conversation about a supposed prophetess with two incomers from Kincardineshire (in the South Northern dialect area), Triptolemus Yellowley and Mrs Baby, who are also her employers:

'I am glad she is gaen, the dour carline,' said Mrs Baby, 'though she has left that piece of gowd to be an everlasting shame to us.'

'Whist, mistress, for the love of heaven,' said Tronda Dronsdaughter; 'wha kens where she may be this moment—we are no sure but she may hear us, though we canna see her.'

Mistress Baby cast a startled eye around, and instantly recovering herself, for she was naturally courageous as well as violent, she said, 'I bid her aroint before, and I bid her aroint again, whether she sees me, or whether she's ower the cairn and awa.—And you, ye silly sumph,' she said to poor Yellowley, 'what do ye stand glowering there for?—You a Saint Andrews student!—You studied lair and Latin humanities, as you call them, and daunted wi' the clavers of an auld randie wife! Say your best college grace, man, and witch, or nae witch, we'll eat our dinner and defy her. And for the value of the gowden piece, it shall never be said I pouched her siller. I will gie it to some poor body—that is, I will test upon it at my death, and keep it for a purse-penny till that day comes, and that's no using it in the way of spending-siller. Say your best college grace, man, and let us eat and drink in the meantime.'

'Ye had mickle better say an *oraamus* to Saint Ronald, and fling a sixpence ower your left shouther, master,' said Tronda.

'That ye may pick it up, ye jaud,' said the implacable Mistress Baby; 'it will be long or ye win the worth of it ony other gate.—Sit down, Triptolemus, and mind na the words of a daft wife.' (Scott 1822 [2001]: 58–9; emphasis in original)

Of course, Mrs Baby in particular is a comic character, and the use of quite dense Scots was often employed by Scott and others to mark this. But the superstitious beliefs of the Shetlander would also have attracted the use of quite dense Scots in the works of writers of the early nineteenth century (Millar 2003; 2004), particularly since the character in question is of the servant class. Yet the language which Tronda employs is quite thin in comparison with her betters. Some of the forms she uses, such as *shouther* 'shoulder', would not be normal phonologically in the modern Shetland dialect. Beyond this, there is little further evidence for Shetland dialect in the novel: just a few examples of *bland*, a buttermilk drink, and discussions of *udal* law, along with other local lexical flavouring which had probably become clichéd even by this point in descriptions of the islands. To be fair to Scott, the novel is set in the seventeenth century, and he comments that 'At this time, the old Norwegian sagas were much remembered, and often rehearsed by the fishermen, who still preserved amongst themselves the ancient Norse tongue, which was the speech of their forefathers' (Scott 1822 [2001]: 17). He may therefore have lessened the density of the Scots of the Shetlanders to demonstrate this second language state. Indeed, Magnus Troil, a local gentleman of Norse descent, who, in keeping with the tendencies and proprieties of linguistic representation of the early nineteenth century, speaks largely in Standard English, uses apparently Norn idioms such as *my heart*, for 'my friend', as in,

> 'Then,' replied Magnus, 'you have no idea of your undertaking. If you think it a comfortable roadstead like this, with the house situated on the side of an inland voe, that brings the herrings up to your door, you are mistaken, my heart.' (Scott 1822 [2001]: 11)

Again, Shetland speech is seen as less 'local' and thinner than other Scots varieties.

Also in the early nineteenth century we gain a few insights into both the way Shetlanders spoke (now that no Norn was spoken in the islands, at least as a first language) and the ways in which outsiders interpreted this speech. For instance, Christopher Thomson, a young shipwright, on his first voyage to the Arctic in the Hull whaler *Dunscombe* in 1820, described a 'whiskey shop' in Lerwick thus:

> Around the glimmer, in the ingle, were seated a troop of crones, attired in coarse grey Woolsey petticoats; over their heads was thrown a dark plaid, just shewing their brown profiles; some of them were knitting; each had a short black pipe, blowing away their ''bacca' and chattering in broad Gaelic. (Flinn 1989: 77)

Of course, it is possible that Thomson *was* hearing Gaelic spoken, since Shetland's connections with the Highlands and particularly Islands of Scotland were long-standing, if not terribly deep at this point; more likely, however, he was hearing a Scots dialect of some sort, so impenetrable that he did not recognise it as a close relative of his own dialect.

Not much more informative are the comments made by Captain James Vetch, of the Royal Engineers, on his visit to Foula in 1821. He notes that 'An elderly man, looking at the great theodolite in its case, exclaimed, "It's a bonny box, but it's no in the poor o' man to take that up the Snuke' [a local rock feature]"' (Flinn 1989: 129). This is certainly Scots, albeit not terribly dense, but it could have been put into the mouth of someone from anywhere outside the *Gaidhealtachd* with the exception of the North-East. More local, perhaps, is his comment that

> probably the omission of native names to minute parts will not be regretted, as many of them can only be pronounced by a native, of which the

> *Snuke* is an instance, as it is somewhat difficult to say whether the concluding consonant should be *k*, *g*, or *d*, though I think the *k* comes considerably the nearest. (Flinn 1989: 130)

These comments are intriguing, albeit difficult to interpret. Low's descriptions of voicing (or lenition) phenomena on Foula cited above might be borne in mind here, as might our knowledge that South-West Norwegian dialects (of which Norn was probably an offshoot) participate with Danish in non-initial consonant lenition. What can be said, however, is that this feature is not present in modern Shetland dialect.

In the *New Statistical Account* of the 1830s and 1840s, most of the comments, as with the original Account, deal with a relatively circumscribed number of lexical items associated with local culture and tradition, such as

> Into the butter-milk, or 'bleddick,' is poured a quantity of boiled water, by which means the curd is separated from the serum. The former, called 'kirn,' is supped with sweet milk; the latter, called 'bland,' is used as drink, and is sometimes kept for several months, when it acquires a strong acidity. (New Statistical Account 1841: Sandsting and Aithsting, 125)

There is only one direct comment on language: 'The language is English, with the Norse accent, and many of its idioms and words' (New Statistical Account 1841: General Observations, 156). Both *English* and *Norse Accent* in these contexts are not, of course, without their own problems in interpretation.

At around the same time (1832), however, Edward Charlton, an eighteen-year-old medical student from Newcastle, makes the following comment: 'I little thought that this day would be one ever-remembered with terror in Shetland, and that da grit gale, as it has always since been termed, was then dealing such destruction among the poor Shetland fishermen' (Flinn 1989: 184). Here, the unself-conscious use of quite convincing Shetland dialect demonstrates that many of the features we associate with the dialect today were already present by the first quarter of the nineteenth century. Certainly, by the time we get to John R. Tudor's book of 1883, the lexis discussed and the examples of dialect given are nearly indistinguishable from the more Anglicised end of written Shetland dialect today, as with this verse to keep off nightmares:

> Arthur Knight,
> He rade a' night,
> Wi' open swird
> An' candle light.

> He sought da mare;
> He fan' da mare;
> He bund da mare;
> Wi' her ain hair.
> An' made da mare
> Ta swear:
> 'At she would never
> Bid a'night,
> Whar ever she heard
> O' Arthur Knight. (Tudor 1883: 161)

By this point, we are of course within a few years of Jakob Jakobsen beginning his fieldwork in Shetland.

3.2.4.1 Possible interpretations of the historical evidence

What are we to make of this evidence? The first thing which needs to be noted is that it is sparse and often confusing. Nevertheless, until we receive direct representation of the dialect essentially as it now stands after around 1830, two contrary descriptions appear relevant. In the first place, there is a view that local people speak a Scots dialect less 'broad' than that found on the Scottish mainland. The other, only encountered at the end of this history, is that the local dialect is so unlike any other 'English' dialect as to be taken for another language altogether.

In addition, we have the two fairly detailed descriptions of elements of the Scots dialect of Foula, where /h/ loss and particular voicing and lenition features, no longer present in the contemporary dialect, are commented upon. There may be reasons internal to Norn why lenition of non-initial consonants took place, but voicing of initial fricatives is most certainly not a North Germanic feature. Indeed, it could, given the history of Shetland, be a feature taken from Low German or Dutch (the 'dropping' of /h/ might also be explained by this or by the influence of southern English sailors and other visitors – although see the suggestion above that /h/ loss may have been a Norn feature). Alternatively, since North Germanic varieties do not have initial voiced fricatives (with the partial exception of a voiced approximant similar to /v/), but Scots and English do, it is possible that there was large-scale voicing by Norn speakers through hypercorrection as they abandoned one language in favour of another. In any event, we probably have an example of the language mixing postulated by Trudgill (2004) and others at the inception of new dialect formation. The fact that these features have not survived into any modern Shetland variety may well be due to their highly marked nature.

How can clarity and incomprehensibility stand side by side? The first explanation for those who heard a relatively thin form of Scots is that the observers involved either did not see, or could not understand, the level of variation in the local dialect. But while this is perfectly likely for particular commentators, it does seem unlikely for such a range of reports, over a lengthy period. The objection could also be made, most particularly with the correspondents to the *Statistical Accounts*, that the observer is reporting what he wants to hear rather than what is actually there. Such a tendency would have been particularly marked in a period when local dialects were beginning to be seen as barriers to progress by some commentators. Yet the opposing tendency, the Romantic desire for linguistic diversity – at least among the rural 'lower orders' – was also present in this period, and could well have affected some correspondents: only it did not. It may also be that the observer's paradox would come into play here particularly strongly. Given that, in Scotland as a whole, and Shetland in particular, literacy was probably more widespread than in many parts of Europe at the time, it is by no means unlikely that local people should shift as close to Standard English as they could when accommodating to the speech either of non-Scots (non-Shetlanders, even) or of those who were socially distinct from them, such as ministers and landholders. Again, however, we have to recognise that this, while not impossible, is unlikely *always* to have been the case.

We are faced, then, with a few intriguing possibilities. It may be that the relatively 'thin' Scots reported for the islands before 1800 in particular was a product of second language acquisition. Perhaps Norn-speaking Shetlanders were exposed almost equally to the various dialects (and languages) of immigrants and the Standard English of the Church. This could be interpreted as an earlier analogue to the development of Highland English in the *Gaidhealtachd* from the eighteenth century on, with the provisos that Scots had not been driven as far underground in the seventeenth century as it had in the late eighteenth; that Scots and Gaelic are distant relatives, while Norn and Scots are comparatively close relatives; and that, except on its periphery, the Highlands did not accommodate the ongoing immigration of Scots speakers which Shetland did (see, for instance, Millar 2010a).

If it is the descendants of Scots-speaking immigrants we are being told about (if we agree that we can actually keep the Scandinavian and Scottish populations separate for any length of time), then might not what is being described actually represent a supraregional koine, created through the mingling of the dialects of a range of immigrants, with accompanying *interdialect development* and *reallocation*? This koine, given the disruption for all settlers of their connection with their homes and home dialects and their connection with trade – often across language barriers, could have resulted in Standard English having a more powerful input into the new dialect's development than would otherwise have been the case.

These views are certainly attractive; they have one glaring problem, however. What I have just outlined is far from being an accurate description of Shetland dialect today. What happened? Let us consider Christopher Thompson's comments from 1820 again, where he appears to identify the local dialect as 'Gaelic'. Of course, he may just have been singularly inept linguistically, and we have to bear in mind that the people he was observing had obviously consumed a considerable amount of strong drink; it may even be that he was making the same mistake that some of my non-Scottish students make of confusing Gaelic and Scots when hearing the latter used by native Aberdonians for the first time, despite the close relationship between Scots and English. The intriguing possibility exists, however, that what he was describing was that this was not the original Scots variety of Shetland, spoken by a population largely separate from the Norn speakers (although the evidence presented certainly suggests some bilingualism), but rather the new Scots varieties of the first or second generation of monolingual speakers from originally Norn-speaking communities, influenced by the earlier Shetland Scots dialect, but incorporating features from their own linguistic heritage. In the first instance, in this uncontrolled environment, the production of a basilect such as the T_A dialect postulated above would be very plausible. There was probably a time – from the middle of the eighteenth to the beginning of the nineteenth centuries – where Norn and Scots features were in competition in Shetland Scots dialect, with Norn features, to use the terminology of the post-creole continuum discussed further in the next chapter, representing the basilectal position associated with the lowest social grouping. The 'Gaelic' Thompson heard in his visit to the 'whiskey shop' may well have been just this basilect. But this dialect is not the immediate ancestor of modern Shetland dialect either.

What we have to envisage, I think, is that a situation not unlike a post-creole continuum existed at this time of shift and transfer, with the supraregional nativised koine acting as the mesolect and the T_A, as we have suggested, as the basilect. With the death of native speaker Norn, the primary non-Scots input to the dialect, this external factor would have ceased to have strong influence upon the basilect's development (although some influence was maintained for a time through the partial, performative, use of Norn in culturally sensitive contexts dis-

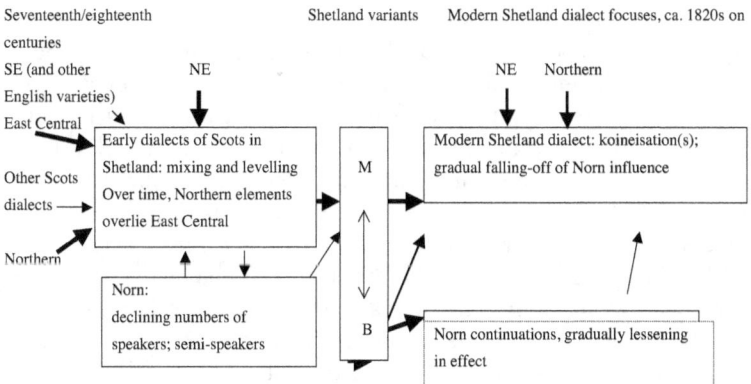

Fig. 3.1 The development of Shetland Scots. The width of the line implies strength of influence. *B* = Basilect; *M* = Mesolect; *NE* = North-East Scots dialects; *SE* = Standard English.

cussed above). As has been shown to happen with post-creole continua, the basilect would have become more mesolectal, with a new basilect being formed combining features from both the basilect and the mesolect, on this occasion fundamentally realigning the nature of this new Shetland dialect. Given the insular nature of the archipelago, we might confidently speak of slightly different examples of focusing in different areas, although a development of this type is certainly in the spirit of Trudgill's *reallocation*.

Throughout this period, the dialects of the North-East in particular and of northern Scotland in general continued to influence the form and development of the dialect. Both the new mesolect and basilect (which, given the egalitarian nature of most Shetland relationships, were, and are, not that different from each other) were influenced by the acrolect, (Scottish) Standard English, although this influence might even have encouraged merger between the two Scots varieties as a symbol of Shetland identity in the face of the 'other'. A more mainstream Scots became the present Shetland dialect because Norn was no longer available. Indeed, a number of features of Norn origin in Shetland dialect, such as the merger of /t/ and /θ/, whose preservation appears to go against the grain of marked form avoidance in new varieties, may owe their survival precisely to their association with the expression of identity.

The complex process can be illustrated as in Figure 3.1.

There are a number of factors left out of this model, primarily for ease of comprehension. The most striking (and vital) of these is the level of dialect diversity to be found in the islands. How can this reality be brought into line with the homogeneity suggested here? Two potential explanations can be put forward. The first is that an initial homogeneity in the late eighteenth and early nineteenth centuries has been replaced with great diversity over the course of the succeeding centuries. This type of change is not unknown – some scholars (such as Bailey 1997) have suggested something similar for the dialects of the American South since the American Civil War – a rather shorter period than the one discussed here. The fact that Shetland was (and to some extent remains) sundered by geography makes this explanation problematical, however. The second explanation is that at least some geographical variation was already present in the 'settler' varieties of Scots spoken in the islands and that the new combination dialects carried out essentially the same process but with slightly different 'ingredients'. It is, of course, possible that the two developmental processes worked in tandem.

Although Orkney resources are not so rich in their discussion of the historical development of the Scots dialects of that archipelago, it seems likely that similar developments would have occurred there, particularly given what we know of the survival of Norn features in the usage of local Scots speakers into at least the nineteenth century. We can therefore tentatively apply the diagram to that archipelago, with the understanding that levels of influence from individual sources would be likely to be different.

3.2.5 Observation on the historical and theoretical dimensions of the study

Of course, something a bit like 'new dialect formation' must have happened in the Northern Isles. I hope that I have been able to tease out some of the forces at work in its development. At least at present, it is not really possible to reconstruct the exact process by which the new dialect was formed in the way that other scholars have followed the creation of 'their' varieties, although certain features of Trudgill's model – particularly those to do with marking and unmarking, reallocation and focusing – are well represented. The creative interaction between continuity, innovation and contact posited by Schneider (2007) also appears well represented. Naturally, given our limited knowledge of settler origins and the depth of time involved, it is impossible to speak in a deterministic way about the development of the dialect, as Trudgill attempts to do for New Zealand English. We can, however, talk in terms of founder effect. Indeed, we can talk about founder *effects*. East Central and Northern (particularly North-Eastern) Scots dialects and Norn have *all* obviously guided the developing variety. Norn seems even to have influenced the development of the Scots variety for some time after its 'death'. Interestingly, the time depth of the dialect allows us to see one founder source – East Central dialects – gradually being displaced by other ones as the orientation of both the settlers and the locals – if they can be distinguished by this point – changed. We might also see some of these founder populations as representing only partly successful examples of *swamping* phenomena. The small population and its relative geographical dispersal may well have contributed to this rather mottled distribution and extent.

Moreover, we can postulate that the absolute native speaker death of Norn in the late eighteenth century led to a realignment of native speaker Insular Scots, with an originally non-native speaker variety being incorporated within it, thus altering profoundly the nature of the dialect.

To some extent, therefore, it is possible to push discussion of 'new' varieties of a language further back to a period where records are not as available as in later periods. Indeed, the process appears to be highly fruitful. What we have to accept, however, is an inevitable loss of focus the further back in time we look. Recognition of this point will continue and deepen in the following discussion.

3.3 New dialect formation: Irish English, Ulster Scots and Ulster English

With the possible exception of northern Scotland, Ireland can be claimed to be the first place where English was brought and diffused *after* the initial settlement and spread of the language in the fifth to eighth centuries.[3] Irish English, emphatically, is the first variety of the language to develop and be spoken beyond the island of Britain. In a number of salient ways, it is the first colonial variety of English.

Because (with the possible exception of residual communities of Norse speakers) only one language – Irish – was spoken in Ireland when the English first arrived in Ireland in the twelfth century (the 'English' themselves, of course, often being speakers of Norman French and sometimes Welsh), it is in some ways relatively straightforward to point to apparent contact phenomena which have been attributed to contact with Irish (although, naturally, the precise nature of these contacts and the extent of their influence are hotly debated issues – the discussion and bibliographies in Filppula (1999) and Hickey (2007) give a sense of these ongoing debates). Given the diversity of Irish English, geographically, socially and historically, it is legitimate to ask whether, in the first instance, it can truly be claimed that the initial English language input was relatively uniform in terms of its origin or not, were there are any specific parts of Ireland where the presumed input and 'mix' were particularly marked in comparison to others.

Naturally, an island the size of Ireland would, in a period prior to the standardisation of the English language, when both communication and travel were arduous and often hazardous, have inevitably received settlement from different parts of England, Wales and Scotland (the last including Gaelic as well as Scots speakers) in a rather patchy way, changing from place to place. The settlers would have developed different linguistic koines, compromise varieties largely based on a combination of the linguistic inputs, the exact 'mix' being determined by a variety of factors, as discussed in Chapter 2, in different locales, in concert with those who were bilingual Irish–English speakers from a native Gaelic background. Indeed, the settlement records we have do, to some extent, support the idea that people from different origins on the island of Britain moved in different proportions to different regions and, in fact, communities.

A further feature which needs to be recognised for Irish English is that, as well as a diverse range of places of origin, there is also (schematising somewhat) evidence for two settlement peaks for English language colonisation in Ireland: the high Middle Ages and also the Early Modern period. Connections between these two sets of settlements and the varieties brought across to Ireland are not entirely straightforward, particularly since there is evidence that English as an ongoing community language was not entirely successful in relation to the first colonisations. The results of this history can be found in the varieties of English recorded in Ireland over the last few hundred years; some medieval evidence also supports this.

3.3.1 Evidence for an earlier Irish English[4]

Throughout the later Middle Ages, evidence presents itself that the English language, brought in by colonists (the *Old English*, as they are termed) in the first century or so after the initial English interest in the island began in the twelfth century, was in considerable decline across large parts of Ireland. The evidence can be debated, but the fact that the Irish parliament on a number of occasions attempted to legislate that 'Englishmen' in Ireland had to speak English at all times does suggest that, at the very least, some Old English were using Irish on a day-to-day basis. The only places where this shift might not entirely have been completed were in the English Pale – the area surrounding Dublin, defended (or at least marked off) by a line of stakes – and also other areas on the east coast of the island, relatively close to Britain (see, for instance, Crowley 2005: Chapter 1).

In one of these enclaves, the Barony of Forth and Bargy, a relatively isolated coastal territory in the far south-east of Ireland, eighteenth- and nineteenth-century evidence suggests that a dialect was spoken which was strikingly different to mainstream dialects in the rest of southern Ireland. When this evidence first began to be analysed systematically in the Victorian period, much was made of the archaic nature of the dialect, with some commentators going so far as to suggest that it represented a Middle English 'fossil'. This conclusion is a little unlikely, however, at least as an intrinsic feature of the dialect as a whole. What is striking, rather, are those phenomena which are widespread in the dialect – such as the voicing of initial fricatives – practically unknown in other Irish English dialects, but formerly commonplace in the Southern and South-West Midlands dialects of England. Since these areas are where many of the Old English settlers in Ireland came from, it is not surprising that features of this type should have survived in the more discrete areas of settlement, as described by Hickey (2007: 71, 79). He notes that

> There are two possible sources for this [initial voicing]. The first being the input dialects of English from the south-west (Wakelin 1977 [1972]: 91ff) which would have had this initial voicing anyway. The second is the (small) Flemish input to this dialect where a similar voicing is found in initial position .... (Hickey 2007: 79)

But, by the same token, there is also evidence for Gaelic influence in the dialect, whether that be vocabulary or phonology – most notably, perhaps, in the sound represented by <fwh> (instead of <wh>) in some texts, probably standing for [ɸ] or [f] (Hickey 2007: 76–7), a feature still commonplace in the dialects of Ireland and northern Scotland, on both occasions places where Gaelic influence has been pervasive and long-lasting.

Other evidence for medieval Irish English and its descendants is relatively uncommon and difficult to categorise. In the Kildare poems of the fourteenth century, whose language might be analysed as a relative of the ancestors of the dialects of Forth and Bargy, there is some evidence for the Irish English nature of the language used, albeit realised in a linguistic setting which demonstrates considerable awareness of what mainstream written (late) Middle English looked like. It is debatable, but it seems likely that at least some of the features found later in the dialect of Forth and Bargy were already present in these early poems. This includes initial voicing of /f/ to /v/, attributed by Hickey (2007:

56, 59) to the influence of the English of south-western England.[5] Beyond this, as McIntosh and Samuels (1968; see also Trudgill 2008) demonstrated, this late Middle Irish English also exhibits examples of koineisation between different Middle English dialects of the Midlands of English, with compromise forms for, for example, 'each' being found in these dialects. What is striking, however, is that this medieval dialect – and its apparent modern offshoot – are not the immediate source for mainstream modern Irish English, although they are likely to have contributed to its development at some level. We could go so far as to claim that a new dialect came into being, as far as we can tell mainly a product of its sources, which was then largely swamped by varieties formed from new sources.

3.3.2 Mainstream Irish English: a brief discussion

The connections between the medieval and Early Modern dialects of Irish English are difficult to delimit accurately. Partly this is due to the lack of useful evidence we have for early varieties, except with what we conjecture to be versions of the early variety which post-date evidence for the later varieties and are very likely to have been influenced by them. There is also the cultural issue that the relationship between the Old English and the sixteenth- and seventeenth-century English-speaking colonists in Ireland was considerably soured by the continued adherence of many of the former to Catholicism, accompanied by closer connections to the Irish-speaking Catholic majority, at variance with the hegemonic Protestantism of the new incomers. Nevertheless, it would be difficult to argue that the descendant dialects of medieval Irish English did not come into contact with, and indeed influence, the later established dialects of the new migrants, possibly on some occasions acting as a conduit for Irish influence upon English, even if it is difficult to find evidence for exact routes through which this influence passed. It must be recognised, however, that, with the exception of the evidence from Forth and Bargy, the natures of the descendants of the late medieval dialects appear to have been *swamped* by new Early Modern varieties, the speakers of the latter becoming a new founder population. Indeed, Hickey (2007) emphasises the point that the vernacular elements of the dialects of the east coast of Ireland provide evidence for an historically decreasing pool of features inherited from the medieval dialects, most of which have been erased by what he terms a *supraregional* variety (or varieties) whose evolution bears comparison with similar developments in the English of England and elsewhere, therefore representing a form of swamping.[6]

Throughout any discussion of this type of influence between close relatives, however, another close-relative input needs to be recognised in relation to Irish English: Scots. This influence would become crucial in the development of non-Gaelic varieties in Ireland from the Early Modern period on, when, we can assume, greater homogenisation was present elsewhere in the island. An exception to the unfettered spread of this koine can be found in the Germanic dialects of the far north of Ireland.

3.3.3 Another angle: Ulster Scots and Ulster English[7]

As far as we can tell, there have been close ties between the northern parts of Ireland and western Scotland since earliest times. Most scholars would, for instance, see the spread of Gaelic in Scotland as the result of Irish colonisation. At other times, however, the traffic was largely in the other direction, whether that be through the active cultivation of political ties between the two countries, as seen with the invasion of Ireland in 1315–18 by Scottish forces under the command of Edward Bruce, or through the individual and group presence of Scottish mercenaries in Ireland throughout the Middle Ages. Almost all of these contacts were between speakers of Gaelic, however, at a time when mutual intelligibility between the two branches, Scottish and Irish, was probably still considerable. Indeed, in the sixteenth century, Gaelic-speaking Scots from the Inner Hebrides managed, probably as a result of the chaotic nature of Ulster at that time, to gain a foothold in the Glens of Antrim. The settlement of parts of Ulster by Scots in the seventeenth century was largely unprecedented, however, since the vast majority of settlers spoke Scots (and only Scots), mostly in the dialects of south-west and west central Scotland.[8]

The underlying reasons for the movement of considerable numbers of Scots speakers into Ulster in the seventeenth century have caused considerable debate among historians and others, often ideologically inspired in their conclusions (for a discussion of these issues, see Robinson 1984, Gillespie 1985, Bardon 1992 and Canny 2001). In brief, however, the province of Ulster was, with the exception of a few settlements along Belfast Lough and around the archi-episcopal see of Armagh, arguably the most Gaelic province of Ireland. Certainly, it was a thorn in the flesh of the English administrators of the island, largely because the best they could make of the situation under normal circumstances was to achieve indirect rule through a Gaelic nobility and gentry who naturally had their own agendas and appeared quite happy to change allegiance when it suited them. Direct intervention in the province's affairs could be nightmarish; while sending armies into northern Ulster occasionally brought about temporary pacification, there was no guarantee that this relative stability would last after troops were withdrawn. By the end of the reign of Elizabeth Tudor, other 'solutions' to the issue were being sought through the process generally termed *plantation*.

Already attempted (with variable success) in other parts of Ireland, plantation essentially involved the clearing from good farmland of the original Irish-speaking tenants (who were then expected to live in more marginal areas or, preferably, take themselves elsewhere), often accompanied by the introduction of 'improved' agricultural practices. Dependable Protestants were then settled on this land. Although generally inspired by central government, the task itself was normally taken on by *undertakers*, who received profits from the land settled in return for their organisation of the settlers and their settlement. Throughout western Ulster, plantations of this type were attempted, in particular in the more fertile territories. In eastern Ulster, however, despite the later demographic dominance of Protestants, no plantation in the traditional sense of the word was carried out. In effect, however, 'free enterprise' plantation took place. Individual landholders in Lowland Scotland regularly straddled the North Channel and brought across those who were connected to them in some way or another; occasionally, this could be on quite a local level, with the holdings involved being much smaller than equivalent holdings taken on by official undertakers in the west of the province. Very occasionally, individual Scottish people came across on 'spec', although they normally had to fit in to the power structures in the part of Ulster in which they found themselves.

In this initial Early Modern plantation of Ulster, the majority of those who moved to the 'official' plantations in western and southern parts of the province came from England (in particular, although not entirely, from the north Midlands of that country). In eastern Ulster, however, Scottish descent was normal – in particular from the counties of the western Lowlands and the south-west (although some settlers came from the Borders counties as well). Almost wholly Scottish were large parts of County Antrim and northern County Down. Eastern County Derry was, and remains, Scots-speaking, as does a section of County Donegal to the south-west of Derry City, the Laggan. It is possible that Scots speakers were at one point settled more widely across these counties (in particular in the east), but that their distinctive dialects were gradually overcome by the English varieties later (or simultaneously) lodged there. By the same token, these English varieties have themselves been influenced by Ulster Scots.

It is interesting to pause for a moment to consider what this type of close-relative contact represents. On the island of Britain, the dominant English sources for the Ulster English and the Scottish sources for the Ulster Scots dialect were situated at least 200 kilometres apart, separated by a considerable number of dialect isogloss bundles. The 'marked' source varieties demonstrate this difference, a difference which could be interpreted as representing – in linguistic terms – the distinction between two languages. In Ireland, however, speakers whose dialects had rarely, if ever, come into contact with each other before, found themselves side by side, in a sense in a relationship not dissimilar to other 'normal' neighbouring dialects, with the proviso that the leap from one to the other was far greater than would normally have been the case in that situation. The situation in which they found themselves, as a settler community at odds politically and philosophically from the majority, would probably have encouraged the establishment of common ground between originally disparate groups. What has happened linguistically since that initial contact tells us a great deal about the nature of the creation of 'engineered' dialect boundaries as well as, perhaps, what happens when close relatives, not directly descended from the same recent ancestor, meet in a zone of settlement. They therefore refer to issues to which we will return in the next chapter as well as here.

It could be argued that Ulster Scots maintained its distinctiveness through a combination of features. In the first instance, while not all Ulster Scots speakers are of Scottish Presbyterian background, many are; the distinction between their traditions and those associated with the state-sponsored Episcopalianism of the Church of Ireland was marked and bitter, even if both traditions were equally opposed to Catholicism. Considerable enmity existed between the two religious affiliations in the seventeenth and eighteenth centuries; this inevitably meant that cultural and linguistic frontiers were less porous than they might otherwise have been (notwithstanding the Protestant solidarity mentioned above). Moreover, northern County Antrim and eastern County Derry in particular are geographically distinct from the territory of their southern and western neighbours, especially in relation to the Mid Ulster English dialects to the south and west of Lough Neagh.

Having said this, there were also reasons why Scots influence should permeate well beyond the Scottish settlement zone: in particular, perhaps into the western Ulster counties. In the first instance, it needs to be recognised that there was a strong secondary diffusion of Scots speakers into these regions in the course of the seventeenth and eighteenth centuries (and, indeed, beyond). Because Mid Ulster appears to have maintained Irish much longer as a dominant language (at least in terms of numbers), it is possible that Scots and Scots-influenced English would have been the variety learned by Irish speakers as 'English' as they switched languages. Despite earlier disagreements, Protestant solidarity and intermarriage across the linguistic/dialectal divide no doubt also encouraged the adoption of Scottish features into the local English varieties, particularly when Irish-speaking Catholics were in the majority (as was the case in many parts of central and western Ulster). What is noteworthy, however, is that while some Scots features – such as the Scottish Vowel Length Rule – were carried over wholesale into some Ulster English varieties and that there was a general adoption of a relatively limited but regularly employed set of vocabulary items, some features of Scots, such as the use of cognates of English *bone*, *home* or *right*, did not cross over, common though they remain in traditional Ulster Scots varieties. Such Scots features were obviously either considered supernumerary or avoided because of their markedness (even foreign nature), as analysed through the model of Trudgill (2004). It is striking, however, that there is an unexpected asymmetry in this northern relationship: Ulster Scots appears to have influenced Ulster English rather more than Ulster English has influenced Ulster Scots. Some attempts at explanation have been provided here, but imponderables are still present.

3.3.4 Irish English: some concluding remarks

In relation to Irish English as a whole, it has to be recognised that the time depth is too great to achieve a fully Trudgillian sense of dialect formation. Some features exist, however, which suggest that people from the Midlands of England represented the core immigrant population, although some features of the Southern and Central dialects of English in Ireland do not derive entirely from these sources.

This account does not pay overt attention to the influence of the Irish language on the developing varieties of Irish English, however. This leads us to the idea of *founder principle*. Might it be argued that *three* founder populations affected the development of mainstream Irish English – the initial English of the medieval settlers, Irish and the English brought by Early Modern settlers? It is the Early Modern settlement which is very likely to have largely *swamped* the other inputs, however.

With Ulster Scots, less time depth is involved (although this is still greater than most contacts of this type discussed in the literature). While dominated by speakers of Scottish South-Western and West

Central dialects, Ulster Scots is more than an amalgam of inherited features from those areas. Indeed, some common features in Ulster Scots (such as the use in all positions of [ɹ]) are unlikely to derive from its presumed Scots 'heartland'. What the linguistic stages were which produced these results would be very difficult indeed – but maybe not impossible – to reconstruct. The level to which Ulster Scots has influenced Ulster English, and in what ways, is also worth pursuing.

3.4 General conclusion

This chapter has demonstrated that a number of theoretical positions created for recent new dialect formation events can be readily applied to phenomena of this type with considerably greater time depth. But several issues none the less stand in the way of our fully being able to plot the inception and development of the phenomena involved in the formation of a particular dialect or set of dialects. An accurate sense of population origins, movement patterns and proportional demographic representation in a particular territory is at best sketchy and may, in fact, often be close to unattainable. Personal and social identities do appear central to the formation of new varieties of a language, a view apparently counter to many of Trudgill's views on the issues involved. It has to be noted, however, that we are obliged largely to imagine the development of these varieties backwards. Their conception and evolution might read differently if considered from the opposite, natural, direction.

One thing becomes clear from our discussion of the development of the Germanic varieties spoken in both Ireland and the Northern Isles: it is quite possible for closely related but distinct language varieties to influence each other's development, in particular in relation to what happens when individuals and groups of people are bilingual. The fact that this type of influence can have an 'afterlife' for speakers with command over only one variety also needs to be recognised, particularly when the two input varieties are close relatives. These issues are of considerable importance and will be developed further in the next two chapters.

4 Linguistic contact and near-relative relationships

4.1 Introduction

In the preceding chapters we have been concerned primarily with the products of contact between dialects of the same language. The next two chapters will broaden this discussion markedly by considering the results of contact and creation between closely related but apparently discrete languages. To what extent can the methodological and theoretical models proposed for the outcomes of dialect contact be applied to contact between near languages? Are further theoretical models necessary for this second set of tasks?

What happens when two (or more) closely related languages come into contact with each other? This is not an easy question to answer, primarily because the study of these contexts has not always been straightforward or, indeed, popular. It would be forgivable to think that the study of near-relative contact was perceived by some scholars as essentially a sideshow to the study of contact between much more distant languages, where a great many examples of these distant-contact contexts around the world have been analysed in major treatments of these issues, such as Thomason and Kaufman (1988). We have touched upon some of these in Chapter 1. The main issue is essentially whether we can say that the developments involved are any different for near-relative contact environments than for other contacts where relationship between the input varieties is either much more distant or non-existent. Carrying this out will inevitably involve discussion of linguistic states which 'bleed into' each other and which do not have absolute boundaries with other postulated linguistic states. In order to give us the greatest chance of developing a systematic sense of the changes involved, therefore, we will analyse contact across a wide range of contexts where discrete languages are involved, often particularly and markedly different from each other, before considering near-native contact. The languages and states analysed will lead to a greater understanding of how close-relative contact works (and does not work).

4.2 Pidgins and creoles – extreme-contact varieties

Let us begin, therefore, by considering the creation of a new language through contact between at least three languages. For such an event (or series of events) to take place, of course, there needs to be a quite drastic breach with what has come before for speakers of all the source languages – to the extent that we cannot analyse (at least linguistically) the new variety as a dialect of any of the source languages (although, over time, the sociolinguistic associations of the new variety bring the reality of such a statement into question). This implies the development of a creole, a form of language which most linguists would believe derives from a pidgin (for discussion of the birth and development of pidgin and creoles, see the essays in Escure and Schwegler 2004).

The language variety we will focus upon is Tok Pisin, one of the two official languages of Papua New Guinea (the other being Tok Inglis, Standard English). Papua New Guinea is one of the most linguistically diverse states presently constituted. Because of its history of imperial exploitation, by Britain and Germany before the Great War and by Australia until 1975, it was inevitable that an imperial language – English – became the main lexical resource for the developing pidgins of the country (although it is worth noting that at least one pidgin, Police Motu, was largely native in its lexical use, as well as being a highly successful lingua franca for a while: see, for instance, Foley 1988). Because of Papua New Guinea's great diversity in culture and language, the need for a unifying language, no matter its lexical background, is paramount and easily overcomes any feeling that the use of an imperialist language as national language is inappropriate.

As matters stand, Tok Pisin represents different linguistic states depending on who is speaking. For some, the language is a basic pidgin, used for outgroup conversation about a limited number of subjects. For others, however, it is a creole, used as a first language (often along with another language or languages). For others still, Tok Pisin is an extended pidgin, a language variety which can be used in practically all the domains in which the creole can be used, but is not the native language of the person speaking.[1] Therefore, when I use the term Tok Pisin it should be noted that I mean the more developed states of the variety – extended pidgin or creole – even if much that is said here can also be said for *all* varieties of the language (for an illustration of the diversity of Tok Pisin, both contemporary and historical, see Mühlhäusler et al. 2003).

What are the primary pidginisation-triggered features which are present in Tok Pisin? Some of these are phonological. In particular, the vowel system is reduced largely to a small number of vowels in a symmetrical pattern, so that, for instance 'to speak' is *toktok* (with reduplication of the root to avoid ambiguity with the homophonous *tok* 'language') Consonant clusters in words from the lexifier language – English – are also generally simplified. At the same time, there is a general 'simplification' of the morphosyntax of the new variety in comparison with the lexifier language.[2]

Different outcomes are, of course, to be found in different parts of the system; what we are discussing here only really acts as a brief introduction to a topic which can fill, and has filled, books. It can be claimed, however, that apparent simplification is also present in morphosyntactic circumstances. In particular, the morphological expression of function – the marking of plurality or the expression of the remnants of case in pronouns such as *him* or *her* – along with morphological marking of verb tense and aspect – has been replaced largely with the use of a rigid word order and, for instance, adverbial particles.[3] In the process, a very different kind of language, not mutually intelligible with English, has come into being.

What is striking about the development of a language like Tok Pisin is that it does not follow the Thomason scale of level of language contact discussed in Chapter 1, primarily because it is not a matter of one language acting upon another language. Instead, overwhelming need for a lingua franca where no valid one existed resulted in the creation of a new language, undoubtedly indebted to its sources, but of its own nature. In order to understand the results of this process in a literate environment, we must consider a telling feature in the life cycle of many (perhaps most) creoles: the *post-creole continuum*. Not all creoles have passed, or are likely to pass, through this process – Tok Pisin and Haitian creole have not, for instance – but most will. Primarily, this process is caused by sociolinguistic forces. Most creole varieties are spoken in something like a diglossic relationship with a language associated with imperialism. Thus Jamaican patois (in origin a creole), for instance, is in contact (and conflict) with Standard English in its native region on an everyday and intimate basis. The dominant language is regularly the *lexifier language* for the creole, providing a large part of its lexis, implying that a degree of knowledge of the lexifier language would be inherent in the creole.

Because of this feature of the relationship between the two varieties,

Fig. 4.1 The post-creole continuum.

along with other forces (such as national educational policy), new linguistic states can develop. The relationship between the varieties can be schematised as shown in Figure 4.1 (it bears some similarities to the schematisation of the origins of modern Insular Scots dialects discussed in the previous chapter):

These new relationships can be analysed in relation to their proximity to the lexifier language. The *basilect* represents the linguistic state most creole-like in the new relationship, while the *acrolect* might be distinguished from particularly prestigious forms of the lexifier language primarily through accent alone. The mesolect lies in between – having some creole features (phonological, morphological and syntactic), while at the same time obviously bearing a much greater resemblance to the lexifier language. It should be noted that, depending on context, native speakers can move along the continuum for a considerable distance in their daily linguistic performance and that the process is not static: what was once the mesolect may eventually become the basilect as the linguistic ecology of the territory as a whole moves towards the standard. Eventually, the local language variety may become decreolised. Elements of this set of relationships can be compared to the *creoloid*, discussed in the next section, not least in the indeterminate nature of these varieties in relation to the lexifier language.[4] Can we find evidence for lesser but similar outcomes in other, not so profound, forms of contact?

4.3 Creoloids

From the 1970s on, it became increasingly apparent that the history of some languages involved developments which were similar to, but not the same as, those which affected pidgins and creoles in relation to the lexifier language and its system. If, as most specialists believe, radical restructuring takes place within a pidgin without reference to the lexifier language(s), the class of varieties discussed here, although bearing similarities to pidgins and creoles in relation to structural 'simplification', have not gone through this rupture, they are still connected to the lexifier language linguistically and sociolinguistically. This set of varieties must represent a separate order of development altogether. A number of scholars, as Long (2007: 9) discusses, use the term *creoloid* for this phenomenon, while others have used *semi-creole* or *partially restructured language* (or *vernacular*) (Holm 2004). I will use the first term largely because it has considerable currency in the historical linguistic literature, although any of these terms has its own value. As Long points out, Trudgill has been able to give a succinct and effective definition of what a *creoloid* is:

> There are many varieties of language in the world which look like post-creoles but which actually are not. Such varieties demonstrate relatively undramatic admixture and simplification relative to some source language but are known to have no pidgin history behind them. Such languages, as I have suggested elsewhere (Trudgill 1983, 102), can be called creoloids, and the process which leads to their formative creoloidisation.
>
> The process of creoloidisation thus consists of admixture and simplification. Unlike creoles, however, creoloids have not experienced a history of reduction followed or 'repaired' by expansion. The difference between a creoloid and a partially decreolised creole is thus a historical one; it is not apparent from synchronic inspection. Creoloidisation is, of course, the result of the influence of imperfect learning by relatively large numbers of adult speakers. However, creoloids are varieties which have never been reduced because they have maintained a continual native-speaker tradition. A good example of a creoloid is Afrikaans, which is clearly a creoloid relative of Dutch. (Trudgill 2002: 71)

Therefore, although there are occasions where the difference between a decreolised creole (created through the workings of the post-creole continuum) and a creoloid is very difficult to map out, there can be little doubt that a state which has creole-like features but where the trauma which brings on creolisation is not present. As we will see, Afrikaans is a particularly good example of this phenomenon. In order to get a full sense of the nature of the creole, however, we will first consider a range of examples of this type of linguistic development.

A useful point of departure relates to the English spoken on the Bonin (Ogasawara) Islands, analysed by Long (2007), as an example of this process. Now part of Japan, these islands lie midway between the Japanese home islands and Guam, in the sub-tropics. In the early to mid-nineteenth century they were settled permanently by a population whose origins were highly mixed, ethnically and culturally, and whose lingua franca was, at least eventually, a form of English. The first settlers spoke, Long demonstrates, a range of languages, many derived from islands in the Pacific; nevertheless, evidence suggests that the creole

Portuguese of the West African coast would also have been present, as well as a range of European languages, of which English (in both British and American forms, we believe, along with one founder who may have spoken an English creole from the Caribbean) was predominant, to some extent due to numbers but also probably through something like the founder effect. Power (symbolic and actual) was vested in the hands of speakers of that language. The community, which was always small in number, developed in near-isolation, with the exception of occasional visits by passing ships, until the last decades of the nineteenth century, when it came under the control of the expanding Japanese Empire; a considerable number of Japanese-speaking immigrants followed.

Given the original make-up of the islands' population (and the fact that literacy in English even declined in the first generations of settlement), it might be assumed that a pidgin would have developed which then became a creole, in the classical manner. This is not the case, however. As Long (2007: Chapter 5; reprinted in a similar form in Trudgill 2010: Chapter 4) and Trudgill point out, fieldwork recordings made in the later 1960s with Charles 'Uncle Charlie' Washington (1881–1972) demonstrated an obvious descendant of New England English, inevitably with a number of non-standard features. In the recollections of Irene Savory Lambert, recorded by Long in 1999, when she was herself a considerable age, recalled (Long 2007: 117) that 'Uncle Charlie' would say to her when she was frightened of *obake* ('ghosts') 'Obake? You no have to worry. You worry about two-legged obake,' which definitely appears creole-like in its use of *no*. This is perhaps even more the case with what she had heard about her great-grandfather, Benjamin Savory (1866–1942), who is supposed to have said (during the period when knowledge of Japanese was beginning to grow) '*Fundoshi kusai. No sit down*' '(Your) loin cloth stinks. Don't sit down' (Long 2007: 93), although on this occasion it is impossible to tell whether the 'simplified' language is for the benefit of Japanese speakers with very elementary English or actually representative of the core dialect. It could therefore be claimed that an essentially 'normal' dialect has apparently creole features due to a particular 'quirk' in that variety's history, predominantly because of the presence in the early development of Bonin English of native speakers of other languages, even if social patterns meant that the latter languages were not competing on an even playing field with English.

A similar set of phenomena can be found in the language varieties spoken on Pitcairn Island and its demographic offshoot Norfolk Island, both in the Pacific Ocean (the generally accepted terms for the varieties being Pitkern and Norf'k). These populations have attracted considerable interest because of the relatively limited size of the population (in particular in relation to Pitcairn Island), as well as the 'romantic' history of the inhabitants, descending as they do from the late eighteenth-century mutineers on HMS *Bounty* and their Tahitian companions. (Amoamo 2013 provides a fascinating cultural history of the islanders; the entire population of Pitcairn Island were rehoused on Norfolk Island in 1856; for a variety of reasons, a minority of the migrants chose to return to their former home in 1864.) With the exception of transient workers, Pitcairn Island remains dominated by the original population, while Norfolk Islanders of Pitcairn descent are now demographically in the minority on their island in comparison to Australian, New Zealand and, to an extent, Melanesian, migrants. Unlike Pitkern, therefore, the prospects for the long-term survival of Norf'k are increasingly doubtful (Mühlhäusler 2007: 215–16; see also Laycock 1989).

Given that, in the initial settlement of Pitcairn Island, 'English' sailors (which included at least one person of West Indies origin) were not numerically dominant in relation to the number of Polynesian settlers (both the partners of the sailors and a number of Tahitian men brought along because of their skills in island life), it might be expected that there would, in the first instance, be a considerable Polynesian presence in the modern dialects derived from this initial set of contacts. Moreover, we might expect that, given the initial impetus to language learning associated in most cultures with contact between children and mothers (who, on this occasion, would *all* have been, at least to begin with, capable of achieving only a limited level of English competence), something like the linguistic disruption associated by most scholars with pidgin creation would have occurred in the first generation of contact. This would seem even more likely, given what we know about the early years of the settlement. By the time connections were re-established with the wider world in the second decade of the nineteenth century, only one mutineer survived; all other adults were Polynesian women, the men of both ethno-cultural origins having died or been killed off in a series of disputes about access to land and, in particular, women. There are a number of features – copula deletion from an early period, for instance – which represent features similar to those found in many creoles, but pidginisation (and later creolisation) did not take place; instead, both Pitkern and Norf'k dialects stand in the uneasy borderland between mainstream 'colonial' varieties – like Falkland Islands English, for instance – and varieties (such as Tok Pisin) where genuine and often radical restructuring has taken place. In many senses this issue is incapable of being resolved; attempts at explanations will be put forward in the following, however.

Perhaps most importantly, the early Pitcairn colony was anything but egalitarian. Both the racial tensions which caused so many difficulties in this first generation and the evidence reported for the views of the second and subsequent generations suggest that 'English' culture, as perceived through the filter of the mutineers' memories (and, no doubt, prejudices), represented the central cultural current of the colony. The English language (in something like its Standard form) was a part of this cultural edifice. Moreover, while literacy was highly limited in the colony (particularly, it might be assumed, after former officers like Fletcher Christian died or were killed), it was, early visitors reported, held in very high regard by all; by the 1820s, external and internal efforts towards literacy had largely been successful, often associated with Christian evangelicalism, emphasising even further the importance of the book. Thus any further drift towards full restructuring was reversed, no matter how strongly later natives of both islands identified themselves with the non-standard features of their by then stabilised varieties. Although knowledge of Tahitian survived into at least the second (and possibly third) generations, it appears it was considered a lesser variety associated primarily with female members of the community (although male inhabitants must have had at least some knowledge of the secondary community variety). Thus the founder effect appears to be supported by this evidence.[5]

4.3.1 Creoloids and near-relative contact

Are phenomena of this type visible in contacts with greater time depth? A number of scholars – most notably Trudgill – have attempted to answer this question. Focusing on language contact scenarios which acted upon the development of three Germanic language varieties of considerable historical depth (English, Continental Scandinavian and Afrikaans), Trudgill (1986) put forward the idea that all three situations led to the creation of a creoloid through language contact. Thus while no abrupt pidginisation event was present with any of these languages, something like a creole was created in a language ecology altered by contact. This sounds reasonable. Is the conclusion entirely tenable, however? The problem lies, I think, in the nature of the contacts involved with each of these languages. At the time, Trudgill would have seen the development of English as having been essentially affected by closely related Norse varieties (a point to which we will return in the next chapter); something similar can be seen with the continental North Germanic languages in relation to Low German, a close relative, towards the end of the Middle Ages. Afrikaans, on the other hand, came into contact with a range of languages during its formative period, whether distantly related, such as the French dialects brought by Protestant refugees, or not related at all, such as the Khoe, San, Bantu, Indic, Dravidian, Austronesian and other languages either spoken by indigenous peoples (or, in the case of the Bantu, recent immigrants by land) or brought to the Cape by slaves and coolie labourers.[6] The result was a language which most scholars would consider to have creole elements.[7]

Normally, when outsiders contemplate Afrikaans, it is the standard variety which is considered, primarily because of its availability in a range of written and broadcast media. This variety may, however, be rather anomalous in relation to the history of the language (see, for instance, Deumert 2001). Due to the history of most of the (white) speakers of Afrikaans, Standard Dutch had an ongoing and pervasive impact on the written nature in particular of the new offshoot of the Dutch dialects spoken at the Cape. Standard Dutch remained the language of Church and State into the 1920s; its presence as the main written variety employed by the Afrikaners was guaranteed under most circumstances until at most two generations before this. Inevitably, Standard Afrikaans remains close to this prestige variety; Afrikaans speakers from a middle-class background in particular would inevitably bring this variety from writing into speech, in particular in formal environments. But other varieties of Afrikaans, spoken by poor, rural whites and by 'Cape Coloureds', are significantly less like Standard Dutch and also exhibit many features which would be considered creole-like at the very least. There is also evidence for some varieties – such as Fly Taal (Mufwene 1997: 58) – which appear to be genuinely pidgin forms of Afrikaans. It is therefore not unreasonable to assume that Afrikaans is, taking speakers of the language as a whole, a language which has features which would normally be considered creole. But given the history of continued contact between speakers of Dutch and Afrikaans, and the long-term prestige of the former for many speakers of the latter, it would be very difficult to say exactly where and when a true pidginisation event took place (or, perhaps better, where a pidginisation took place which had a profound and lasting effect on the development of Afrikaans as a whole). Considerable evidence exists for the development of 'broken Dutch' among servants and slaves in the early days of the colony. *Creoloid* appears to be a particularly appropriate term for the status of Afrikaans. This still leaves unresolved the issue of the natures of the contacts between West and North Germanic mentioned, however. We will leave the contact between Old English and Viking Norse to the next chapter; here, however, some discussion of the contact between Middle Scandinavian and Middle Low German is necessary.

How do we compare the 'distant contact' phenomena and their results found in Afrikaans with those found in contacts where the inputs are largely close relatives?

In late medieval Scandinavia, trade routes became increasingly difficult to maintain through native labour, perhaps due to the virulent nature of the Black Death in that region and the subsequent and overwhelming loss of population, but also because of the economies of scale which large countries with small populations often face. One result of this crisis was the loss of contact between the doomed Norse Greenland colony and Norway; another was the moves towards political unity between the constituent parts of Scandinavia (successful with Norway and Denmark, less permanent between these two countries and Sweden); the third was the rise of the Hanseatic League as chief carrier and trader along the coasts and, eventually, a major political force in Scandinavian social, political and economic development. The Hanseatic League was a trading confederation of cities with considerable German-speaking populations, largely based on the southern Baltic and North Sea littorals, such as Riga, Danzig (modern Gdańsk), Lübeck, Hamburg and Bremen, along with some inland cities, such as Cologne. In Scandinavia, the effects of its infiltration and conquest of markets can be found in almost all coastal settlements, with population centres such as Bergen, Oslo, Gothenburg, Copenhagen and Visby (the capital of Gotland, the Swedish island in the middle of the eastern Baltic) being particularly influenced. Indeed, the city of Stockholm is practically entirely a German foundation (see the discussion in the papers collected in Harreld 2015). In all of these settlements (and many more), speakers of (Low) German were found in considerable numbers; bilingualism was common and most native Scandinavians had knowledge of some words and phrases.

Although, eventually, Scandinavian interests (and culture and language) reasserted themselves in their native territories, the influence of Low German on the local languages was intense and long-lasting. This is probably most readily visible with vocabulary, where Low German influence is all-encompassing, to the extent that it might be said to be the Scandinavian equivalent of French influence upon English lexis (with the proviso that the near-relative status of Low German in relation to Scandinavian meant that word formation processes in the two languages were rather more similar and that therefore the borrowing of 'foreign' vocabulary was much more straightforward). In terms of structural influence, while it is always difficult to find a 'smoking gun' in circumstances of this type, it is very striking that a large part of the changes which affected the Scandinavian languages, but not Faeroese and Icelandic, such as the loss of plurality and number concord in any part of the verb, or the loss of practically all case marking in the noun phrase (although grammatical gender was maintained – gender assignment in Low German and North Germanic are very similar, which may explain this survival), passed through the systems of the Scandinavian languages during the period of highest contact. That coincidence does not necessarily mean that these developments were caused in the first instance by the contact – there is some evidence suggesting that many of the changes involved were already present in incipient form in the Scandinavian dialects *before* the contact began in earnest. It can be argued, however, that they were encouraged and transmitted through the dialects in a situation where large-scale 'simplification' brought on by the need for understanding in the wake of contact was prevalent – even dominant. Something like the koineisation which will be discussed for north Indian varieties in Fiji below can also be seen here.[8]

The language states brought about by contact between near relatives and those which contact has produced as creoloids are likely to be similar but not the same, primarily because of the question of mutual intelligibility between the initial contacts. This means that the products of near contact are rather less likely to be thoroughgoing in its 'simplification' and move away from the dominant source language variety than is the case with a creoloid. This is demonstrated forcefully through the development of koines. We will see in the next chapter if this conclusion can be supported. To begin explaining this, I will now turn to the nature of *convergence*, which, it can be assumed, has a particular role to play where near-relative contact takes place.

4.4 Convergence

All languages change all of the time. The traditional genetic analysis of change (see 1.5), so central to historical linguistics, somewhat distorts this truth by canonising divergence as the central, evolutionary trajectory for change. It would be difficult to argue with the idea that divergent change is the most common kind of development; it is unlikely, however, that it is the sole process at work in linguistic variation and change. Convergence is also a very real possibility. A striking example of this is the history and present state of Okinawan in relation to Japanese. For a considerable period prior to the mid-nineteenth century, the Ryūkyū Islands, centred on the island of Okinawa, developed independently from the Japanese archipelago to the north and east, their culture affected directly by Chinese models through trade and political relationships in ways in which their northern neighbours could not participate. Over the last two centuries, however, the islands have been brought under the control of the central Japanese authorities, with the exception of a relatively lengthy occupation by American forces in the aftermath of the Second World War (although, even then, the territories were largely administered at a local level by ethnic Japanese). These changes had linguistic consequences. At the start of the nineteenth century, Okinawan was, in many ways, as discrete from Japanese as English is from Dutch: they shared a common, relatively recent, ancestor but were barely mutually intelligible, if at all. The imposition of Japanese as the language of mass literacy, its presence as the sole code of the powerful administration, its association towards aspirations to a better life led to the language's hegemonic omnipresence over the whole territory. Okinawa in particular was affected by these changes because of its ongoing industrialisation and urbanisation. Over the last few generations, it has become apparent that the dialects of Okinawa have been so affected by Japanese that they can now be taken as dialects of that language, with which they have now a far higher level of intelligibility than was previously the case (Dixon 1997: 60–1; for a discussion of the historical factors involved, see Kerr 2000).

More can be said about the results of convergence between close relatives. A number of convergence zones present themselves in relation to contact between Spanish and similar varieties, both in Europe and elsewhere in the world. Fronterizo[9] (otherwise known by locals as *Portuñol* or *Portunhol*, a blend of *Portuguesa* and *Español*, following the spelling conventions of either Spanish or Portuguese), for instance, is spoken in different ways by different groups along large parts of the long border Brazil shares with officially Spanish-using territories; its best-covered and most striking examples are to be found on the present boundaries of Uruguay and Brazil, where contested frontiers meant that a considerable number of originally Portuguese speakers found themselves in a Spanish-dominated polity over a hundred years ago. As our understanding of the matter stands at present, it is difficult to say whether Fronterizo is a Portuguese variety which has been heavily Castilianised or a largely Spanish variety which has gone through intense Lusification. Confusingly, we could actually have an example here of both processes at work at the same time, given how close (to the edge of mutual intelligibility) the two source languages are; Spanish speakers could have moved towards more Lusophone models just as Portuguese speakers travelled in the opposite direction.

What appears certain is that, while there are many Portuguese lexical items in Fronterizo, the general tenor – in so far as we can tell with such close relatives – is towards Spanish being lexically dominant. Morphologically, however, many Brazilian Vernacular Portuguese features have been maintained. These include plural marking on only the first declined feature in a noun phrase, rather than the strict number concord marking across the phrase expected in both standard varieties, as in, following Carvalho (2006: 154),

> Loh sueldo [no plural marking] son bajos
> 'the salary [sg., but plural in original] is [literally, 'are'] low',

used by a middle-class adolescent female in Rivera, right on the Uruguay–Brazil frontier. But morphosyntactic convergence is not merely a matter of transfer. Mixtures of forms, including in the article paradigm, Lipski (1994: 343–4) demonstrates, is also common, suggesting that native speakers do not distinguish, even when this is possible, between the source varieties. Other near-relative contacts associated with Spanish include Cocoliche, discussed briefly in Chapter 1.

Closer to (linguistic) home is the apparent ongoing convergence between Low and (Standard) High German in northern Germany. Höder (2014) demonstrates the nature of the convergence between the two systems, paying particular attention to those situations where the spoken Low German of individuals and groups has moved towards the standard variety. Most of these examples are lexical or phonological, but he presents one example which is morphological in nature.

The Germanic languages do not have a dedicated future tense (in marked distinction to the western Romance languages, for instance). In Standard High German, futurity is often expressed using the verb *werden* 'to become' (although the verb also takes on other grammatical functions, in particular in relation to the expression of passive voice), as illustrated by Höder (2014: 52):

> Er   wird   Kaffeetrinken
> 3SG.M.NOM become-IND.PRS.3   coffee drink-INF
> 'He will drink/will be drinking/is going to drink coffee [future]'
> 'He is probably drinking coffee [epistemic]'

In traditional Low German, Höder reports, a formally exact equivalent can be given:

> He   ward   Kaffe drinken
> 3SG.M.NOM become-PRS.3SG   coffee drink-INF
> 'He is probably drinking coffee',

where only the epistemic associations of *werden/warrn* (the latter the Low German equivalent of the former), and not those of the future, are present. More modern forms of Low German have converged with High German, with *warm* being used in essentially the same way in Low German as in High. It should be noted, however, that on no occasion does Höder describe the breakdown in whole categories found, it will be suggested in Chapter 5, between the close relatives Old English and Old Norse.[10]

It is noteworthy that neither of these contacts, while causing some issues with morphology, has anything like the scale of change associated with the products of the contact between Scandinavian and Low German. This might have something to do with higher levels of literacy in the target variety, a point to which we will return in the following, where we will consider further the development of a common linguistic variety through the contact of near relatives. Linguistic distance might also explain it. Low and High German are much closer linguistically than were the late medieval dialects of Scandinavia and Low German.

4.5 Koineisation

Throughout this book reference has been made to *koines* and *koineisation*; an introductory discussion of dialect koineisation was given in Chapter 2. When two language varieties come into contact with each other they may form a *koine*, a compromise variety sharing elements from all the inputs, but presenting innovations which come, in the main, from these compromises. The term itself derives from the Greek *koine glossa* 'common language, speech', the name given to the language variety associated with the exploitation of Hellenistic culture and values into South-West and South Asia in the aftermath of the spread of Macedonian power in the late fourth century BCE. Immediately prior to these events, Greek was found in widely divergent dialects; there were no dominant varieties, even if some dialects had accrued a great deal of prestige. Nevertheless, given the cultural predominance of Athens in the Greek world, it is not surprising that Attic should have formed the basis of the *koine*. Attic had a number of linguistic eccentricities, however: eccentricities which might have affected comprehension for other Greek speakers. Less difficult or contentious material was also therefore incorporated from Attic's close relative Ionic, spoken both in the islands of the Aegean and on the mainland of Asia Minor. The new language variety was used in trade and in government, and eventually became the native dialect of many speakers (only one modern Greek dialect – Tsakonian, spoken in the Peloponnese – is not descended entirely from the *koine glossa*) (Horrocks 1997: 33–45). In its development, the koine had been spoken by a wide range of speakers – both native speakers of Greek and second language users (including a number of early Christian writers), all of whom made an impact on the final form of the common language. An understanding of this process helps us follow the development of similar phenomena recorded in recent times (although it has to be recognised that the different kinds of varieties termed *koine* in the scholarly literature do sometimes make defining the central characteristics of the phenomenon difficult to put together. That does not mean that it is impossible, however).

Throughout his work, Siegel (see, for example, Siegel 1985 and 2001) has attempted both to describe the phenomenon of koineisation as a whole and to analyse the in-depth nature of particular contacts. It is striking that, from the beginning of his analysis of these topics, Siegel places the nature of koine development in many ways in opposition to the development of pidgins and creoles (see Siegel 2001 for further details); something similar can be seen in the debate over the nature of the development of English as well. While Mufwene among others has questioned such a stark and absolute contrast, it is still a useful way of starting a discussion, in particular in terms of what constitutes koineisation. At its heart is convergence, an issue we have already discussed. How far can the ideas of koineisation and convergence be taken? A good example of this can be found in relation to the Indo-Aryan variety spoken in Fiji.

4.5.1 Koineisation in Fiji Hindi

While koineisation regularly involves, as we have seen, contact and compromise between dialects of the same language, the process can also be constructed through interrelationships between close relatives which might be considered discrete languages. A striking example of this process can be found in Fiji.

Following the abolition of slavery in the British Empire in 1833, the need for labour on plantations in particular led to the reinstitution of indentured servitude as a means of making up shortfalls in finding labour for the most physically exacting and repetitive tasks. Perhaps the largest single group of non-white British imperial subjects in the nineteenth century were to be found in the Indian Empire. In this territory, economic forces, along with a population subject to exponential growth, led to a considerable number of supernumerary members of the peasantry. With considerable hucksterism and probably some degree of force, many thousands of people of South Asian origin moved as indentured servants to a range of places within the sub-tropical and tropical parts of the Empire, including the Caribbean, East Africa, South Africa, and Fiji and other southern Pacific islands, where plantation economies had been established. As well as being employed in large-scale crop production, South Asian migrants were also used to build railways and other public works.[11] Some Indians did return to their homeland, although most, for whatever reason, stayed on in their 'temporary' residences. Unlike the earlier white indentured servants, however, South Asian migrants of this sort could not readily blend into colonial society, being physically different from both the ruling and the ruled in the various colonies. Indeed, many of the tensions sometimes still encountered between locals of South Asian origin and the present majority in a given territory can be traced to these initial contacts.

These migrants came from a range of backgrounds within South Asia. Most were Hindus, although a large minority were Muslim. Many languages were spoken – Indo-European, Dravidian and a range of other varieties were (and are) to be found in the diaspora. The distribution of these languages was different in different colonies, so that, for instance, as Mesthrie (1991) points out, the Dravidian language Tamil had more speakers in KwaZulu–Natal in South Africa in the early days of the diaspora than any other South Asian language. In Fiji, however, where migration was so great that people of South Asian descent have at times come close to making up the majority of the inhabitants of the country, most migrants spoke an Indo-European variety as their first language.

Although all descended from a common ancestor (which lay behind the written construct Sanskrit), the diversity of the Indo-Aryan (or Indic) languages is considerable. Someone speaking Dhivehi, spoken in the Maldives off India's south-west coast, for instance, would have little more chance of understanding Nepali, spoken on the edge of the Himalaya, than an English speaker would Lithuanian. But the languages and dialects which run from the Punjab in the eastern Indus valley to the mouths of the Ganges and the Brahmaputra – several months' journey apart using traditional forms of transport – form a dialect continuum. This does not mean that someone from the Punjab can understand someone from Bengal when using their native local languages, but it *does* mean that there are generally no major distinctions, represented in dialect atlases as bundles of isoglosses, between varieties, with difference gradually increasing across space. These possibilities of connection are particularly likely in the central Ganges valley, in those areas where, no matter the differences, the local varieties are generally classified as dialects of Hindi. It is in relation to these dialects, exported to Fiji, that Siegel (1987) takes particular interest.

In the often difficult circumstances of the early part of this migration, many people from South Asian backgrounds would have been faced

Table 4.1 Indian Hindi dialects and Fiji Hindi definite future suffixes (from Siegel 1987: 115).

	Bhojpuri	Avadhi	Braje	Fiji Hindi
1 sg.	bō, ab	bū	ihaū, aūgau	egām
1 pl.	ab, bī, iha	ab	ihaī, aīgai	egā
2 sg. (masc.)	bē, ba	bē, ihai	(a)ihai, (a)igau	egā
(fem.)	bī, bis			
2 pl. (masc.)	bâ(h)	bō, bau	(a)ihai, (a)igau	egā
(fem.)	bū			
3 sg.	ī	ī, ihai, ē	(a)ihau, agau	ī
3 pl.	ih, ē, ihen	ihaī, aī	(a)ihaī, aīgai	ī

with people speaking varieties which were on the edge of understanding for them. People from other backgrounds were not entirely incomprehensible, but full comprehension would have taken considerable effort. In a situation where most people were at best semi-literate, there was no written standard to employ as a reference point. Instead, attempts at finding common denominators by trial and error were made.[12]

In his description of the development of Fiji Hindi, Siegel discusses a great many examples where compromise (or, indeed, new) forms and structures have been created through compromise. One must suffice for the present (see Table 4.1).

This paradigm demonstrates considerable simplification of the forms found for the various north Indian dialects from which the Fijian variety has been created. This is not only a matter of differences between the divergent Gangetic varieties; many of the dialects involved are themselves highly variable. This cannot be said for the language variety as it developed in Fiji, however. It is relatively straightforward to recognise from this paradigm that the Fiji Hindi forms derive from forms found in the 'mother country' (whether directly or apparently in a compromise between different forms). But whereas in the original dialect most gender and number distinctions are expressed, in Fiji plurality and gender are no longer marked.[13] We will have more to say about features of this sort when we consider the development of English in the late Old English and early Middle English periods in the next chapter.

It could be argued that what marks off the evidence from Fiji from the modern Romance and Germanic near-relative contacts described above is the level of diversity of language varieties in the original mix. Literacy is an equally important factor, however, since it demonstrates that most modern speakers caught up in near-relative contact have an idealised sense (as well as something you can 'point at') of how the target written variety behaves linguistically. This was not the case for speakers of Indic varieties spoken on Fiji during the critical period of development for the new variety. It also was not the case with English some thousand years ago.

4.6 Conclusion

This chapter has touched upon a number of themes related to near-relative contact between discrete language varieties, concerned with both the development of creoloids and the achievement of koineisation. It has demonstrated that near-language contact seems likely to be a phenomenon (or set of phenomena) largely discrete from other language contact events. Some reference has also been made to the ways in which near-language contact relates theoretically to the new dialect phenomena discussed in Chapters 2 and 3. In the next chapter, we will focus on an extended example of many of these processes: the morphosyntactic development of the English language in the period 900 to 1350.

5 English in the 'transition period': the sources of contact-induced change

In Chapter 4 we considered a number of theoretical and methodological insights which feed into our understanding of what happens when closely related but linguistically discrete varieties come into contact. In this chapter we will consider in more detail this type of development, focusing on one particular set of contacts in the history of the English language. The theoretical positions discussed and assessed in this book will be regularly measured against the evidence presented here.

5.1 English and typological change

The English language as it now stands is strikingly different typologically from its earliest recorded ancestor, Old English. Of course, this is true for many language varieties when we either have texts dating from earlier forms of the language or can reconstruct ancestral forms consistently. What is striking about English, however, is that many of these profound changes were primarily confined to a particular stage in the language's development – the late Old English and early Middle English periods (roughly, 950–1300) – and that, when evidence is available, the actual changes involved took between two to three generations to pass through any one dialect. The level and speed of change involved are considerable.

A particularly apposite example of this can be found in the two continuations of the *Anglo-Saxon Chronicle* produced in the monastery at Peterborough in the south-east English Midlands in the first half of the twelfth century (as discussed in Millar 2012: 115–18; see also Watts 2011: 8). The two monks who wrote the continuations were, we can surmise, relatively old. It is tempting to see the creation and continuation of the *Peterborough Chronicle* as essentially representing use close to home or even primarily by the writers.[1] We have no way of knowing the extent to which the birth dates of the two continuators differed, but it does seem likely, given the linguistic contrasts between the sections, that a gap of at least one generation was present. The differences in language between the two writers are unlikely to be due to provenance since, underlying the continuing influence of the Anglo-Saxon *Schriftsprache* 'literary language' in their written idiolects, evidence suggests that both were speakers of the same dialect, which appears to be essentially identical with what would have been expected in the Peterborough area at the time (see also Millar 1997 for a discussion of the native idiom of the scribe providing additions in earlier parts of the Peterborough copy of the *Anglo-Saxon Chronicle*, again demonstrating a more 'modern' language than that of the surrounding text he also reproduces). Both continuators had considerable knowledge of Old English scribal and linguistic practice, quite likely derived from reading the manuscript which they continued (as well as other texts their monastery possessed); they were in no way novices in relation to the written language towards which they aspired. They could not fully reproduce it, however.

Similar issues can be found in relation to one of the last pieces of Anglo-Saxon writing copied in post-Conquest England: the version of Ælfric's *De Initio Creaturae* 'on the beginning of creation', found in London, British Library, Cotton Vespasian A.xxii and dated to around the beginning of the thirteenth century. It was probably copied in Kent (further discussion of these issues can be found in Millar and Nicholls 1997). With this text we are blessed in having, at the very least, a manuscript witness which is very close to the original: London, British Library, Royal 7 C.xii, dated to the end of the tenth century and with direct connections to Ælfric himself (Eliason and Clemoes 1966: 28–35).

It needs to be recognised, however, that, no matter how steeped these scribes were in both Anglo-Saxon scribal tradition and language, what they produced was *not* Old English. A few brief examples from *De Initio Creaturae* must suffice. While, for instance, the Royal manuscript has *buton ælcum eorðlicum fæder* 'without any earthly father', Vespasian has *buton elce eorðlice federe*, the apparent falling away of word-final inflectional morphology between (near-)original and latest copy is immediately observable. Equally striking is Vespasian *se eorðe his awirigd on þine weorce* 'the earth is cursed in your work' as compared with Royal *seo eorðe þe is awyrige on þinum weorce* 'the earth which is accursed in your work'. As well as the apparent simplification of endings morphology, the later version appears to use an 'incorrect' demonstrative for the noun in relation to gender use – *se* (originally nominative masculine) rather than *seo* (originally – and correctly – nominative feminine).

When faced with a rather limited amount of information, such as that presented here, it is quite tempting to throw up our hands and declare that what is in front of us, while interesting and indicative, can only be regarded as inconclusive. But while the *Peterborough Chronicle* Continuations and the Vespasian *De Initio Creaturae* are particularly apposite reflections of ongoing linguistic change, they are most certainly not unique or unrepresentative of the considerable structural variation and change in English witnessed during the period across England (and the Anglian-speaking areas of Scotland, we assume, although we have little or no evidence for this from the period). Indeed, in original texts from the period we often find more radical manifestations of the same features, since the written form is not immediately braked by any inherited practice. In the following sections I will therefore discuss the presiding issues of the period in relation to morphosyntactic change (phonological change during the period follows its own path and logic, only occasionally being affected by the contacts discussed in this chapter).

5.1.1 Change in the English noun and verb phrases

Over a period lasting some 350–400 years (roughly 900–1300), and for considerably shorter periods in its spread within and between dialects, English significantly changed its typological status from one which had many synthetic tendencies – something it shared with its near relatives – to a rather analytic one (an alternative, although complementary, analysis would be a move from fusional to isolating typologies). In concrete terms, this implies the following changes with the noun phrase[2]:

1. The loss of grammatical case, except for its partial retention with some personal, interrogative and relative pronouns (although the latter category in particular has not survived well). Demonstrative pronouns are marked now only for plurality (with even this category being lost in the Northern and Insular dialects of Scots: Millar 2007: 86). What case marking on nouns themselves which survived from Indo-European into even the earliest attested Old English was among the first victims of these changes, as we will see in 3 below. One exception remains: the survival of -'s as a marker of possession.
2. Grammatical gender was entirely lost, with its morphological expression barely remembered in some of the surviving pronoun forms, where it now refers to natural sex divisions. Until the 1960s, the prevailing explanations for breakdown in the English grammatical gender system was *Genuswechsel* 'gender shift', a view that the 'incorrect' use of originally gender-sensitive relationships represented the transfer of items from gender to gender, often under the influence of the gender assignment of other words (sometimes including French

and Latin lexical items in their source languages). Despite the manifest issues with accepting this view – not least that it did not really explain the loss of grammatical gender – it had considerably longevity. This was to end with the first publication of Charles Jones's work on the topic. According to Jones (1967ab, 1983 and 1987), originally grammatical gender-sensitive forms came to be reinterpreted as markers of function. Thus *þone*, originally associated solely with masculine contexts with the accusative case, came to be used regularly in all direct object contexts, no matter the original gender of the noun.

3. To some extent due to these structural changes (but also as part of the process which caused the major typological shift), the relatively rich noun class inflectional morphology system, based to a considerable extent on inflectional suffixation (as well as vowel alternation), quickly became confined to a very small number of plural marking strategies: in particular (in Modern English), *-(e)s* (as in *stones*), *-en* (as in *oxen*), zero plural marking (as with *fish* 'a number of fish') and vowel alternation (*men*).[3] But even this highly limited level of variety masks a situation where practically all native words, no matter their original declension, have gravitated towards the *-(e)s* paradigm. Although some dialects have preserved a little more diversity (in traditional dialects of Scots, for instance, the plural of *ee* 'eye' is *een* while the plural of *coo* 'cow' is *kye*), this is really only a matter of a few words. As with both 1 and 2, many of the issues which caused this apparent simplification were due to a falling together of a number of the unstressed final vowels; this cannot be seen as the only reason for the change, however, since the breakdown also involved final consonant inflections.

4. Of course, the adjective paradigms, whose inflectional morphology patterns were based on the noun declensions to a considerable extent, also fell together; neither case nor gender (or, moving beyond these, function) could be marked any more. The distinction between 'strong' and 'weak' paradigms of adjectival use (a system which still survives to a lesser or greater extent in many Germanic dialects and is based, essentially, on the amount of functional information carried by the definer – or equivalent, if there is one) naturally fell victim to these changes, particularly since little or no information was now being carried by any element of the noun phrase, bearing in mind the exceptions discussed in 1 and 2 above. Although Northern dialects lost this distinction early, forms of London English in the late fourteenth century still continued to use alternating forms descended from the strong/weak distinction. They also generally realised noun plurality on the adjective (Samuels 1989b). These distinctions were

then wiped out in the following generation by the absolute and terminal loss of final -*e* as a functional marker.
5. As part of the same series of changes, the original bipartite demonstrative distinction between a simple demonstrative paradigm, probably distal in orientation (and carrying article function), and a compound demonstrative paradigm, probably proximal in orientation, was replaced by a tripartite distinction between a discrete definite article (*the*), a distal demonstrative (*that/those*) and a proximal demonstrative (*this/these*) (Millar 2000).

With the verb phrase the changes involved are, perhaps, not quite as clear-cut as with the noun phrase. Nevertheless there is considerable evidence that tangible instability existed formally and conceptually within the verb paradigm over essentially the same period. These issues can be broken down in the following ways:

1. With the exception of *be*, where the difference between *was* and *were* was maintained, the distinction between past tense singular and plural verb forms was lost. This change also had the effect of simplifying considerably the strong verb paradigms by, under normal circumstances, removing one of the Ablaut distinctive forms around which the paradigm was constructed.
2. From as early as the writing of the English gloss to the *Lindisfarne Gospels* (dated to the first half of the tenth century; for these features, see Cole 2014), distinctions between the singular and plural in the present tense of the English verb were beginning to develop away from the previous norms, where each number in the singular was distinguished formally in the present tense (and the second singular in the past), as well as there being an absolute distinction between singular and plural in both tenses. Although, unlike the modern Scandinavian languages, almost all dialects of English make some distinction between singular and plural in present tense contexts, these paradigms were often strikingly different from those realised in both Old English and present-day Standard English. In some dialects, including my own, mainstream plural forms are used when there is a simple subject, but singular forms when the (plural) subject is a complex one (the *Northern Subject Concord Rule*). Thus I would naturally say *we* were *walking along the road* but *the men we saw yesterday* was *walking down the road*. In other varieties, plural forms may regularly be used in singular contexts and vice versa. Some dialects (largely, but not entirely, of creole origin) regularly realise no singular and plural distinction at all. What can be said when considering

this diversity is that a straightforward relationship between number and form based upon historical models is no longer possible for most non-standard varieties.
3. The subjunctive, a central feature of the Old English system (as it remains today in, for instance, German), with a paradigm largely formally discrete from the indicative and imperative, collapsed (see, for instance, Mustanoja 1960: 452–8). As a result of many of the changes described in 1 and 2, the paradigm became largely incapable of, in the first instance, retaining a formal distinction between singular and plural in the subjunctive and, secondly, maintaining a formal distinction between subjunctive and indicative in the plural. Thus, in Modern English, it is possible (at least in those varieties which distinguish between singular and plural in the indicative) to maintain a formal distinction between indicative *he goes* and subjunctive *if he go*. This cannot be achieved in the plural, however. A distinction which only works some of the time is not really worth maintaining and, indeed, beyond a few fossilised phrases, like *God save the King*, the subjunctive is essentially moribund in all but the most formal speech (and writing). Many – perhaps most – speakers of English never use the formal expression of that mood, beyond these fossilised phrases (see Denison 1993: Chapter 11 for a discussion of these issues).
4. Connected to the verb phrase are the changes in element order rules during the period, one of which being an element order SOV (Subject Object Verb) becoming SVO (Subject Verb Object) and SvOV (Subject Auxiliary Verb Object Main Verb) where auxiliary verbs were used) to one where SVO and SvVO (Subject Auxiliary Verb Main Verb Object) dominated. It is also worth noting that the later dominant word order pattern existed as a minority usage when the earlier order was the norm. For a discussion of these changes, see van Kemenade (1987) and Pintzuk (1999). Van Gelderen (2011) presents a broad-based analysis of these and related developments. Ringe and Taylor (2014) provide an overview.

It will be the overriding theme of this chapter that linguistic contact is at the heart of any explanation for these changes. In the interest of fairness, however, the issue of whether system-internal explanations can be central in any explanation of this type will be given primary focus to begin with. As will become apparent, however, while convincing in many ways, these theories cannot be said to suffice; further, extra-systemic, explanation is necessary.

5.2 Explanations of change not involving contact: a nil hypothesis

Is anything particularly surprising happening to English during this period? It will be the contention of this chapter that this is indeed the case. But we need to consider whether such a statement is actually true. In general, scholars investigating this set of changes tend to compare what happened with English during this period with retention and change in other Germanic varieties. If similar changes have taken place in all the sister languages, it might be necessary to consider revising the viewpoint that contact lies at the heart of change in English.

To begin with, however, we need to reach further back in time. We believe that proto-Indo-European was typologically a rather synthetic (and fusional) language. In relation to the noun phrase, the language had seven grammatical cases and three grammatical genders, interacting with a range of noun and adjective inflectional morphology classes. With the verb phrase, indicators of tense, mood, voice and aspect, along with a range of declensional patterns, were represented by a diverse range of inflectional morphology.

This system was not replicated in full by even the earliest recorded daughter languages, such as Greek or Sanskrit. Although these varieties apparently maintained a large part of the original distinctions, at the same time the languages' 'collapsed' a number of earlier inflectional features into pre-existing and originally discrete categories (see Beekes 2001: Chapter 8). To some extent, these changes can be attributed to an ongoing move towards a less synthetic typology among proto-Indo-European's descendants, although it must be recognised that each of the daughter varieties appears to have 'cherry-picked' individual features of the inherited system to retain or discard; in other words, change is peculiar to each language sub-family or, indeed, language, with no apparent inherited patterns in relation to which features should be kept and which jettisoned, even when many of the daughter languages appear to be developing essentially in the same direction.

Not all sub-families of Indo-European have changed in the same way and at the same speed in relation to inflectional morphological marking, even if the same time depth must be assumed from ancestral form to modern descendants. The Slavonic languages (with the exception of Bulgarian and Macedonian), for instance, maintain a great deal more of the ancestral inflectional morphology than have, for instance, the Romance languages. It is necessary to provide an explanation for why these apparent discrepancies have occurred, although it may not be the place here to discuss these changes fully. What we will focus on, however, is the nature of change within the Germanic languages.

To begin with, however, what is striking about the alterations which affected English was not so much the nature of the changes involved as the speed with which they passed through the various English dialects. It is this speed which makes us want to find a specific sense of the causation and explanation for these changes. But this still does not explain why the Germanic languages appear to have developed in such similar ways.

5.3 *Drift* and the Germanic languages

5.3.1 *The 'Lord's Prayer' in the Germanic languages: an historical survey*

Since we have over 1,500 years of recorded evidence for the sub-family, the Germanic languages are particularly conducive to the study of long-term patterns of linguistic change, with both English and High German having around 1,300 years of continuous recording. What is very striking is that these early attested varieties are both similar to each other in morphosyntactic terms and not at all exceptional developmentally in relation to other early Indo-European varieties (this is in considerable contrast to their phonological development, which marks them off in comparison to most of their contemporary sister varieties).

This conservatism is no longer the norm, however, at least not with every member of the sub-family. What has happened to the daughter Germanic languages in relation to their development is very striking, particularly because originally quite close relatives appear to have developed severally in strikingly different directions. Some preserved something essentially similar to (or at least obviously descended from) the inherited inflectional system while others have moved a considerable distance typologically from the ancestral language and use little or nothing of the ancestral inflectional marking material. Yet underlying these different trajectories are striking similarities.

To illustrate these issues, in the following we will consider a range of (short) texts – translations of the same text (the 'Our father' or 'Lord's Prayer'[4]) – which exemplify different stages of some of the Germanic varieties. A present-day direct English translation of the original Greek is

> Our Heavenly Father, may your name be honoured; May your kingdom come, and your will be done on earth as it is in Heaven. Give us this day the bread we need, Forgive us what we owe to you, as we have also forgiven those who owe anything to us. Keep us clear of temptation, and save us from evil.

It must be remembered throughout this analysis that there are gaps in our knowledge of the textual history of some Germanic languages. With Faeroese, for instance, we have evidence for what is likely to be the language's ancestor, Old (West) Norse, largely from documents written in either Iceland or Norway. We have little or no evidence for Faeroese as a written variety until the eighteenth century; it is only in the nineteenth century that the language 'takes off' as a literate and standardised variety. We *can* reconstruct what developments Faeroese went through during its non-literate period, but these are educated guesses. Therefore the choice of which early varieties to consider is not entirely free; it is based primarily upon the availability of material.

In the following, the earliest witness analysed is Gothic,[5] an East Germanic language, originally written in the fourth century in a unique, Greek-based, script. Its version of the 'Lord's Prayer' runs as follows:

> Atta unsar, þu in himinam, weihnai namo þein, qimai þiudinassus þeins, wairþai wilja þeins, swe in himina jah ana airþai. Hlaif unsarana þana sinteinan gif uns himma daga, jah aflet uns þatei skulans sijaima, swaswe jah weis afletam þaim skulam unsaraim, jah ni briggais uns in fraistubnjai, ak lausei uns af þamma ubilin.

Even without in-depth knowledge of the early Germanic varieties, it is almost immediately apparent that Gothic is inflectionally rich. If we accept – correctly – that most final suffixes at least are inflectional morphemes, the relationship between function and form can be analysed as complex and highly nuanced, even in such a small space.

With the noun phrase, grammatical case marking is immediately evident. Accusative case contexts along the lines of *Hlaif unsarana þana sinteinan* 'bread-our that of today', where the *-na* would have told a native speaker that these refer to masculine nouns with the accusative case, are present in some numbers, as are dative case expressions, such as *in fraistubnjai* 'in temptation' or *af þamma ubilin* 'from that evil'. Nominative case contexts include *namo þein* 'name-your' and *þiudinassus þeins* 'kingdom-your', where, in the latter case, *-s* implies nominative masculine contexts. As the last two examples demonstrate, noun class and, in particular, grammatical case affect the type of endings (and, indeed, form) which nouns, adjectives and determiners realise even when the same case is being represented. In this text, moreover, case is expressed both through noun (and adjective) ending morphology and the form of determiner realised. Impressionistically, the former might exert more force than the latter; this is not fully the case in later Germanic varieties. Like all early Germanic languages (and most contemporary ones), Gothic made a distinction between *weak* adjectives, where gender, case and number information is carried by a determiner, not the adjectives, as with *Hlaif unsarana þana sinteinan*, where the *-na* on the pronouns carries sufficient information that the adjective does not need to express grammatical relationships morphologically, and *strong* adjectives, where gender, case and number information is carried by the endings on the adjective. No strong adjective forms (or, indeed, contexts) occur in this passage, but they are as common in the Gothic corpus as a whole as in any of the later Germanic languages which have maintained the distinction.

In relation to verb use, less can be said based upon this brief excerpt. We can see that a subjunctive mood existed, with distinctive endings for second (*ni briggais uns* 'may you (sg.) not bring us') and third person singular present (*qimai þiudinassus þeins* 'may your kingdom come'). Imperative forms, such as *gif uns himma daga* 'give us this day' are also present. Only one indicative form is triggered – *weis afletam þaim skulam unsaraim* 'we give forgiveness to those debtors-our' – but information from the whole Gothic corpus tells us that discrete forms for these moods are found for both singular and plural in all persons and most numbers, as well as for gender in third person and dual number in first and second persons.

Some 200–250 years later, the West Germanic languages began to be recorded in Roman script, with Old High German and Old English being used in a considerable number of contexts, including the production of a translation of the 'Lord's Prayer'. We will begin by considering the Old High German version, recorded in a ninth-century variant written in a southern (Upper German) dialect:

> Fater unsar, thû pist in himile. uuihi namun dînan. qhueme rîhhi dîn. uuerde uuillo diin, sô in himile sôsa in erdu. prooth unsar emezîch kip uns hiutû. oblâz uns sculdî unsarô, so uuir oblâzem uns sculdîkêm. enti ni unsih firleiti in khorunka. ûzzer lôsi unsih fona ubile.

As with the Gothic version, morphological expression of function with the noun phrase, including noun and adjective class, number, case and gender information, is complex, whether that be in the nominative case, as with *rîhhi dîn* 'kingdom-your' (where lack of endings on noun and pronoun informs us that this is nominative neuter) or dative, as with *sô in himile sôsa in erdu* 'as in heaven as on earth' (where *-e* and *-u* represent dative forms for different noun classes and genders). Indeed, it is striking that, unlike in the Gothic, no determiners are used to express functional relationships. This does not mean, however, that Old High German is as close to having a form to function relationship as Gothic. Accusative phrases with neuter nouns like *prooth unsar* 'bread-our' cannot be distinguished morphologically from nominative equivalents. A great deal of the information a native reader or hearer would receive from the text in relation to syntactic role was already carried by *where* a phrase was placed in the syntax rather than *how* it was represented.

Similar points might be made about verb use. Subjunctives are prevalent, such as *uuihi namun dînan* 'may hallowed-be name-your' and *lôsi unsih fona ubile* 'may you protect us from evil'. Strikingly, however, person no long appears to be represented morphologically for this context. Imperative forms also occur, as with *kip uns hiutû*, 'give us today'. Indicative forms are represented by *uuir oblâzem uns sculdîkêm* 'we forgive our debtors', with the *-m* on the verb marking the first person plural indicative present. Indeed, the corpus of Old High German as a whole demonstrates that person, number and gender marking (when appropriate) is largely discrete in some moods and tenses, while they have been conjoined in others.

The Old English version is somewhat later (tenth or eleventh century) and recorded in West Saxon dialect (from the south-west of England):

> Fæder ure þu þe eart on heofonum; si þin nama gehalgod; tobecume þin rice; gewurþe þin willa, on eorðan swa swa on heofonum; urne gedæghwamlican hlaf syle us to dæg and forgyf us ure gyltas swa swa we forgyfað urum gyltendum and ne gelæd þu us on costnunge ac alys us of yfele soþlice.

Many similar issues could be addressed here. With noun phrases, dative case is expressed inflectionally, as with *on heofonum* 'in (the) heavens'. Accusative contexts can also be expressed by form, even if this is largely carried by modifiers rather than the noun itself, as can be seen with *urne gedæghwamlican hlaf* 'our daily bread', where the use of the *-ne* ending would have told native speakers that accusative masculine contexts were being represented. But the ancestral distinction in form between the (originally noun class-marking) *-e* in the nominative form *rice* 'kingdom' and the (originally gender- and case-sensitive) *-e* in *of yfele* 'from evil' is no longer possible. With the verbs, a fully functioning subjunctive mood is present, even if the endings used do not express number or person in the ways found in Gothic. It is also striking that *si*, the subjunctive form of 'be', is being used as an auxiliary in *si þin nama gehalgod* 'may your name be hallowed' (the fact that this is a passive construction would encourage this).

Although not shown fully here, however, position in the clause is obviously of considerable importance for both noun and verb phrase contexts, suggesting a move away from a fully synthetic typology; nevertheless, a great deal of information related to noun phrase relationships is carried by Old English determiner use (earlier varieties of Old English, most notably early Old Northumbrian, had a richer endings morphology inventory than had late West Saxon). For Old Saxon, the ancestor of Modern Low German and a close relative of the ancestor of Modern Dutch, no straightforward translation of this prayer exists. Instead, a poetic paraphrase is found in *The Heliand*, a heroic life of Christ:

> Fadar usa firiho barno, thu bist an them hohon himila rikea, geuuihid si thin namo uuordo gehuuilco, Cuma thin craftag riki. UUerða thin uuilleo obar thesa werold alla, so sama an erðo, so thar uppa ist an them hohon himilo rikea. Gef us dag gehuuilikes rad, drohtin the godo, thina helaga helpa, endi alat us, hebenes uuard, managoro mensculdio, al so uue oðrum mannun doan. Ne lat us farledean leða uuihti so forð an iro uuileon, so uui uuirðige sind, ac help us uuiðar allun ubilon dadiun.

> 'Our Father of the children of earth, you are in the high kingdom of heaven, hallowed be your name in such words, may your mighty kingdom come. May your will be worthy over all this world, the same on earth, as it is up there in the high kingdom of heaven. Give us today some counsel, lord the good, your holy help, and forgive us, guardian of heaven, our manifold sins, just as we do to other people. Do not let us be led away by evil creatures to do their will, as we deserve, but help us against wicked deeds.'

Despite the lack of exact concordance, essentially the same features and tendencies as analysed for Old English and Old High German can be found in this text. These include dative marking, whether without prepositions, as in *al so uue oðrum mannun doan* 'just as we do to other people' or as part of a prepositional phrase: *an them hohon himilo rikea* 'in the high kingdom of heaven'. We also find the use of other cases, such as the genitive, as in *Fadar usa firiho barno*. In relation to the verb, subjunctive forms are prevalent, whether through the use of a periphrasis, such as **geuuihid si thin namo** 'hallowed be your name', or where the subjunctive is marked on the main verb, as with **Cuma thin craftag riki** 'may your mighty kingdom come'. But the verb 'let' is also used to express future possibility, as in *Ne **lat** us farledean leða uuihti so forð an iro uuileon* 'do not let us be led away by evil creatures', which may be taken as a forereckoning of periphrastic usage in a number of later Germanic varieties. This must be weighed up alongside the considerable inflectional conservatism of this piece, however, particularly in comparison to Old English.

The extent to which this was also true for North Germanic, here represented in a twelfth-century Icelandic version, will now be considered:

> Faþer vár es ert í himenríki, verði nafn þitt hæilagt. Til kome ríke þitt, værði vili þin sva a iarðu sem í himnum. Gef oss í dag brauð vort dagligt ok fyr gefþu oss synþer órar, sem vér fyr gefom þeim er viþ oss hafa misgert. Leiðd oss eigi í freistni, heldr leys þv oss frá öllu illu.

Despite being somewhat later than the West Germanic examples discussed above, the Old Norse represented here is, in fact, quite conservative morphosyntactically in comparison to the contemporary West Germanic varieties. Dative case contexts are particularly well represented, as with *í himenríki* 'in heaven kingdom' and *a iarðu sem í himnum* 'on earth as in (the) heavens'. On the other hand, unlike Gothic and Old English, the accusative phrase *brauð vort dagligt* 'bread-our daily' is not morphologically marked as being distinct from the nominative. This is largely related to noun choice: Old High German *prooth* and Old Norse *brauð* are members of the neuter-gender class and therefore, from early times, did not distinguish between nominative and accusative case contexts. Elsewhere in the considerable Old Norse corpus the distinction between nominative and accusative cases is highly marked, however. As we might expect, the potential morphological distinctions in the verb paradigm is considerable – very much in line with Old English, even if not on the same level of discrete formal realisation, as with Gothic.

Let us now analyse modern translations of the prayer into varieties of the Germanic languages (with the exception of Gothic, which disappeared as a written language after the East Roman conquest of the Gothic kingdom of Italy in the sixth century; we can tell that the language continued to be spoken from a fragmentary sixteenth-century recording from Crimea). In the first instance, let us consider the Modern Icelandic translation:

> Faðir vor, þú sem er á himnum. Helgist þitt nafn, til komi þitt ríki, verði þinn vilji svo á jörðu sem á himni. Gef oss í dag vort daglegt brauð og fyrirgef oss vorar skuldir, svo sem vér og fyrirgefum vorum skuldunautum. Eigi leið þú oss í freistni, heldur frelsa oss frá illu.

This version is strikingly similar to the translation made in the Middle Ages. To some extent, this is due to the reverence Icelandic language planners and educationalists feel towards the ancient variety of their language. This explanation can only go so far, however. If the morphosyntax of the modern language had changed significantly from its ancestor, it would have been quixotic to remain too close to the ancestral model in the written form. It is apparent, therefore, that the grammatical structure of both noun and verb phrase has remained (essentially) the same, with the exception of the grammaticalisation of the archetypically North Germanic 'medio-passive' construction in *Helgist þitt nafn* 'your name being hallowed', in comparison with the *verða* periphrastic construction found in the Old Norse version, representing an earlier Germanic passive construction pattern.

This conservatism is in marked contrast to the Modern English equivalent, as demonstrated in the Authorised Version's translation (1611) of this prayer, which has been particularly influential on later versions of the text:

> Our father which art in heauen, hallowed be thy name. Thy kingdom come. Thy will be done in earth as it is in heauen. Giue us this day our daily bread. And forgiue us our debts as we forgiue our debters. And lead us not into temptation, but deliuer us from euill.

In terms of the verb, the formal distinctions between the subjunctive (*Thy kingdom come*), the imperative (*lead us not into temptation*) and the indicative (*we forgiue our debters*) have been, to a considerable degree, neutralised. The overt expression of the subjunctive is prevalent in this text perhaps because of the learned background of the translators, but relatively uncommon overall in the language, thus suggesting that the distinction between subjunctive and indicative has become essentially an artificially maintained one. The slide away from the use of an inflectionally marked subjunctive was already well under way. The reality of this partial coalescence between indicative, subjunctive and imperative forms was that its weakest link – the subjunctive – had been replaced largely by the use of modal verbs.

With the noun, even less of the inherited 'machinery' survives. Indeed, beyond plural marking on the noun (but not on the adjective, a central feature in other languages), it is only with the relative and personal pronouns that function marking (and, to an extent, 'gender' marking with the latter) has maintained its presence, with the exception of the possessive marker -*s*. English has become largely divorced from its inflectional ancestry.

It is worth comparing this state to the situation in Modern High German, here in a 1975 version (although the Martin Luther translation of 1522 underlies this text, making it perhaps rather more conservative in its usage than would be the case with a translation based solely on a modern and idiomatic interpretation of the original Greek):

> Vater Unser im Himmel, Geheiligt werde Dein Name, Dein Reich komme, Dein Wille geschehe, wie im Himmel so auf Erden. Unser

tägliches Brot gib uns heute. Und vergib uns unsere Schuld, wie auch wir vergeben unseren Schuldigern. Und führe uns nicht in Versuchung, sondern erlöse uns von dem Bösen.

In relation to the noun phrase, it is striking how little inflectional morphology is maintained on the noun itself, with the exception of *auf Erden* 'on earth' and a few other instances (most of which are related more to the expression of plurality than grammatical case). Up to this point, Modern English and Modern High German are similar. Unlike English, however, German maintains case, plurality and gender information on determiners (for example, *im Himmel* – *im* an abbreviation of *in dem* – 'in [the] heaven' or *von dem Bösen* 'from the wicked one', both representing dative masculine or neuter usage). Strong adjectives (the distinction is maintained) also carry this information, as *Unser tägliches Brot* 'our daily bread' (with *-es* representing accusative and nominative neuter contexts) demonstrates. The same is true for personal pronouns (for instance, *unsere Schuld* 'our debt' – accusative feminine – and *unseren Schuldigern* 'our debtors' – dative plural). With English it could be argued that a central spur for the breakdown in grammatical case and grammatical gender marking was the loss of noun endings except in relation to plurality; it would be difficult to argue against this as at least a contributory factor to the breakdown, as we have seen. But although the change in inflectional suffixes has been almost as great in German, the language continues with a conceptual structure not that different from its ancestor, through the maintenance of already extant inflectional morphology with determiners and modifiers of the noun phrase being employed.

German verb morphology has been maintained in rather more ways than was true for the noun, with subjunctive, imperative and indicative forms being continued as discrete entities. There has been one syncretism in the indicative plural, with the original *-m* of the first person plural present being replaced with the *-n* of the third person plural, as with *wir vergeben unseren Schuldigern* 'we forgive our debtors'. Both being nasals, of course, *-m* and *-n* often fall together naturally, particularly in word-final unstressed positions.

With Dutch – a close relative of both English and in particular German – something like a typological half-way house between the patterns for those languages can be seen, however:

> Onze Vader in de hemel, laat uw naam hierin geheiligd worden, laat uw koninkrijk komen en uw wil gedaan worden op aarde zoals in de hemel. Geef ons vandaag het brood dat wij nodig hebben. Vergeef ons onze schulden, zoals ook wij hebben vergeven wie ons iets schuldig was. En breng ons niet in beproeving, maar red ons uit de greep van het kwaad.

With the noun phrase, plural (*onze schulden* 'our debts') and grammatical gender marking (*het brood* 'the bread' – neuter gender-class) are maintained. No trace of case marking is visible, however, even in such archetypal 'dative' contexts as *van het kwaad* 'from the evil one' (compare the Modern High German equivalent *von dem Bösen*, with dative case marking), although this text does not provide evidence for an interesting historical fact: until recently, Dutch maintained some case marking in the standard form, and many family and place names perpetuate these 'fossils'. The verb system is rather similar to the German, with the exception that *laat* 'let, allow' is preferred as an auxiliary in contexts associated with the use of the subjunctive in earlier varieties.

At surface level, the Afrikaans version of the prayer looks very similar to Dutch:

> Ons Vader wat in die hemel is, laat u Naam geheilig word; laat u koninkryk kom; laat u wil ook op die aarde geskied, net soos in die hemel. Gee ons vandag ons daaglikse brood; en vergeef ons ons oortredings soos ons ook dié vergewe wat teen ons oortree; en laat ons nie in die versoeking kom nie maar verlos ons van die Bose.

When we move beyond this similarity, however, largely caused by there being considerable historical influence from Standard Dutch directly on the Church language of many of the speakers of Afrikaans (as touched upon in Chapter 4), as well as the two languages' descent from a common ancestor in the quite recent past, it quickly becomes apparent that Afrikaans has lost grammatical gender marking (as can be seen with the invariant determiner *die* in comparison with the Dutch distinction between 'common gender' *de* and neuter *het*). As it stands here, Afrikaans seems to be at the same stage as English in relation to the inherited inflectional system. If we had a text which was more idiomatic, however, it would be apparent that Afrikaans, like English – perhaps more markedly than the latter – has assumed a radical analytic stance morphologically and typologically in comparison with the other contemporary Germanic varieties.

Modern Norwegian (on this occasion the Bokmål version of 2005) appears rather similar to Dutch in terms of development:

> Vår Far i himmelen! La navnet ditt helliges. La riket ditt komme. La viljen din skje på jorden slik som i himmelen. Gi oss i dag vårt daglige brød, og tilgi oss vår skyld, slik også vi tilgir våre skyldnere. Og la oss ikke komme i fristelse, men frels oss fra det onde.

As with Dutch, grammatical case has apparently been jettisoned. Gender marking is maintained, however, generally through the use of enclitic definers (*i himmelen* 'in the heaven' – masculine), determiners (*fra det onde* 'from the wicked one' – neuter) or personal pronouns (*vårt daglige brød* 'our daily bread' – neuter). Plurality is also marked on the noun (although not the verb). But unlike in Dutch, little is left of the inherited verb system. Like in Dutch, subjunctive usages have been replaced by the verb 'let'. Unlike in Dutch, underlying this is the fact that, as we saw in Chapter 4, there has been a complete breakdown of number and person marking in the verb paradigm to the Scandinavian languages. In Norwegian (and, indeed, in Danish and Swedish), little distinction between the moods is possible. Although a few fossilised phrases, such as *Gud velsigne deg* 'God bless you' or *leve Kongen* 'may the king live [for a long time]', survive, it could be argued that the Scandinavian languages have (as discussed in Chapter 4) gone further in this matter than has English.[6] Nevertheless, English and Afrikaans stand out as being the only Germanic languages which have lost grammatical gender and – to a large extent – case entirely.

5.3.1.1 Summary: Morphological change in the Germanic languages

A strong tendency therefore exists for all Germanic languages to move from a synthetic to an analytic typology, although the extent to which this has happened is different from language to language.

In the noun phrase, this set of changes led to a general move away from the foregrounding of noun inflections as markers of grammatical case and gender associations (this point with the exception of Icelandic, which has maintained a considerable amount of its ancestral morphological inventory). A continuum exists between those languages, like German, which have retained the original case and gender distinctions, largely, although not solely, through the use of differing forms of the determiner, through to Afrikaans and English, which demonstrate little or no continuity with the ancestral system. In between lie languages such as Dutch and Norwegian, where grammatical gender has been maintained to a considerable degree, but not case, except in essentially fossilised contexts.

With the verb phrase, the situation is rather more complex. As we might expect, only limited, generally phonologically triggered, changes are to be found with the verb paradigms of (Standard) High German and Icelandic; the same can be said for Dutch, even if dialectal usage provides a rather more simplified paradigm. English has – at least in the standard variety – maintained the singular–plural third person split found in Old English (the North Sea Germanic languages did not, from ancient times, express a distinction between the persons in the plural;

although dual pronouns existed, plural morphology was employed, rather than discrete endings). The first person singular form gradually fell into line with most plural endings; the spread of *ye/you* at the expense of *thou* meant that the same forms were also found with these numbers (these changes took place, of course, much later in at least the written form than was the case with equivalent noun phrase change).[7]

5.3.2 Sapir's drift

With some qualifications we can state that all of the Germanic varieties are moving in the same direction. We thus have evidence of something rather like Sapir's *drift*. This represents the understanding that all languages have a propensity towards *drift*, a metaphor Sapir derived from what we now call plate tectonics (Sapir 1921). As is the case with many brilliant ideas, this seems obvious after it has been described. Sapir demonstrated that there was an ongoing series of changes taking place in the English pronoun systems. While Old English had a fully-fledged demonstrative paradigm distinguished by number, gender and case relationships, Modern English only formally distinguishes number (Northern Scots dialects do not even do that). The personal pronouns distinguish number, person and – to a degree – function, with third person singular forms distinguishing between natural sex divisions. There are a number of occasions where this is not as straightforward, however. In all varieties, subject and oblique functions have *you* (or *ye*). Many dialects of English use historically oblique pronouns in subject contexts and often historically subject pronouns in oblique; many creole-based varieties do not distinguish between the functions. These are not recent developments. All English speakers are inclined towards producing structures of the *me and him went to the pictures* and its subsidiary, but perhaps more common, *between you and I* types, despite well over a century of prescriptive grammar teaching to all (for a minimalist take on this issue, see Sobin 1997). It could be argued, again, that the system is 'frayed around the edges'. Sapir brings these ideas into focus by discussing change in the English interrogative/relative pronouns. The function-sensitive form *whom* is now used primarily in writing or in planned speech (particularly in the British Isles; the distinction between *who* and *whom* appears to be far more prescriptively guarded in North America: see Millar 2005 for a discussion). Even in these circumstances, however, many native speakers get the rules 'wrong', with constructions along the lines of *whom is at the door?* not being uncommon. Sapir claims that all of these tendencies appear to be working in the same direction – ongoing loss of overt function marking. Indeed, they are part of the same process where a language follows the same track across similar features, over time achieving the same or similar results.

A number of issues might be raised about *drift*. It does seem, for instance, to anthropomorphise language, giving it desires and a sense of itself and what it is 'doing' which appear very close to mysticism to many scholars (see the discussion in Malkiel 1981). None the less, it appears to *work* across languages and times. One way of looking at it, perhaps, is that all varieties of a language or closely related languages, at all times, are the product of the same or similar 'genetic material', so that many of the same features will occur at different times and in different places in different varieties, just as they would with an extended family. Other images designed to illustrate and explain, from biology, genetics, geology and perhaps even musical improvisation, have been proposed.

Sapir did not, at least overtly, consider *drift* a feature shared by closely-related languages, although the example he uses certainly begs the question in that direction. Many historical linguists have employed it with this intention, however (see Malkiel 1981 for a discussion), and it is to this point I will now turn.

5.3.3 Drift and the speed of change

If we consider the evidence as a whole, it is apparent that, while all appear to be moving in the same direction, some Germanic varieties – Afrikaans, English and, to a lesser extent, the Scandinavian languages – have travelled further along the continuum of *drift* from synthetic to analytic structures. Their association with the latter typology is not as advanced as that to be found in pidgins and creoles, but the change is still impressive. At the other extreme lie Icelandic and High German, where, particularly with the former, only a small number of changes have taken place. With German, the inflectional richness of Old High German has been substantially lost, in particular in relation to the noun phrase, but the actual system remains essentially intact conceptually (although many, probably most, German dialects have ceased to use the genitive case, preferring a dative-based structure instead). In between these extremes is Dutch, where change has meant the loss of, for instance, grammatical case, but other aspects of the inherited Germanic morphosyntactic patterns, such as those associated with the verbs, have been maintained intact. These changes and distinctions can be represented diagrammatically (Fig. 5.1).

This analysis leaves out an important point, however. While German, Icelandic and Dutch have taken all of the last thousand years to 'travel'

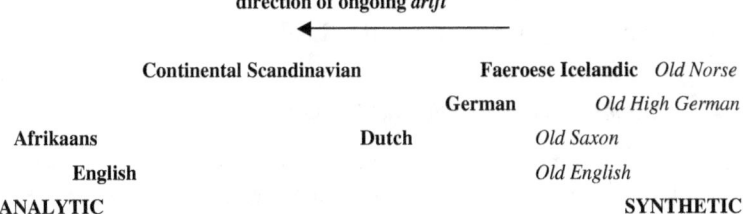

Fig. 5.1 Typological *drift* in the Germanic languages. Languages in *italics* = the earliest recorded form of a language. Languages in **bold** = modern varieties, descended from the italicised variety to their right.

relatively circumspect distances in their drifts, English, Afrikaans and the Scandinavian languages have travelled much greater distances relatively rapidly. We must therefore consider it likely that drift can *accelerate*. It is the argument of this book that language contact is a primary means by which this acceleration can be explained, a point already briefly considered in our discussion of the development of Afrikaans and Scandinavian in Chapter 4. The following sections will consider these processes in relation to the history of English. Can a connection be made between these typological changes and language contact?

5.4 Contact in early English

It has long been recognised by scholars that the set of typological changes described in section 5.1 for English may have been triggered to a lesser or greater extent (depending on viewpoint) by contact between English and other languages. Until recently, the languages most discussed by scholars as potential influences were Old Norse and (Norman) French. In recent years, however, the Celtic dialects of post-Roman Britannia have been added as potential influences by many. Some scholars have taken a position that at least downplays the contact phenomena earlier scholars had associated with the influences of French and/or Norse. The other external input which influenced Old English considerably was Latin. Unlike these other languages (with the exception of words borrowed along the former Roman imperial frontier, such as *wine*), Latin influence tended to be of an initially literate sort which was unlikely ever wholly to affect everyday interaction (or, at least, this is the mainstream viewpoint). It can therefore be ignored in this discussion. In the following I will give a brief summary of the historical developments by which English speakers came into contact with speakers of these other languages, before turning to the nature of

5.4.1 Contact between Celtic and English speakers[8]

Speakers of Germanic dialects had probably lived in south-eastern parts of Roman Britannia for a considerable period before links between that province and the Roman centre were permanently severed around the beginning of the fifth century. Some Germanic speakers were there as mercenaries; others had probably infiltrated coastal regions to settle. In the aftermath of the Roman withdrawal, however, something of a veil descends over Britannia, with little documentary evidence for who ruled and what language was used until around 150 years later. When contacts with continental Europe were fully restored towards the end of the sixth century, a very different situation was in place: most of the south-east of Britain was in the hands of English rulers who were well on their way to becoming kings. The coast of the island up to the mouth of the Tweed (and increasingly to the Firth of Forth) had also fallen under English control. Beyond these undoubted facts, however, a number of issues remain to be settled: issues, moreover, which cannot be answered entirely from the archaeological record. Central to these is the question: what happened to the indigenous people of south-east Britain?

In the nineteenth century, when these issues were first considered in a systematic manner, the general view was that most, although not necessarily all, of the Britons (if they can be termed such) fled from the invaders before finding sanctuary in the highland fastnesses of Wales, Cornwall and what would eventually become the north of England and Brittany. Genocide, this view would have it, may also have been committed in certain areas. War and retreat are indeed described both by native historians, such as Gildas and Nennius, and in English accounts, such as those of Bede and the compilers of the *Anglo-Saxon Chronicle*. But many of these resources are quite late in relation to the English settlement. If a witness lived through the events, as with Gildas, we cannot be sure of the extent to which his ideological position – the Britons were suffering destruction and the loss of their land because of their terrible sins – intensified his description of the violence and chaos of the English settlement period. To a large extent, therefore, according to this viewpoint, the Anglo-Saxon 'conquerors' inherited a *tabula rasa*; the new polities possessed little or no continuity with the old settlements.

A small amount of evidence supports this idea of catastrophe, in fact. Perhaps the most important of these is the status of Brittany in relation to Britain. Breton is a close relative of Cornish and an ancient tradition links the continental territory with the emigration of a range of (possibly high-status) natives of the south-western part of Britain to Brittany during the final (probably chaotic) years of Roman rule in Gaul. Moreover, it does appear as if a number of Roman urban centres – London being the largest – were barely inhabited, if at all, in the early Anglo-Saxon period. Medieval Welsh traditions suggest, furthermore, an awareness that a lengthy period of war and resistance had been a reality for their ancestors.

Linguistic evidence, at least at first glance, provides evidence for the violent seizure of territory with limited contact between invaders and dispossessed. A rather small amount of British vocabulary has been transferred to early English, suggesting a lack of contact between the two peoples (although, as we will see in the following, a counter-argument could be made, based on the same evidence). These borrowings are overwhelmingly onomastic in origin and are reminiscent of later imperialisms, where river names in particular were preserved as part of a general transfer of property rights and defined boundaries.

But these points are greatly outweighed by evidence that a violent rupture between Romano-Celtic and Anglo-Saxon dominance was at most localised. From this viewpoint, most 'British' people stayed on in the territories they had originally inhabited and eventually became 'English'. The archaeological record appears to provide some support to this position. In a number of places where Germanic settlement was early – on the coastlines and up the major river valleys – there is considerable evidence of peaceful cohabitation between the indigenous population and the incomers. In the St Albans region, for instance, Christian and apparently non-Christian burials took place near to each other at roughly the same time. While it is not impossible that some of the Germanic settlers had converted to Christianity before their arrival on Britain, continuities of practice suggest that the people carrying out the burials in the fifth and sixth centuries were, at least in terms of tradition, descended from those who had been carrying out burials a century before.

Moreover, there is evidence for group and individual movement between the different peoples. For instance, Cerdic, the semi-legendary founder of the West Saxon royal house, had a Celtic (Modern Welsh *Caradog*) rather than Germanic name. A number of other 'English' rulers, in particular in northern England, also had names with a Celtic origin. In addition, the Hwicce, a tribal grouping who were in possession of the lower Severn valley in the early Anglo-Saxon period, appear originally to have been a Celtic people. Even in the south-east of England, the names *Kent* and *Canterbury* (Old English *Cantwarebyrig*, 'the fortress of the people of the Canti(ac)i/of Kent') may well mark a continuity between Celtic and Anglo-Saxon rule.

In fact, the negative linguistic evidence for contact between the indigenous language(s) and English can possibly be given a positive spin. In his seminal study of linguistic change and use in Britain in the post-Roman period, Jackson (1953) convincingly argued that this dearth in transfer of British lexical items was not due to *lack*, but rather *because*, of close and long-term contact. People who live side by side will inevitably develop a degree of bilingualism. If there is social inequality between the peoples, bilinguals who speak the low-status variety are likely to avoid using vocabulary from that source when speaking the high-status variety. A few generations of this type of linguistic behaviour is likely to codify it.[9]

The question of how long Celtic dialects continued to be spoken in what was becoming the Anglo-Saxon heartland is a highly vexed one. Evidence such as that of the ethnic background of the Hwicce, touched upon above, suggests an early and relatively straightforward cross-over from Celtic to English at a formative stage in the Anglo-Saxon settlement. It is striking, moreover, that the Hwicce actually lived in the Welsh marches rather than in the English 'heartland' previously defined; they could have had more reason or opportunity to maintain their ancestral language than would, for instance, someone in the Thames valley. On the other hand, some evidence appears indicative of a long-term British presence on Anglo-Saxon soil; law codes in particular seem to suggest a niche (or set of niches) which the British inhabited in the new order. The possibility of a client–patron relationship between British noblemen and the Anglo-Saxon leadership presents itself, suggesting the survival of pockets of Celtic-ruled land within England, at least in the first few centuries of the settlement. This is supported by our awareness of the presence of Celtic kingdoms such as Elmet, situated in what is now southern Yorkshire, well into the period of historical record. Considerable room for manœuvre exists in relation to the length of time Celtic and English were in regular contact with each other, a point to which we will return in 5.5.3 below.

5.4.2 Speakers of English and Norse in direct contact

Anglo-Saxon England possessed considerable connections with Scandinavia long before the Viking period. The Angles, according to ancient tradition, had originated on the edge of Scandinavia in what is now Schleswig–Holstein; Anglian dialects *may* share features – such as, perhaps, the use of what is now *are* (rather than the undoubtedly West Germanic *sind(on)*, also recorded in Old English) – with the North Germanic languages, which are not found in other West Germanic varieties. The epic *Beowulf* is set in Scandinavia and displays a considerable understanding of heroic-age politics and history in the basin of the western Baltic. Some archaeological evidence appears to connect parts at least of eastern England to Scandinavian trade routes and practices (see Sawyer 1997a). But the contact between speakers of English and Norse from the eighth century on was of an unprecedented type. There is a sense, therefore, in which the later contacts between speakers of Old English and Old Norse essentially continue and deepen earlier avenues of contact: only a sense, however, as we will see.

There is long-standing debate over why Scandinavians first began to raid, and later settle and trade in, the British Isles (for a recent discussion of these issues, see the papers collected in Brink and Price 2008). Push factors, such as the growth of population in regions with limited soil fertility and available land, undoubtedly carried some importance, as did political centralisation and instability in the home countries (see Sawyer 1997a: 3–8 for a discussion of these matters); and pull factors, such as the growing wealth of monasteries and other Church property, often located in readily accessible coastal sites, must also have been involved.

While raiding remained a central form of wealth acquisition from the beginnings of the Viking period in the late eighth and early ninth centuries, petering out in the late eleventh century, trade and farming were also central to the Norse contact with English speakers (and, indeed, with Celtic speakers in other parts of the British Isles). Given the fertility of large parts of the soils of England, it is unsurprising that Scandinavians settled down in many places, no doubt regularly from an early period along with English-speaking partners. The centrality of settlements like York to trade throughout northern Europe was also quickly appreciated by the settlers. To lump all people of Scandinavian origin together is, of course, unfair and unrealistic. It may distort our view of the period: a period, as has already been noted, of considerable duration. It is likely, for instance, that Norse speakers who either had themselves been settled for a long time in England or were descended from Scandinavian settlers would have had limited sympathies for later raiders who happened to speak the same language (although it is also likely that opportunism encouraged the occasional decision by settled farmers to become part of major raiding enterprises; see Keynes 1997 for further discussion of these issues).

What is striking about Norse settlement and linguistic influence is that they are regional. While it is true to say that at particular crisis points, such as the near-collapse of the West Saxon kingdom in the late ninth century and the elevation of a Danish king to the English kingship in the early eleventh century, Scandinavian influence was appreciable throughout England, a number of factors – lack of geographical proximity to Scandinavia and the growing influence of Wessex over large parts of southern and western England being the central catalysts – made the Norse influence on the customs and language of southern England and the West Midlands relatively limited. The East Midlands, East Anglia and pre-eminently the north of England were ruled for considerable periods by speakers of Scandinavian dialects. They appear to have attracted considerable Norse settlement, to the extent that some scholars – for instance, Lutz (2012) – have claimed superstratal status for Norse in the region.

Samuels (1989b) put forward the idea that within this general Scandinavian settlement a 'Great Scandinavian Belt' existed, a region which had particularly dense settlement of Norse speakers who continued to speak Scandinavian dialects for a number of centuries. This area was, Samuels claims, marked to the south by the Rivers Humber and Ribble and to the north by the River Tees and what would eventually become the western Scottish border. A number of linguistic features mark off the Belt from surrounding areas (themselves Norse-influenced to a considerable extent); these include lexical items such as *laik* 'play' and *leet* 'look', not found anywhere else in the English-speaking world.

One of the puzzles which remains from this analysis is the amount of time for which Norse was spoken in this region. Most scholars would be happy to see a continuation of use up to a point somewhere in the eleventh century; Samuels places the moment of final shift in the twelfth century. This second dating does not imply, naturally, that Norse continued to be spoken by *all* people of Scandinavian descent in the north to that point; knowledge and use of Norse possibly would have been confined eventually to rural and even marginal regions towards the end of its life. The question of how English and Norse speakers interacted with each other socially and linguistically is also one which has engendered a considerable amount of scholarly debate. A number of these issues have considerable impact on how we assess the contributions Norse made to the development of English. They will be discussed in greater depth below.

5.4.3 Contact between speakers of English and speakers of French[10]

The French influence upon English is, in many ways, easier to demarcate. We can set a date – late 1066 into early 1067 – when the Norman Conquest looked likely to be permanent. We can also easily prove what type of relationship – socially and politically – speakers of Norman French and English had. Given the growing prestige of French culture across Europe, it is likely that at least some of the French influence upon English would have happened in any event.[11] But the social relationships between users of French and English, with many speakers of the former being in positions of political, intellectual and economic power (and Anglo-Saxons quickly being placed in the minority – if present at all – in the upper echelons of lay and ecclesiastical society) meant that, in many senses, the status of French in England was unassailable for a number of centuries.

Perhaps ironically, this status existed side by side with the slow shift away from French towards English by descendants of the Norman conquerors and later well-heeled French-speaking immigrants (for evidence of how this happened, see Coleman 1995). In part this changeover was due to conscious choice of English nationality by a considerable number of landholders of Norman descent after the loss of Normandy in 1204; it is likely to have started somewhat before this, however. From an early period, most French speakers would have been obliged to develop a 'kitchen English' in order to communicate with their servants, particularly when they lived far from the political centre of the kingdom. For a long period, a bilingual diglossia (Fishman 1967) must have existed, with Anglo-Norman as the High variety. Over time, however, the latter variety increasingly became a marked social code which may not have been used much and eventually became an identity marker.[12] The last few decades of spoken Anglo-Norman in England in the early to mid-fourteenth century evidence a variety which was lexically French but structurally English.

5.5 A sifting of the evidence: language contact and the early history of English

5.5.1 French influence

Until the last fifty years of scholarship concerned with the history and development of the English language, it was French which was often analysed as the presiding catalyst for the typological change which affected the language during the late Old English and early Middle English periods. To a degree this does, of course, make sense. The importation of French vocabulary is more than considerable and has altered the nature of the language's lexical structure permanently (although, as Thomason and Kaufman (1988) point out, the proportion of French borrowings any individual uses depends on her background, education and the context; they are not always central to the language's expression). Knock-on effects have included the phonemicisation of the previously allophonic voiced fricatives and a far less rigid word stress pattern than was previously the case. If we consider the structural influence French might have had upon English morphology and syntax, however, it does become quickly obvious that little concrete evidence for influence can be found. One feature which is occasionally mentioned (including in popular histories of the English language) as demonstrating French influence upon English is the preponderance of *-(e)s* as a plural marker in Modern English (also the dominant plural marker in French), in comparison with the position of this 'strong' noun plural in Old English in proportion to the 'weak' noun *-an* ending, omnipresent in German and Dutch. But a plural ending in *-s* was already common in Old English and can be seen, essentially, as merely becoming more prevalent.

While there may be some influence from French on the regularity or prevalence of these features, it would be quite plausible to envisage exactly the same change without any external influence at all; indeed, it is difficult to produce reasons why French morphological patterns should have had such a profound influence upon this feature and this feature alone, ignoring all other features of the noun phrase. Otherwise, the sensation of clutching at straws can be considerable, when reading arguments supporting this view. The impersonal pronoun *one*, for instance, may be derived from French *(h)on*, itself originally grammaticalised from Latin *homo* 'man, person'. On the other hand, a number of Germanic languages – particularly North Germanic ones – use their form of the numeral 'one' in just such contexts. Moreover, the social contexts in which *one* can be used are limited: for many – perhaps most – English speakers, the pronoun is probably barely within their use patterns, if at all. Other features, such as analytic prepositional possessive constructions along the lines of *the house of Robert*, may well be influenced by similar French constructions of the *la maison de Robert* type. Analogous constructions can be found in other Germanic languages, however, largely due to the loss or marginalisation of the inherited genitive constructions, as discussed in footnote 6. In other words, French influence may well have been at work in these examples, but not normally as the sole or even central impetus for adoption or change, a point to which we will now turn.

5.5.1.1 French as an ancillary force in linguistic change

Might the French influence upon English have been ancillary or auxiliary rather than primary? This can be analysed from a largely sociolinguistic viewpoint. With the Norman takeover of all (or practically all) central governmental and ecclesiastical roles in England within a generation of the Conquest of 1066–7, French had, as we have seen, become the primary (if not sole) language of the governing class. While it would be misleading to say that, in the aftermath of these changes, English ceased largely to be written, it is true that its use is rare, except for primarily functional purposes (as is the case with the homiletic material discussed above) or as something approaching a hobby. The lack of an elite versed in poetic technique and, if not literate, at the very least highly receptive to the literate reproduction of their native language, is likely to have loosened the bonds connecting English to what would have been a rather conservative model for representing itself (although see the discussion below on this matter). It also succeeded in rendering the West Saxon *Schriftsprache* roleless.[13] Although some influence from this writing system can still be perceived in thirteenth-century works such as the *Ancrene Riwle* or Laȝamon's *Brut*, this tends to be rather peripheral to the linguistic and dialectal nature of the texts themselves. French did not cause these changes, but it certainly encouraged them.

A further example of this kind of influence might be visible in the final stages in the complete loss of grammatical gender in southern English in the High Middle Ages, as I have pointed out in Millar (2000) and (2002). French did not cause the environment which brought about the breakdown of this feature, since this started well before the Conquest in at least some dialects. But, while a language with a fully functioning grammatical gender system is capable of incorporating a considerable number of borrowings within that system, assigning appropriate grammatical gender to each item, as can be seen with a range of immigrant languages spoken in North America in relation to their borrowing of English lexis (see, for instance, Haugen 1950), an already shaky system may fail to process a large number of borrowings and assign them to the existing grammatical gender system, just as Middle English was obliged to do with French lexis. This overload may have been the 'straw which broke the camel's back' in relation to the survival of any element of the system. Again, French provides the final blow to an already threatened feature (or set of features).

5.5.1.2 French and English 'creolisation'

But this view of a rather muted form of influence from French was rejected entirely by a marginal but still vocal group during the 1970s (see, for instance, Bailey and Maroldt 1977 and Dominigue 1977). Although these scholars differed considerably in their analyses and conclusions, the school's argument was that the abrupt need for French speakers to learn English created a pidgin (and eventually a creole). French influence could thus be classified not by direct transfer of material but rather through interference. This event (or series of events) therefore explains the typological changes which affected English during this period. While attractive in many ways, this explanation has a number of issues associated with it. The most important of these is that the influence French exerted on English must have been considerable if it could produce change in the language at least 150 years before the Norman Conquest and the introduction of fully-blown French-medium secular and ecclesiastical government in England. That is not to say, of course, that pidgins, or closely related phenomena such as 'foreigner talk', did not exist among speakers of Norman French as they attempted to assimilate a new (and low-status) language in the first generations after the Conquest. Any such set of developments could only have had, at most, a marginal influence on the development of the language, however. Norse influence appears rather more likely to be a major factor in typological change in English.

5.5.2 Norse influence

Creolisation arguments have also been used to explain the English typological shift, but with the proposed creole being brought into existence by interaction between Old English and Old Norse, a viewpoint supported – with differing emphases – by Poussa (1982), Rot (1984) and Hines (1991).[14] This argument is particularly focused in the debate over the extent to which English and Norse were mutually intelligible at the time of the Scandinavian settlements (see, in particular, Townend 2002, Þórhallur Eyþórsson 2002 and Moulton 1988). It is likely that the two varieties had been essentially dialects of the same language some 300–400 years before the Viking period; moreover, as we have seen, the ancestor (or one of the ancestors) of Old English was probably situated at or near to the boundary between the West and North parts of the postulated North-West Germanic unit. But a number of changes which affected either Norse or English separately (or, indeed, jointly but with different results) had ramifications in relation to the development of the morphology which carried functional information, as seen in the following versions of 'the man had two sons':

Old English: *se mann hæfde twegen suna*
Old Norse: *maðrinn (manninn) hafði tva sǫnu*.

Considerable issues existed in the comprehension of grammatical structures, even if the lexis of the two languages was very similar (albeit with some phonological divergence). These problems were not due to differences in the fundamental morphosyntactic distinctions expressed in these languages – these generally were very similar for both, with Old Norse being a little more conservative (and therefore inflectionally complex) in this matter than Old English (the concept of *complexity* will be returned to on a number of occasions below), but differences are distinctly limited. Rather, it is the outward expression of these distinctions which caused the problems in moving from one language to another.

These changes are, proponents of this viewpoint would suggest, essentially equivalent to those found with creoles (and, indeed, pidgins); less convinced adherents would analyse the set of changes as being similar to creolisation, but with the proviso that an abrupt historical breach with input varieties had not taken place. Most scholars appear to feel that the use of the term *creole* (and its conceptual underpinning) for what happened to English is unsustainable in relation to the evidence we have before us. In particular, there is no evidence for there being a period during the development of English when a radical breakdown in communication made the development of a 'simplified' variety an absolute requirement of societal and personal needs. Most creolists would consider this breach as underlying the development of a pidgin, and therefore of a creole. A number of scholars have pointed this out – Mitchell (1994) and Görlach (1986) being among the most eminent commentators – with Allen (1997) erring, perhaps, on the side of caution within the debate (see George 2013 for a discussion). This still leaves us looking for explanatory models, however.

5.5.2.1 English a creoloid?

A related issue can also be brought into play: if English is not a creole caused by contact with Norse, can a category be put forward for a situation which bears many resemblances to, but is not exactly the same as, creolisation? Could it, in other words, be what was discussed in Chapter 4 as a *creoloid* or *semi-creole*, in essence similar to varieties like Pitkern and Norf'k patois? In work from the 1980s, Peter Trudgill (1983 and 1986) built upon these ideas with specific reference to English, comparing the development of that language under the influence of Norse to that of Continental Norse in relation to Low German and Afrikaans in relation to its range of contacts. In Millar (2000) and Chapter 4, I critiqued this equation, suggesting that *creoloid* was better suited to Afrikaans, with contact developing between a range of different languages within a continuum between Standard Afrikaans, to a considerable extent mutually intelligible with Standard Dutch, until fairly recently the language of Church and State, and the non-standard varieties spoken by poor rural whites and 'coloureds', which contain many features analogous to those found with creoles. Middle Scandinavian and Low German, along with Viking Norse and Old English, were involved in close-relative contact; this distinction is very likely to have influenced the ways in which the various languages developed.[15]

At essentially the same time as Trudgill was working through his initial ideas on how to approach this set of changes, Thomason and Kaufman developed their own response to the issues, in particular in relation to the Norse-influenced creole hypothesis.

5.5.2.2 Thomason and Kaufman: 'Norsified English'

The publication of Thomason and Kaufman's *Language Contact, Creolization, and Genetic Linguistics* in 1988 is seminal to our present understanding of how language contact affects the nature of languages. The scales relating to the level of contact given within the book have been reproduced, both by the authors and by their admirers (which includes the present writer), on a number of occasions. Indeed, Thomason and Kaufman's views have become something like a prevailing orthodoxy among those who study contact. And yet, on rereading the book more than 25 years after its publication, nagging doubts about some of the points made remain, in particular in their treatment of the development of English under Norse influence, a sense of unease already expressed in Millar (2000).

Essentially, this discomfort derives from a single point, central to their analysis: the idea of structural borrowing and transfer (phonological, morphological and syntactic, as well as of lexis) as representing the primary means by which large-scale contact affects languages involved in such a relationship. That contact phenomena of this type are common cannot be doubted; they may indeed be the central by-product of the process. Other phenomena are also regularly present, however: phenomena which do not involve borrowing. Instead, they demonstrate interference and 'simplification'. Thomason and Kaufman analyse these phenomena as a product of creolisation (particularly what they term *abrupt creolisation* and language shift). Little discussion is afforded to those situations where the varieties in contact are close relatives of each other and where there might be some degree of intelligibility, as discussed above.

Possibly the best place to see where the problems with these issues lie is in their discussion of the 'simplification' processes through which English passed in the late Old English and early Middle English periods. Thomason and Kaufman make a case for there being a regular set of changes in the morphosyntax of English which are, in the first case, not at all 'dramatic' or 'traumatic', and which are also mirrored in many of the other Germanic languages (and, indeed, beyond). At a surface level this is, of course, correct. The typological changes through which English passed, while probably not commonplace, are also, as we have seen, certainly not rare either. Almost inevitably, some isolating languages will move towards fusional or agglutinative states (as can be seen to some degree in Chinese today); as was the case with English, languages with considerable synthetic tendencies can easily move towards analytic patterns. Moreover, as we saw earlier in this chapter in our discussion of Sapir's *drift* and in the illustration of that process in a range of Germanic varieties at the beginning of this chapter, *all* Germanic languages have followed essentially the same path over the last thousand years or so; even morphosyntactically conservative varieties like High German and, to a lesser extent, Icelandic are notably more analytic in their organisation than were their ancestors. There is no need to invoke language contact to explain these changes, as Thomason and Kaufman quite rightly point out; a view of this sort does not necessarily discount contact from having *any* effect on changes of this nature, however.

Thomason and Kaufman trace a change moving from the north of England (or, from their point of view, the north Midlands) into more Southern dialects. As transfers between dialects take place, the effect of these changes is lessened (a point to which we will return shortly). At a global level, therefore, it is not at all unlikely that changes caused by Norse should be equivalent to other contacts normally considered to be lesser, such as the influence of Low German upon English in the later Middle Ages, a comparison which Thomason and Kaufman make much of. But it should be noted that the latter influence, rather than being diffused across England, is largely confined, according to this analysis, to East Anglian dialects; the influence of Norse within and beyond its original 'Great Scandinavian Belt' is rather more potent than what is suggested by them, even with Britton's (1991) downplaying of some of the more marked elements of Samuels's original argument. But there remains a suspicion that, in concentrating on transfer, these scholars may be missing something.

Moreover, possibly because neither Thomason nor Kaufman has taken the historical development of the English language as her or his specialisation, their analysis, while rarely wrong when discussing English, occasionally feels lacking in nuance to those who have made the history of that language their specialism. I have critiqued aspects of their views in Millar (2000: Chapter 2). What needs to be recognised, however, is that Thomason and Kaufman are often too content to take evidence from later witnesses of a dialect as representing evidence for an earlier variety. Issues such as these inspired Millar (2000).

5.5.2.3 Millar (2000): koineoid

Basing itself on discussion of change in the English demonstrative systems during the late Old and early Middle English periods, Millar (2000) attempted to ask whether we should look towards convergence as a means of explaining change involving the radical simplification of inherited material which did not help encourage easy communication. This is in line with the development of koines of various types around the world, as we saw in Chapters 2, 3 and 4, including the original Greek variety and, for example, Fiji Hindi. Because Viking Norse and Old English were more distant from each other than many other contacts which produce koines, the simplification involved in the linguistic marriage of the two would have been considerable. This simplification would also have been inherent and partly latent in the input varieties, represented by the *drift* phenomena in the Germanic language discussed at the beginning of this chapter. In a sense, therefore, what happened to English could be envisaged as an acceleration of *drift*.

This view that koineisation and convergence need not be mutually exclusive is not, of course, a new matter; Millar (2000) does at least attempt to view the changes involved as part of a greater set of modifications associated with the dialectal development of language. Perhaps primarily the change is not seen as representing a single and unalterable process but rather a situation where elements are spread independently of each other. This process would build similar but not identical subsystems in the newly affected dialects.

A central feature in our understanding of the development of English morphology during this period is how the grammatical gender system of English collapsed. As we saw, Jones demonstrated, in work spanning three decades (Jones 1967ab, 1983, 1987), that in between the possession of a fully functioning grammatical case and gender system and one where little, if any, such concept existed there were one or two generations where a sub-system developed where originally case- *and* gender-sensitive forms were used to express *only* functional information. Thus a form like *þæm*, originally associated exclusively with members of the masculine and neuter gender classes in dative case contexts, came to be connected to all nouns in indirect object and most prepositional contexts. A change of this sort would be in line with Kuryłowicz's (1949: 31) fifth formula: 'In order to re-establish a difference in a central function, the language abandons a difference in a more marginal function' [my translation]. Millar (2000) described the process as *conservative radicalism*, the use of innovative features to shore up as much as possible of the inherited system.

The problem with such a process from the point of view of any survival of the inherited system, as Millar (2000) claimed, is that at the time, due to *drift*, even the most conservative southern dialects were beginning to move towards inflectional simplification. At the same time, the radical features created in the primary contact areas in the Great Scandinavian Belt were answering this need for change and being exported south (and also north into Bernicia and Scotland, although we have practically no evidence for this). Once one set of changes was carried through, however, this created new issues which had to be answered by further northern importations. This process could be seen as a form of capillary action involving the movement of features (each perceived, perhaps, as a means of maintaining the system in as 'ancestral' a form as possible). Ongoing change, often demonstrated in the rather chaotic inflectional morphology found in many texts as the changes passed through, meant that a full set of most developments had to pass through all varieties before full stabilisation could take place. This 'capillary action' in the spread of features from north to south is well documented in medieval English, as Samuels (1989a) demonstrated.

Because, in contradiction of the deeply flawed arguments of Emonds and Faarlund (2014) that Modern English is actually a North Germanic language, English has remained *English* in its solutions to these problems, rather than borrowing from Norse or other sources, Millar (2000) described the language as a *koineoid*, basing the new coinage on the distinction between *creole* and *creoloid*. An original *koine* was created in the north of England where primary contact between Norse and English took place, convergence between two highly distinct varieties and simplification producing a new variety. These compromises over what parts of the original koine 'package' were brought into other dialects meant that the results were lesser events; convergence between two relatively similar varieties where developments derived from the original contact was now present only as a secondary feature (something, as we have seen, also suggested by Thomason and Kaufman 1988). To distinguish between the two similar but different sets of contacts, the product of the latter was termed *koineoid*, based on the word formation underlying *creoloid*. This gradualness, which can be illustrated using examples from

Samuels (1989a), also counts against Faarlund and Emonds's argument that Modern English is a descendant of Norse which replaced English in the East Midlands in the early Middle English period, as discussed in footnote 14.

In retrospect, *koineoid* is a term too far, since, as we saw in Chapters 2 and 4 and elsewhere, *koine* can be used to describe a wide range of convergence phenomena from contact between essentially discrete languages to contact between very similar dialects. What it is necessary to bear in mind is that not all the contacts involved in the changes in late Old English and early Middle English were of the same type or involved the same distance between the different inputs, however. The changes involved were quickly nativised, primarily because lesser but similar changes were already to be found in the more southerly dialects before contact took place. This is also in line with our understanding of long-term drift in both the north and more southerly regions. Fischer (2013) supports the idea of the koineisation of English and Norse as being a central impetus behind these changes.[16]

5.5.2.4 Discussion

Despite these scholarly disagreements, however, it would be fair to say that, at the end of the last century, the general consensus on the typological changes in the late Old English and early Middle English periods was that the primary contact between Norse and English in the 'Great Scandinavian Belt' during the Scandinavian settlements was the fundamental catalyst for the change involved. This orthodoxy has more recently been challenged by scholars advocating alternative contact scenarios as catalysts. Strikingly, these views are now supported by a scholar who formerly endorsed the Norse origin hypothesis.

5.5.3 Trudgill and the Celtic contact hypothesis[17]

As we have seen, in the 1980s, Peter Trudgill considered the typological change in English in the late Old English and early Middle English periods as being primarily derived from contact between Viking Norse and Old English in the north of England, ploughing essentially the same furrow as Thomason and Kaufman (1988) and (later) Millar (2000). In the last thirty years his views on this matter have altered, however. He now considers the contact between English and the Celtic varieties spoken in what became England in the early Anglo-Saxon period the catalyst for typological change in English (Trudgill 2010 and, in particular, 2011). In order to understand his argument, however, we need to consider how Celtic influence – previously interpreted by many, as we have seen, as being of little importance to the development of the language – should have assumed such centrality to some scholars.

5.5.3.1 The Celtic catalyst?

If, as we have previously discussed, there is general scholarly consensus that large numbers of speakers of Celtic dialects remained in those parts of Britain where Anglo-Saxons established local and (eventually) regional hegemony, we are obliged to consider what effects speakers of these languages might have had upon the target Germanic dialects as language shift took place. What would be the results of such a socially unequal bilingualism? Many scholars concerned with this time period – often, but not exclusively, historians rather than historical linguists – tend to see Celtic influence as lying at the centre of the typological changes which have affected English, making the case that the mass unequal bilingualism just described would have caused a general 'simplification' of the English they used in comparison with native speakers. This is, of course, a fair argument, but one which sidesteps one particular but vital issue. If the changes involved were entrenched during the period of greatest contact effects – which, we might assume, was the fifth to seventh centuries – why does it appear first in the tenth century in the north of England? Why does evidence not first present itself in the English Midlands, where the largest number of people speaking *any* language lived?

This is a difficult issue to address and implies (although it might not be stated as) a considerable leap of faith. Essentially, a diglossia is assumed where speakers of English who either remained bilingual in a Celtic dialect or were descendants of such bilinguals, using the Celtic-influenced English variety (or varieties) postulated, were subordinated, despite the fact that they were quite possibly in the majority, to an Anglo-Saxon ruling class which used 'classical' Old English. Because of the last group's stranglehold on literate use of the vernacular, this 'classical' form remained the sole written variety except where there was a breakdown in societal structures, as was the case in the north of England during the Viking period.[18] Some scholars have gone so far as to describe the relationship between 'Celtic' underclass and 'Anglo-Saxon' rulers as being an example of *Apartheid*, with the majority forced to remain mute and disenfranchised. It is from these sets of views that Trudgill (2010 and 2011) derives much of the impetus for his new viewpoint, although he does not endorse some of the more extreme views of some proponents of the Celtic hypothesis.

5.5.3.2 Trudgill and the Celtic consensus

Trudgill's revised argument runs in the following way: when prepubescent children learn a language, they tend, if anything, to make the acquired language more complicated, particularly, perhaps, if there are no linguistic standards or fully encapsulated norms of usage available to the child, as would have been the case with most users of English during the Anglo-Saxon period. Thus the Norse influence upon English developed primarily in households where high tolerance levels existed in the use of the close relatives English and Norse by members of the nuclear family, with children growing up exposed to both. Situations like these would have been more likely, so the argument goes, to produce complexification phenomena in the English target variety than it would simplification. Initially, at least, however, speakers of Celtic varieties beginning to use English (not, it should be noted, a close relative) would largely have been adult; in a situation not unlike that of both contemporary indigenous minorities and immigrant populations, the youngest children in a family would, for some time, have remained the least likely to have full bilingual competence. Under these circumstances, simplification of the structural features of the language would have been more likely than complexification, given that adult learners rarely achieve complete control over a language.

Trudgill adds a further feature to his argument, again based on his reading of the theoretical nature of the distribution of complex and simple structural typologies within languages, following in the main Dahl (2004), McWhorter (2007)[19] and Kusters (2003). From this point of view, languages which have complex structural features – depending on the region, this might include ergative syntax, a large number of grammatical cases, a complex grammatical gender system, a plethora of consonants produced in many different places in the mouth and beyond, and so on – tend to be used in inward-looking communities where there is a limited amount of contact with external languages and cultures, and the overwhelming majority of children grow up with the community language as their sole everyday language. Comprehension is not, therefore, imperilled by there being considerable numbers of non-native speakers of the language. Basque, before the modern period, is an appropriate representative of a language of this type.[20] Languages with structures which are relatively straightforward to learn are, on the other hand, Trudgill claims, more likely to be found in situations where a language community is highly receptive to external influence, where network ties are generally loose and where a considerable number of adult learners of the language are present. Examples of languages of this type could include present-day French and English. The latter in particular also documents a relationship between standard and modern, largely urbanised, dialects fundamentally different from those found in the past between a standard or prestige dialect and traditional dialects. Therefore, Trudgill would argue, the necessity for communication in the early Old English period between native speakers of English and Celtic-speaking learners of the language would inevitably have led to a situation of simplification. This would have particularly been the case during a period when stable political structures were barely known.

5.5.3.3 Discussion

To what extent are Trudgill's arguments tenable? In the first instance, it makes sense to consider some of the wider arguments and assumptions made by some adherents of the Celtic catalyst hypothesis. Can we maintain the idea of there being two largely separate groups, one dominated by the other, within the framework of early Anglo-Saxon England?

Finding answers to this type of question is, of course, problematical, not least because a large part of the evidence is more limited and open to interpretation than would be preferred by any scholar. As we have already seen, there is some archaeological evidence which suggests a Christian presence deep in the heart of the Anglo-Saxon settlement area. Early historical accounts describe battles between Anglo-Saxon forces and British ones (or between Anglo-Saxon forces, but with considerable and organised British support) in areas which are generally supposed to have been Anglicised considerably earlier. The surviving early law codes also seem to envisage the British residents in English-ruled regions as being 'second-class citizens'. The *wergild* 'blood money' stipulated for a British nobleman was less than that for his Anglo-Saxon equivalent, for instance. Human societies being what they are, moreover, it would be unsurprising to hear that many of the large numbers of slave and unfree inhabitants of early Anglo-Saxon England had been put in this situation by their or their ancestors' being on the wrong side in one quarrel or another; many of these quarrels must at some point have derived from struggles between speakers of Celtic and Germanic dialects over possession of land and power. But does all of this imply *Apartheid* (Woolf 2007) or even a lengthy separation of social groups along ethno-linguistic lines within one community?

Let us return to the differentials in *wergild* cited above. This does suggest a situation where prejudice (or at least its judicial expression) was embedded in Anglo-Saxon society, possibly with the final goal of transferring capital from Celtic into English hands (each of these terms, of course, comes with something of a health warning) and thus producing, at the very least, a more homogenous ruling group. But we cannot say that British noblemen were not accorded some worth in the community: quite the opposite, in fact. Their presence within the wider English-speaking environment is also likely to imply the existence of organised pockets of British leadership on a par with, but not of the same number as, the English 'nobles' who financed and assembled the levees called for by a king in time of war. While appearing to support the hypothesis that English and Britons were kept separate, evidence of this type actually suggests the opposite. A crude bipartite analysis of the social and political relationships between natives and incomers is not representative of the documentary evidence. Most importantly, the idea of (near-)complete ethno-linguistic separation which the hypothesis requires in order to explain the length of time between inception of the changes and their introduction into written English is rendered decidedly dubious.[21]

Considering the issue with a more linguistic focus, there are also problems with the dating of the initial contact-induced changes in the early Anglo-Saxon period and their expression only in the later Anglo-Saxon period (and then just in northern England). Why was the new, 'Celtic', variety not recorded at all in writing? It is likely that scribes, generally, if not universally, recruited from the ruling classes, would, for a variety of reasons, have preferred more conservative writing styles. But would this always be true? More importantly, would the linguistic conservatism of the scribes always be represented in the codes of their equivalents and contemporaries?

An interesting case in point revolves around Bede's account of the poet Cædmon. Cædmon worked in a menial capacity for an Anglo-Saxon monastery, whose monks and nuns would largely have come from rather more elevated social backgrounds than did he. Yet not only was he able to produce 'classical' Anglo-Saxon poetry, but also his work was taken seriously by his superiors, who encouraged him to compose more in the same vein. There *is* a long-standing debate about the extent to which Cædmon's poetry is represented in the extant Old English versions of his 'Hymn to God the Father', with some critics seeing the extant version as being a translation of the Latin, the original being entirely lost (see O'Brian O'Keeffe (1987) for a discussion of some of these issues). But it is the social relationships between elite and lowly described which cut against the idea that there were social (and, more importantly, linguistic) barriers of some strength and standing within the community, even if *Cædmon* is itself in origin a British name.

5.5.3.4 Complexification *and* simplification: *some further thoughts*

The notion of *complexity* also needs to be unpacked. To a native speaker of Modern English, Old English appears structurally complex. In fact, the use of categories such as grammatical case and grammatical gender may appear unnatural or even meaningless to a modern reader. This cannot have been the case for native speakers of Old English, who probably did not think in terms of these categories at all unless they had been taught to do so, instead using them in relation to appropriate 'complexities' in the combinations of endings and forms. Taken cross-linguistically, these concerns become rather more clear-cut.[22] For instance, speakers of most Western European languages find the inflectional morphology of the Finnish noun phrase daunting. But, from what I understand, Finnish speakers find the English (or, for that matter, the French) prepositional system, with its concentration on idiomatic associations in relation to usage, confused and confusing in comparison to their grammatical case system. These apparent anomalies in viewpoint can be multiplied in a variety of ways. At certain levels of understanding, complexity can be in the eye of the beholder. This is not to say that typologies of complexity cannot be constructed. We have to be careful over how we begin, and carry through, categorisation, however.[23]

Some apparent simplifications may even cause complication. One example in English from the period under discussion is the development of a discrete definite article from the detritus of the collapsing simple demonstrative paradigm. The distal 'pure demonstrative' *that* derives from the same trauma. It is not that the semantic roles these forms now have developed with the forms; instead, Old English, like Modern High German, supplied both article and demonstrative function through the use of forms from the same paradigm. The split which altered a bipartite to a tripartite pattern cannot really be analysed as anything other than a complication or complexification of a previously more simple system; it also may well be the product of direct Norse influence (see Millar 2000).

This issue is further reflected in the development of English syntax. As this chapter has demonstrated on a number of occasions, the English morphosyntactic means of representing functional relationships have become considerably less complex since the early Middle English period in comparison with what they were before. That does not mean, however, that English syntax has become less complex. Indeed, the opposite could be argued, in particular in relation to hypotactic expressions of subordination. Structure of this type is likely, of course, to have come into the language as a result of influence from Latin stylistic patterns. But the fact that Modern English can handle a fair amount of hypotaxis (even if less than German, perhaps, with a richer inflectional morphology, can – or its readers will – tolerate) demonstrates the extent to which the language as a whole can deal with complexification.

5.5.4 Contact and the survival of diglossia

As we have already touched upon, time is also a factor in relation to the profound Celtic influence suggested by Trudgill and other scholars. How long can a variety spoken by a majority (albeit oppressed) remain 'underground'? If we believe that large-scale Germanic–Celtic contact in Britain must have started, at the very latest, by the second half of the fifth century, could this apparently strict separation of native-origin and Celtic-origin Englishes have remained unnoticed in the written record until its first occurrence in early tenth-century texts?[24] Even if we assume that most contact phenomena were created in the apparent hiatus in the westward and northward spread of English in the late fifth and early sixth centuries, we are still left with a considerable period of occlusion, an occlusion a critic might see as the flaw in a conspiracy theory.

It is true that Low varieties can remain outside the written record for a considerable period. A case could be made for Modern Standard French in relation to its colloquial forms representing just such a phenomenon. Written Arabic is an even more apposite example: although Modern Standard Arabic is not identical to Classical Qur'anic Arabic, it is much more closely connected to the latter variety than it is to any of the modern colloquial varieties (even if, from what I understand, it is normally possible to ascertain someone's origin from the written form through lexical choice and a number of other morphosyntactic features, in a way not dissimilar to the means by which users of British and American written forms of Standard English can work out relatively quickly the geographical origin of the writer in relation to these variants).

But these examples are not really comparable with the linguistic ecology of Anglo-Saxon England. The linguistic situation in France has been created by mass education and male military conscription over the last 150 years, along with centripetal forces related to linguistic homogenisation since at least the Great Revolution well over 200 years ago. Standard French has also been focused in the main on the language of the savants and not dissimilar Paris-centred language attitudes and practices dating from at least the Early Modern period, based on aristocratic models and notions of language purity and appropriateness (Millar 2005). With Arabic, the split is considerable and apparently permanent; the status of Classical Arabic as the revealed word of God in the view of Muslim believers is what gives the present written–spoken split its force (for a recent discussion, see Amer et al. 2011). In neither event can it be said that Anglo-Saxon England reflects similar divisions, as was suggested in our discussion of Anglo-Saxon '*Apartheid*' in the above. The presence of anything like a 'governmental' system, as we would understand it, is most unlikely.

5.5.5 Where were the first 'simplified' English texts written?

There is also the issue of where the first breakthrough texts representing the supposedly underground variety first appeared: northern England. Given what we know about proportions of population in the various parts of England now (and, indeed, then), the largest proportions of the postulated Celtic underclass must have been found in Southumbria (and, in particular perhaps, in the Midlands). Why, bearing in mind the one exception analysed by Roberts (1970), was the new system not found equally in that area rather than the north? The only way to answer this is to look to the disordered nature of Northumbria during the Scandinavian settlements. But this does beg a number of historical and linguistic questions. It is likely enough that there was an ongoing Celtic language presence in parts of the north (particularly, perhaps, in Bernicia). We can only assume, therefore, that any influence this Celtic contact variety, spoken by a relatively small population at the edge of England, must in some way be connected to the interference in social structures developed during the Viking period.[25] It seems, therefore, that we must argue for the centrality of contact with Norse as the primary catalyst for typological change in English.

5.6 Comparison with new dialect formation

How do we, moreover, bring into line the means by which contact between different varieties of the same language participates in the creation of new varieties of a language – theoretical and empirical discussion of which being one of Trudgill's primary research routes over the last thirty years – and his view that the contact between Old English and Old Norse would primarily have caused complexification? It is, after all, with this type of close-relative contact, where mutual comprehension is to a degree possible, that, Trudgill claims, complexification is most likely; early learners and users would work in this way, with simplification being associated essentially with the learning processes of adults. Is it possible to square these two sets of views?

Koineisation has, at its heart, compromise. It is not only a matter of ease which works upon the processes by which some variants within a dialect continuum are preferred over others. As Trudgill has pointed out in his work on dialect development, the proportion of a population using a given form, how different (and therefore marked) a form is in relation to all other choices, and perhaps also prestige and identity (although here Trudgill would disagree with other scholars) matter. Each of these is a powerful impetus in a particular linguistic direction; it is certainly common for less complex paradigmatic relationships to be preferred over others as a new variety comes into being, as our discussion of Fiji Hindi in Chapter 4 suggests. Given the differences (masking inward similarity) in outward expression of morphosyntactic relationships between Viking Norse and Old English discussed above, would we not have expected convergence encouraging similarity of this type to be the final result of contact of this sort in any event? Two issues need to be addressed if we are to weigh up this viewpoint: what distance must exist between language varieties before koineisation is no longer possible? And to what extent is what we have in later Old English and early Middle English *really* the result of these compromises?

The first of these issues is problematical, since it is not always possible to interpret exactly how linguistic distance affects comprehension; this is also the case with how native speakers cope with the combination of difference and similarity which exists between linguistic relatives. A good example of these issues can be demonstrated when we compare the Germanic and Slavonic languages. A native speaker of a Scots dialect from north-east Scotland – where this book was written – would recognise relatively quickly that the German dialects of northern Switzerland contain lexical features shared with her native dialect. But even with an in-depth knowledge of the comparative phonologies of the two varieties, she would not be able to build up sufficient comprehension ability without first actively learning the other variety. Even on an idealised desert island it seems unlikely that a koine would readily leap into being from the relationship between speakers of the two languages. This would not be such an issue with at least most of the Slavonic languages. Full comprehension would be impossible between, for instance, a speaker of Montenegrin and a speaker of Russian; more would be recognised than cognate forms, however, to the extent that, with good will on all sides, speakers of different languages could develop a compromise variety, making themselves understood without interpreters or special knowledge of the other language with the exception of a rough awareness of useful comparative indices. Thus an awareness of close genetic connections can mean strikingly different things for speakers of different linguistic (sub-)families. Nevertheless, we can safely say that the language boundaries which we consider central to our understanding of the linguistic universe may, in fact, be considerably more porous than might normally be thought and that koineisation – at least between near-relatives – is eminently possible.

A further possible connection to the theory of new dialect formation can be seen in a feature of some of the written language we possess from late Old English writing and much we have from the early Middle English period in that its realisation is on the borderline of being chaotic, particularly in relation to the expression of inflectional morphology. This goes well beyond the natural variation of a language. Old English, at least to begin with, had gone through some standardisation without full focusing (with the product being the result of contacts between the West Saxon *Schriftsprache* and the spoken (sometimes written) dialect of the scribe) and which later was subject to the normal patterns of a variety of relatively localised norms. As we saw earlier in this chapter, the variation involved appears to set up what were once discrete forms as mere variants of each other; 'new' forms which do not directly descend from the ancestral usage are in variation with this ancestral usage.

Of course, the variation described here, being written and therefore lacking in the immediate connection of usage and underlying interpretation which oral use presents in a much more straightforward way, is not necessarily representative of how the authors and scribes spoke. Nevertheless it gives some sense of the extent to which the inherited system has been devalued. Realistically, such a partial and broken inheritance veers toward the complete jettisoning of what has come before. As the failure of Jones's function marking sub-system illustrates, the sub- or semi-conscious defence of elements of the inherited structures was impossible (or, at the very least, unlikely). Does this represent rather more than the features we generally associate with koineisation? Or is it a matter of the actual process appearing nonsensical or chaotic up close, but its processes appearing much more logical when observed from further away? If that is the case, then another point of contact with the theory behind new dialect formation could be possible, with specific relations to the first-generation mixing Trudgill observed in his New Zealand materials. Interestingly, McMahon and McMahon (2006), taking a starting-off point derived from a cross-pollination of the theories and methodologies of computational genetics and historical linguistics, portray an English whose history is formed by sets of contacts far more chaotic than any of its close relatives. This 'chaos' accentuates the language's unique position in the Germanic language sub-family.

5.7 Discussion: towards a consensus

How, then, can we envisage the coming together of the two language communities – Norse and English – in the north of England both at the time of Viking settlement and in the period that followed? In the first instance, we must accept that the written evidence we have for the change is in many ways only partial and quite possibly unrepresentative of the language in its various forms as a whole. If we could see what was happening at relatively lowly levels in society, we might be able to say something more concrete. This opportunity is denied us, however; we are obliged to reconstruct from an informed understanding.

There is a literature extant – albeit of a rather limited extent – which describes what happens when speakers of different languages, who have at least passive understanding of their partner's language, settle down and have families together (see Baron 1971 for discussion[26]). Their children are likely to grow up in a situation where an 'imperfect' (or, rather, a simplified or koineised) variety of one (or, indeed, both) of the parental varieties is produced. In a situation where there is limited or no literacy, there is a good chance that the conservative 'braking' features which a standard written variety of a language possesses through prestige (and, also, inertia: a well-established standard variety may make it difficult for native speakers to think of any more appropriate way of saying something) will not affect these speakers. While it is true that in relatively stable situations where 'the elders' have considerable control over the practices of a non-literate traditional people, considerable power might be exerted over oral language use and what is appropriate, what we have here is something rather different: anomie and change would render the potential primary slowing mechanisms on language change of this type powerless.[27]

This is not a single-stage process, however. In the communities we envisage, this or similar processes would be at work in a considerable number of households. Again, similarities to the states described for New Zealand English in Trudgill (2004) are present, at least at a global level. What actually happens at ground level would be different – subtly or otherwise – from family to family. In the *second* generation, therefore, two different new varieties of the language would be likely to come into intimate contact with each other; new koineisation processes would then come into play, in order to bridge the differences between the varieties. Since it is not only within family units that these differing varieties were coming into contact (although this would be where they would be at their most intense), ongoing accommodations would be present throughout the community. Under these very fluid circumstances it would take no more than three generations (and perhaps only two) for a new and quite radical variety to come into being. Norse influence therefore lies near the centre of these typological changes. In many ways this resembles a much-enhanced version of the processes described in Chapter 2 for the first generations of New Zealand English.

The fact that the koine which developed in northern England was an English-based variety suggests an analogy with Myers-Scotton's (2002) argument that, in code switching, every complementiser projection (CP) has a 'matrix language'. No matter the level of contact, the local language remained dominant and supplied the essential building blocks for the new variety as it came into being. That this new variety is different from earlier local varieties demonstrates how profound these changes were, however.[28]

5.7.1 A return to the Celtic hypothesis

This discussion has still not answered all possible questions about the development of English during this period, however: in particular why the proposed koine took such a radical turn in its development. For this I believe we must turn to the 'wild card' of the linguistic relationships described in this chapter: Celtic influence. If you believe that Celtic influence lies at the heart of these changes, it is enough to say that the breakdown in social cohesion in the north of England in the course of the late Old English period due to Scandinavian settlement was the reason why the already existent Celtic-influenced English (that is, following this interpretation, essentially Middle English) first became visible in the written form. If, however, you believe, as the argument here suggests, that what pushed Old English in the typological direction at the speed it developed described in this chapter was primarily near-relative contact between Old English and Viking Norse, it might be possible to pinpoint Celtic influence in the north and west of Northumbria in particular – where the takeover of English was recent and relatively shaky – as being the catalyst for the broadcasting of change originally brought into being by other contacts. (For a further discussion of Trudgill's interpretation of these issues, see above.) It might even be the case that this extra influence acted as the tipping point which created momentum for the acceleration of *drift*. It is possible that, at some level, this 'virus' was at work on all varieties of the language, but that it was only where another major (and vital) contact – with Norse – took place that its potential effects were made real. We return here at some levels to the *founder principle* as proposed by Mufwene, discussed in Chapters 2 and 3. What marks off these lower-status Northern English varieties is the presence of a somewhat different set of founder 'DNA' (linguistically at least) from those found elsewhere. Without the societal breakdown envisaged, however, it is unlikely that such an effect could have developed, at least not at the speed and intensity suggested; near-relative contact lies at its heart. Essential to these analyses is the spread of innovation by the 'capillary action' described above. Variants of koine formation created largely by contact between discrete but closely related languages led to smaller-scale, but still fundamentally system-altering, forms of koine formation.

Contact between Norse and English is likely to have caused the formation of a koine in the north of England between speakers with limited but negotiable mutual comprehension of each other's varieties. Elements of this koine may, however, have been borrowed from 'foreigner talk' phenomena developed by Celtic speakers for speaking English on the edge of the areas of Anglo-Saxon dominance.

6 Conclusions

In this book we have discussed and analysed a range of language contact situations. Most of these dealt with circumstances where closely related varieties have come into contact with each other. Our focus has been primarily, but not solely, upon the English language and its history. In this final chapter a number of the issues which have been raised earlier in this study will be considered. From this it is hoped that consensus can be reached over some of the processes and outcomes involved in close-relative contact, whether the original inputs are considered dialects of the same language or as discrete, but related, languages.

In the first part of the book we concentrated on contact between dialects of what would normally be analysed as the same language. Various theoretical models were introduced, most of which were found to have a genuine bearing upon many of the issues involved. No one model could explain all of the features involved in the process of new dialect formation, however. The founder principle proposed by Mufwene, for instance, is an intriguing concept which helps explain the nature of the development of many new dialects. The problem comes, however, when we find that multiple founder populations appear to have made distinctive contributions to the development of a variety; moreover, initial founder impulses may be replaced by later forces. By the same token, *swamping* as an explanation is not entirely convincing (although nor is it anything near worthless). Indeed, at first glance the opposite of the founder principle, since swamping assumes that the influence of earlier linguistic inputs on a new variety can be erased by a (metaphorical) flood of speakers whose language is either nearly or wholly homogenous, the two theories are actually fairly compatible. As Mufwene has constructed his theory, it is not the *first* population which necessarily provides the blueprint for the new dialect; rather, it can be the *first significant* population which acts as the founder. A swamping event is perfectly in tune with such an analysis, yet it cannot be said to be applicable to all situations.

The most striking explanation for the mechanisms of new dialect formation is that developed by Trudgill over the last thirty years and more. Basing his observations upon ideas derived from sociolinguistic theory, Trudgill has set up a scale by which we can see progressive movement towards what might be described as colonial linguistic homogenisation. What is striking about this model is that it allows for considerable – indeed, sometimes apparently overwhelming – variation in the early years of the settlement, even when homogeneity later becomes the norm, a point supported by the recorded evidence of early New Zealand speech discussed in Chapter 2. Trudgill deftly demonstrates that this move from great diversity to considerable homogeneity is a completely natural part of the development of a new variety; in a sense, the one is impossible without the other.

Trudgill also puts forward a more striking but also controversial idea: that there is a connection between the dialects of the places of origin of settlers and the final result of the contact found in a given territory. In some ways, a viewpoint of this type is not controversial; it is only reasonable to assume that the linguistic backgrounds of the pioneer generation will affect the result of the contacts between people of different origins. What is striking about Trudgill's views, however, is that they involve a degree of determinism (or *inevitability*, as Trudgill terms it) in the construction of a new variety. Essentially, if a majority of the settler population exhibits a particular feature, this feature will inevitably become part of the new variety. This is a view which, in its most pronounced form, many scholars find difficult to accept, primarily because it denies individuals and groups much in the way of agency in the construction of a new variety; perhaps most strikingly, it appears to question the contribution of identity construction to language use, a cornerstone of sociolinguistics and of the sociolinguistic analysis of language. To be fair, Trudgill argues his position well; many of the points he makes are well founded in the evidence. He also makes a strong argument for there being occasions when even a majority form is so marked that it cannot survive in the competition between less marked (and therefore more 'natural' – or even acceptable – for greater numbers of speakers) and more marked features. Nevertheless, the apparently mechanistic nature of Trudgill's model is troubling.

This leaves us in something of a quandary. Each of the models presented has considerable merit, but none is fully satisfactory as a universal model (something to which at least Trudgill aspires). It may be that a full explanation for the phenomena associated with new dialect formation will remain beyond our reach. What Chapter 3 demonstrated, however, is that a combination of the founder principle, swamping and many of Trudgill's views can produce a preliminary archaeology of a dialect's development. Whether we can provide all of the answers from a broad-based analysis of this type is beyond the present book's competence; it does seem unlikely, however. What is certain, none the less, is that koineisation is a central feature in the development of new varieties, whether this be in a *tabula rasa* island settlement, such as Tristan da Cunha, or an urban centre during a period of mass immigration, such as Glasgow in the nineteenth century or Milton Keynes in the latter part of the twentieth century.

In giving the analysis of new dialect formation considerable historical depth, Chapter 3 also contributed to a broader debate on how far this analysis is possible. With most scholarly discussion of these phenomena, a large part of the evidence comes from the nineteenth century at the earliest. With American English we can look back to the seventeenth century on occasion, although the linguistic developments of the first pioneer generations are difficult to analyse in a systematic manner; the evidence is extremely hazy on occasion and often apparently contradictory. In Chapter 3 of this book, in our discussion of the development of the modern Scots dialects of Orkney and Shetland along with that of the English of Ireland, at least as great a time depth was presented in the case studies (with Irish English deriving, at least in part, from sources in the high Middle Ages). Again, much more debate in relation to the origins and development of these varieties is possible than with varieties whose origin is more recent; the evidence we have is also open to a range of interpretations; none the less, it is to be hoped that some contribution to the debate has been made. In addition, the Shetland and Orkney case studies demonstrated a connection to the second part of the book through the inclusion of a closely related but discrete language variety – Norn – in our narrative of the development of these dialects.

The book then considered what happens when two or more closely related varieties come into contact with each other where the linguistic distance between the varieties is considerably greater than among the dialects previously discussed but still not as great as would be found between most languages in relation to *Abstand*. Many of the same points applied, however, although inevitably with differing emphases. Certainly, *koineisation* was a central feature in our analysis of contacts such as that between Scandinavian North Germanic varieties and Low German in the later Middle Ages and Early Modern period. The results of this koineisation were more striking (perhaps even radical) and thorough-going than anything found in the first part of the book, however. When dialects of the same language come into contact with each other, there is often some simplification (a term which seems to be interpreted in a number of ways, depending on theoretical persuasion and, perhaps, the evidence) of, for instance, inflectional morphology. This is rarely all-pervasive and generally does not inhibit understanding by speakers of other dialects for the variety produced by the contact. With those situations where two more discrete varieties come into contact, however, the effect of the contact upon the variety which is created from it can be very striking indeed; so striking, in fact, that we can actually begin to talk on occasion – as with Fiji Hindi – about a new discrete variety being produced. Some commentators on these phenomena have gone so far as to compare the changes involved with creolisation; such an equation cannot be taken to its logical extreme, however (nor, to be fair, would all but a few linguists actually suggest such a complete equation).

The section – indeed, in many ways, the book – was dominated by a multi-layered discussion of the development – in particular in relation to inflectional morphology – of the English language from around 900 until about 1350. While it was recognised that the considerable – in fact, in many ways, revolutionary – changes through which English passed could (indeed, can) be explained as being due to system-internal developments or through the process of *drift* across a range of Germanic (and other Western European) languages (if the two explanations do not amount to essentially the same thing), system-external factors were necessary, it was argued, to give a full explanation of *why* and *how* the changes happened. Given the level of cultural and linguistic contact English sustained during the period, the obvious place to look for explanations is in connection with language contact.

As Chapter 5 demonstrated, the question of *which* contact – Celtic or Norse – most affected the development of the English language has dominated recent debate about these changes. While one influence can be viewed more favourably than the other, it is difficult, in fact, to see how they could have acted completely independently of each other. As I hope I have demonstrated, the origin of the change itself in contact between English and Norse may have been at least amplified by contact between English and Celtic.

A number of scholars have made much of the contact between Celtic and English as essentially the sole source for the great changes which affected English in the early Middle Ages. There is much that is attractive in an argument of this type, not least its apparent simplicity. As we have seen, however, there are serious issues with its complete acceptance. This is particularly visible in relation to Trudgill's views on what *simplification* and *complexification* actually mean. The argument that simplification comes largely through the imperfect learning of a language by adults (or at least anyone who has passed the 'critical threshold') obviously carries some weight, as does the argument that languages with 'simple' structures tend to be spoken in situations where there is considerable need for outward communication in ways which are readily comprehensible to as wide a set of users as possible. Concomitant with that view is its opposite: *complexified* languages tend to be spoken in tightly networked and essentially inward-looking communities, while *complexification* takes place in terms of language change when children under the critical threshold combine their native system with the newly acquired one to produce structures – phonological, morphological and syntactic – which retain the complexity of both systems. Again, it would be difficult to argue that this is not the case under certain circumstances; too much evidence can be used to support these hypotheses.

Yet the particular context in which arguments of this type have been used in relation to the history of English is problematical. As we have seen, for the argument to work in its entirety we need to assume that a Celtic-speaker variety of English survived for a number of centuries without being described or influencing the assumed acrolect, before finally breaking through the dissipating, conservative 'standard' in the aftermath of 1066–7. This seems dangerously close to a conspiracy theory. That does not mean, however, that elements of the Celtic influence scenario are not useful to our understanding of systemic and radical variation and change over the period.

It needs to be recognised, in fact, that the typological changes involved apparently began in the north of England – essentially what the textual evidence indicates. Given the history of that region, this suggests that Norse had an important (and probably central) part to play in spreading the changes developing in that part of the world. I would go further, however. The near-relative status of Norse and English is very likely to have created a koine where the lexical similarities between the two inputs were stressed (quite naturally and without conscious decision) over the inflectional differences. Although this development would have been on an individual or family basis on most occasions, the act of creation would have been shared across communities and therefore have become the force behind the development of a more general radical dialect in many ways similar to the processes illustrated by Trudgill in relation to the early period in the development of New Zealand English.

This view does not rule out Celtic influence as contributing to these developments, however. As has been demonstrated, the presence of Celtic speech 'islands' in the north of England is practically certain until a relatively late date, in particular, perhaps, on the northern and western fringes of Northumbria, close to the centres of power in

Bernicia, in comparison with more southerly Anglo-Saxon kingdoms. A situation where a somewhat 'simplified' version of English was used in the north, a variety which was replicated across a significant period of time because of the ongoing border experience of (partial) bilingualism, is easy to envisage. No 'underground' Celtic code needs to be proposed, however. It seems unlikely that the proposed dialect underlay the eventually universal set of changes which affected all dialects of English over the following four centuries, though; it is much more likely that developments in the Celtic-influenced variety helped replicate and transmit changes similar to those found in the Norse-influenced variety. The contact between near relatives is likely to have been central, at the very least, to the development of the koines described above and of the overall koineisation process.

There are many themes running through this book. These are largely focused upon the nature of the contact process itself when associated with closely related language varieties. As we have seen on a number of occasions, the details of these contacts do not necessarily refute some of the theoretical concerns embodied in particular in Thomason's schematisation of language contact; it is necessary, however, to bring a number of other factors into play to explain the changes involved in our specific types of change. Central to this is the idea that a degree of system simplification rather than actual borrowing of material from one language variety to another is a necessary outcome to near-language variety contact. This inevitably feeds into ideas concerned with the nature of koineisation.

In a sense, all forms of koineisation are fundamentally the same, primarily perhaps because they involve the same types of relationships at ground level and also at the macro level involved with how communities work. There are obvious differences between the relatively small-scale negotiations necessary in the creation of a new dialect in Milton Keynes, where most of the inputs were quite similar, and the leaps necessary to bridge the gap between discrete languages, such as Old English and Viking Norse or Scandinavian North Germanic and Low German. The processes involved remain essentially of a single type, however. Indeed, most koine-like events fall between these two stools. The development of New Zealand English can act as an epitome of this type of koine formation; a number of the sources from which the variety derives were quite divergent from the metropolitan varieties stemming from the south-east of England. Remnants of this diverse pattern of origin can be found in contemporary New Zealand English. But the input from the metropolitan sources eventually won out in the main, possibly, through the predominance of settlers from that region (I say this without entering fully into the debate about whether such an outcome was inevitable). No matter the level of divergence between varieties, however, the same basic principles are visible: (unconscious) compromise, accommodation and some degree of simplification (or, perhaps more appropriately, 'rationalisation') visible in the final product. Inevitably, of course, the level to which the last feature is brought to bear depends strongly upon the level of linguistic distance between the input varieties. The apparent blind spot some scholars have in seeing the different types of near-relative contact not as representing a continuum across the supposed dialect–language divide but rather as entirely different states and ecologies to be analysed using essentially different theoretical paradigms is an unfortunate one. I hope that this book may go some way towards redressing the balance.

Naturally, this book and the research which lies behind it cannot be the final word on these matters. In all honesty, it may just be the beginning. I would welcome any attempt to continue the study of near-relative contact, in particular beyond English (taken in its broadest sense). It would be particularly interesting to compare widely distributed and hegemonic languages with the contact between lesser-used close relatives in particular. What a koine is (and what it is not) seems to me to be at the heart of the debate.

Notes

Chapter 1

1. As has already been stated, some linguists believe strongly in a fundamental difference between internal and external forces in relation to change in language. From this point of view, the internal workings of a linguistic system should be the primary focus for an historical linguist (rather than a linguistic historian) with external forces being relegated to the background in which change takes place (this is, of course, a caricature, but it does bear some resemblance to reality). The problem with a viewpoint of this type, however, is that it ignores the fact that apparently external features – social background, contact and a number of other contributory factors – *do* affect the linguistic system and how that system develops over time, as we will see on numerous occasions in this book. For these and other reasons, *internal* and *external* are generally avoided in this book, to be replaced by *linguistic* and *sociolinguistic*. This terminological distinction is also not without its issues, albeit of a different and rather lesser type, but it serves the purpose of describing a difference between linguistic change, which happens directly and exclusively within a language, and social change, which might (indeed, often does) affect language use. Thus gender is a sociolinguistic factor which might affect the expression of social deference in some languages; changes in the social and sociolinguistic situation in relation to this variable could bring about change in, for instance, the pronoun system, with new gender-free pronouns being promoted or women beginning to use forms of language previously confined to men and there being a reaction in use by men.

Chapter 2

1. Given Schneider's interest in post-colonial English, it is unsurprising that it is towards that language's varieties that his focus lies; practically the same points could be made, with a degree of modification, about the languages of other European imperialisms.
2. Similar points have also been argued in relation to the origins and spread of Latin American Spanish. It has long been a commonplace to claim that the features which most Latin American varieties share with the dialects of Andalusia in Spain, such as the lenition of /x/ to /h/, in words such as *Juan* or *junta*, are the product of a common origin. A degree of logic underlies this connection: the ports of Andalusia were early on closely connected to the new American colonies. Lipski (1994: 38) observes that

   > The fact that Andalusians represented 30%, 20% or even 10% of a given colonial population does not preclude a significant Andalusian influence in the developing colonial dialect. This is especially true if the remainder of the population was divided among diverse regional dialects, each of which represented a smaller proportion than the Andalusian component. Conversely, a numerical majority of Andalusians in a particular zone does not automatically entail an Andalusian cast to the regional dialect. The sociolinguistic prominence of regional varieties in the colonial setting is an important detail, often overlooked in tracing the development of Latin American Spanish.

   This is not, as we will see, in line with the views of Peter Trudgill. It points in a similar direction, however: origins (indeed, a founder population) do matter in the development of a new variety, even if later in the same book Lipski is careful not to rule out influences from the language of later migrants (1994: 52). But the origins of the founder population may not be the sole reason for the eventual nature of a variety. This could be said to be particularly apposite when discussing the relationship of some varieties of Spanish spoken across the Caribbean to the dialects spoken in the Canary Isles.
3. It would be tempting to see the *swamping* event as being connected to the mass immigration of English speakers associated with the gold and diamond 'rushes' of the late nineteenth century. This ignores, however, evidence from 'naïve' testimony for archetypically South African features being present earlier in that century (see, for instance, Lass 1987). As we will recognise below, what

may seem to be *swamping* can also be analysed as the workings of a founder effect.
4. Macafee (1983 and 1994) provides an excellent survey of the language and sociolinguistic history of Glasgow; this section is indebted to both sources.

Chapter 3

1. American English, whose development we have touched upon on a number of occasions in this book, fulfils many of the criteria for deriving from a deep time-depth dialect formation. But the very size of the territory (meaning that we probably have to think in terms of multiple new dialect formation events), the relative paucity of records and the fact that North America has remained a major and ongoing focus for mass immigration makes the variety (or varieties) less than straightforward in providing a clear narrative for the process. It is also worth noting that American English largely derives from mainstream varieties relatively close to Standard English; this is not the case with many of the varieties discussed in this chapter.
2. The following is based primarily on the discussion in Millar (2007: Chapter 5).
3. The early history of English in Scotland beyond the south-east is a complicated issue which does not really concern us here. It is discussed to some extent in Macafee (2002).
4. Findings in the following are based primarily on material from Hickey (2007: Chapter 2). Elements of the interpretation are mine, however.
5. Hickey notes that 'if the language of the *Kildare Poems* is a genuine representation of medieval Irish English, then it would seem that an amalgam of the different varieties which were spoken by English settlers had arisen by the thirteenth century' (Hickey 2007: 49). In other words, a koine of sorts had come into being in Ireland, sharing elements with many of the input varieties, but not representing all of the features of any one input variety.
6. This analysis ignores the influence which bilingualism in Irish and English and language shift from the former to the latter has had upon the English varieties of Ireland, a central theme of Hickey (2007). This influence is, of course, considerable. It would render Irish English a more discrete derivative of the English of southern England than is the case with many other such 'colonial' developments from around the world; they are not the concern of the present discussion, however.

7. The following is based upon the linguistic findings in Adams (1948, 1958, 1986), Barry (1981a), Corrigan (2010), Gregg (1972 and 1985), Henry (1995), Kallen (1999), Kingsmore (1995), McCafferty (2001) and Montgomery (1992 and 2006). Again, interpretation of findings may reflect my own analysis, however.
8. This is the scholarly consensus. In a rather naïve article, Hill (1993) argues that many of the settlers from these parts of Scotland were Gaelic speakers. This seems unlikely: there would still have been Gaelic speakers in Galloway at that time; some Gaelic knowledge was also possible in the less populous regions of Ayrshire, such as the south-west of the county, or close to the Highland *Gaidhealtachd* (such as Largs, in the north-west of the county). The chance that the language was spoken by a majority of the settlers from these regions in Ulster seems counter-intuitive, given what happened linguistically relatively rapidly after the settlement.

Chapter 4

1. It is not unusual for languages to be known in different forms by different people in the same basic environment. Kiswahili, for instance, can be found in parts of east and central Africa as a mother tongue for some, a somewhat simplified lingua franca for others and a pidgin for still others (for a relatively recent discussion of these matters, see Drolc 1999). The Papua New Guinea context is somewhat different, however, since the language in question is itself a recent product of contact, via pidginisation and creolisation.
2. It should be noted, however, that, in particular with the creole state, complication of the grammatical structure of the language is possible. See Romaine (1995) and (1999) and Sankoff (1990) for some discussion of this phenomenon.
3. These changes are not always a matter of simplification. Tok Pisin marks transitivity on the verb overtly, something which only a very few mainstream dialects of English do.
4. It should be noted that the contact between lexifier language and creole enshrined in the post-creole continuum could itself actually be analysed as a form of near-relative contact.
5. At first glance, this example (and that of Bonin Island English) share much with apparently more mainstream varieties like Tristan da Cunha English. This is undoubtedly the case. The inputs into creoloids as they develop must, however, have been more divergent from each other, both linguistically and sociolinguistically, than is the case with 'normal' new dialects.

6. English, which is, of course, a *close* relative of Afrikaans, was not really in a position to influence the development of Cape Dutch in any profound way until around the beginning of the nineteenth century, by which time Afrikaans had, we think, developed to a form essentially in line with what we have now.
7. It should be noted that some scholars would analyse the loss of, for instance, present tense number and person verb morphology marking as being a result of *koineisation* among Dutch speakers, without any input necessarily from non-native speakers. It is not impossible, however, that one force acted in tandem with the other. Indeed it could be argued that the need for such radical simplification would have been particularly noteworthy in the multilingual context of the new colony. Roberge (2004) is dismissive of Dutch-based koineisation being the primary explanation for the present state of any form of Afrikaans, however.
8. For a discussion some of these features, see Wührer 1954, Dahlberg 1954/6, Haugen 1976: 5.2, Ureland 1986 and 1989, and Jahr 1995.
9. The following is based primarily on Lipski (1994: 342–5), as well as Lipski (2006 and 2013), with cross-reference to, among others, Carvalho (2006).
10. Indeed, in another essay in the same collection (Berg 2014), Berg describes the 'borrowing' of the dative case – in particular when used prepositionally – from Standard High German to Low German, where syncretism of accusative and dative cases had happened considerably earlier. The level at which a written and spoken standard can influence less prestigious and largely spoken forms must be borne in mind on this occasion. For many of the varieties discussed in this book, literate appreciations of levels of written appropriateness in a language are largely irrelevant.
11. It was not, of course, only South Asians who were moved around in this way. Natives of Papua New Guinea and the inhabitants of a range of Melanesian islands served seasonally in the sugar plantations of Queensland in Australia in the late nineteenth and early twentieth centuries. Interestingly, it was these contacts which helped to bring into being Tok Pisin and a range of other English-based pidgins and creoles in the region (see Crowley 1990 for a discussion).
12. It should be noted that today's Fiji Hindi speakers are often literate in Standard Hindi. This happened *after* the creation of the local variety, however. It is with this earlier period that this discussion is concerned, although we have to remember that the mesolectal and, in particular, acrolectal varieties now spoken in the islands are very

likely to demonstrate contact between the local varieties and the standard form.
13. Fiji Hindi is by no means unique. As Mesthrie (2004a: 268–9; see also Mesthrie 1991) demonstrates in his discussion of what he terms South African Bhojpuri, considerable amounts of morphological koineisation (including, on occasion, simplification) can be teased out from the language of the descendants of north Indian immigrants into South Africa in the nineteenth and early twentieth centuries.

Chapter 5

1. Treharne (2012) and the essays in Swan and Treharne (2000) make a strong case for the continuation of interest in English writing after the Conquest. Most of this interest appears focused on the copying and interpretation of a relatively small number of Anglo-Saxon authors, however, writing about a limited number of topics. The scholars' analyses appear unfortunately blind to ways in which the language of the pieces copied was becoming confusing, perhaps even opaque, to the copyist and his assumed audience, a point to which we will return shortly.
2. A discussion of these features can be found in Hotta (2009); Lass (1994) presents an overview of the Old English system.
3. This narrative does not take into account the foreign plural morphological patterns incorporated with greater or lesser success into English since the Early Modern period.
4. The earlier translations of this text given here (with the exception of the Gothic) derive from the classic Latin Vulgate translation of the original Greek, while most modern versions will have the Greek version as their ultimate authority (although the Renaissance translations – themselves heavily influenced by Latin models – associated with the Protestant Reformation have such a force of tradition behind them that they continue to influence the wording of more modern versions of this prayer). But while there are regular issues of exact translation between the two 'originals', these are not vital to the argument here.
5. The North West Germanic runic corpus is earlier, but does not contain a version of this prayer. Given the materials normally used in the writing of the runes, moreover, genuine issues concerned with that writing system's idiomatic nature and over whether it necessarily represented anything like the oral norms contemporary to its writing make its full acceptance as equivalent to later texts written in alphabetic script problematical.

6. What is striking is that English, in other ways less synthetic than many other of the Germanic languages, has retained a descendant of part of the Old English noun phrase paradigm, masculine and neuter *-es*, in *-'s*. This form, while it cannot exactly be described as a genitive case marker (the Old English genitive case marker could be used in functions well beyond the expression of possession), certainly represents a morphological means for expressing possession. The analytic equivalent – *the house of Robert* rather than *Robert's house* – would often sound forced and stilted to a native speaker's ears. Its Germanic sisters, on the other hand, are more analytic, since they have replaced or are replacing the Germanic genitive case. Thus in Norwegian it is possible to say *Roberts hus*. Much more common, however, are the structures *huset til Robert* or *Robert sitt hus*. In some varieties, such as German, these changes remain non-standard; they are rarely seen in writing. In others, such as Luxembourgish, they have replaced the inherited genitive structures entirely. For a preliminary discussion, see O'Neil (1982).

There are, however, some signs that structures similar to those found in the other Germanic languages were also developing in varieties of English. In early Modern English, for example, constructions such as *Sejanus his fall*, 'Sejanus' fall', were common (see Mustanoja 1960: 70–93). There is even some evidence from Northern English dialects of constructions along the lines of *Robert house* for 'Robert's house' (Klemola 1997).

7. This argument could be taken beyond (close) genetic relationship, in fact. As Heine and Kuteva (2005 and 2006) have pointed out on a number of occasions, something like a *Sprachbund* development has been at work for some time upon the languages of Western and West Central Europe in relation to an analytic approach to the expression of functional relationship, no matter the nature of the ancestral language (on this occasion, Latin and proto-Germanic – as with so many other developments, both the Celtic languages and Basque follow their own particular paths). Thus French and Dutch share much which was not present (at least as the dominant pattern) in their separate ancestors. These developments could also be analysed as a form of *drift*, although its implications take us far beyond what has been discussed here.

8. For a range of references to the sociolinguistics of this period, see Millar (2010b: 117–32).

9. A further complicating factor is the recent scholarly debate over what language(s) were spoken in Roman Britannia. In a range of publications, Schrijver (2002, 2007, 2009 and 2014) has argued

that, at least in the south-eastern and heavily Romanised parts of the province, Latin may have been the most widespread language (rather than its being confined largely to the urban areas and the middle and upper classes of rural areas, as scholarly orthodoxy has held). He also claims that the primary Celtic language spoken in the lowlands of Britain was Q-Celtic rather than P-Celtic (a relative of the modern Gaelic languages rather than their Brittonic cousins), a conclusion he derives primarily from the phonology of Old English. This particular argument need not concern us tremendously here, since the structural features which some scholars claim to have either been brought across from the indigenous languages into English or been caused by the interference between the two languages would have been likely to be similar, no matter the specific Celtic catalyst.

10. For a discussion of the historical and cultural background behind the Conquest, see Chibnall (2000). Ingham (2012) presents a description of Anglo-Norman which also provides an analysis of the language's decline and demise in England.

11. Some evidence for this can be found in the fact that a number of French words, including the ancestor of *pride*, are recorded, as the *Oxford English Dictionary* demonstrates, in English *before* the Norman Conquest. The fact that Edward the Confessor had spent his formative years in Normandy, had a Norman mother and may even have been, at least by choice, a Francophone, along with his favouring of French speakers over English after he acceded to the English throne, probably explains developments of this type, although these personal relationships and connections may well be indicative of the ways in which the (cultural) winds were blowing at the time across Europe, so that French influence would likely have affected English even without the Conquest, although perhaps not to the same extent.

12. The English royal family is unusual in relation to these changes, largely because of its possession of large parts of France over the period and its close personal ties to Gascony in particular. Although, from the thirteenth century on, knowledge and use of English were the prevalent social pattern, use of French as an everyday language among at least the close relatives of the king was probably normal until at least the end of the fourteenth century.

13. Of course, linguistically, this set of norms, if it had continued to be used as it was before the Conquest, would have had to be revised significantly to deal with the rapid changes through which English passed during the next two centuries. This was not the reason

why the use of West Saxon was discontinued, however. See Millar (2005) for further discussion.

14. In the last few years, a rather more extreme analysis of this contact has been proposed by Jan Terje Faarlund and Joseph Embley Emonds: that Modern English is actually a North Germanic, rather than West Germanic, language. Until recently, the only fully available discussion of this research was a minor paper by Emonds (2011); a more substantial discussion is now available in Emonds and Faarlund (2014). There are a number of reasons why theirs is an unlikely claim, however. Essentially, a case is made that not only is English somewhat influenced by the North Germanic languages, but also that it is itself a North Germanic variety whose origin lies in contacts in the late Anglo-Saxon East Midlands of England. Since this variety is the ancestor of Standard English (so goes the argument: there are serious misunderstandings of earlier scholarly analysis underlying this), it was able to overcome the 'native' forms of English. As evidence for this, the North Germanic languages are compared to Old English and Modern English. The argument is made that English now shares more features (such as SvVO rather than SvOV element order: compare English *I have **done that*** and German *Ich habe **das getan***) with the Scandinavian languages morphosyntactically than with its supposed near West Germanic relatives.

There are, of course, considerable structural similarities between the North Germanic languages and English; many of them may be due to contact. But I believe that Faarlund and Emonds have fallen into a particularly invidious trap for comparative linguistic analyses. Similarities do not always (or even regularly) prove relationship. Some of the connections proposed happened much later than the supposed contact and appeared first in the 'wrong' part of England. Other archetypal North Germanic features which probably *are* as old as the contact proposed do not appear in English – the enclitic definite particle or the 'medio-passive' being particularly good examples (strangely, Emonds and Faarlund actually claim that both of these features were lost in the general loss of inflections; this does not explain why the native English *the* definer and the periphrastic passive survived, however, if English is North Germanic). None of this even begins to approach the question of why a fully North Germanic variety should have an overwhelmingly West Germanic phonology, moreover. Their thesis, as it now stands, is untenable.

Critiques of the proposal can be found in Thomason (2012), Stenbrenden (2013) and Pereitsvaig (2014). Criticism can be made of Faarlund and Emonds's methods, use of materials and knowledge of advanced secondary literature. Perhaps the worst example of this is one which is all too common for outsiders to the field: the assumption that nothing was written in English after the Norman Conquest and that, during this occluded period, the 'new' language was able to develop in secret, coming into writing after the hidden period. This idea is not based on fact. Moreover, throughout the Middle English period, we actually see Northern innovations spreading in quite normal ways from one dialect to another. There is no abrupt break. It is a great pity that such a controversialist stance was taken; many (but by no means all) of the features they describe could well represent transfers from Norse to English.

15. It is worth noting that, while Trudgill has now abandoned these views in relation to English, he has retained them in connection to the Scandinavian dialects. This is likely to be the case primarily because no other obvious contact which could have effected the changes was present in late medieval Scandinavia. The Finnic dialects were just too marginal and Latin too literary at the time to act as catalyst to explain the changes through which these languages passed.

16. It should be noted, however, that in the same volume Mufwene (2013) appears to support the Celtic hypothesis (although he does not attempt to define the extent to which that contact can be felt). Surprisingly, he does not mention Norse influence at all.

17. A thoughtful analysis of these issues can be found in Schrijver (2014); it should be noted that he treats the changes discussed in relation to the English grammatical case system as if Celtic influence (through the lack of case in Brittonic) were so obvious as to need no further discussion, however. How this can be brought in line with his belief that a variety much more like – case-intensive – Old Gaelic was spoken in lowland Britain (and therefore most likely to influence English) is not made entirely clear.

18. Nowhere is it discussed whether there would have been any use of the Low 'Celtic' variety of English by members of the privileged overclass, although our knowledge of the nature of diglossia in other situations would support such a supposition. How such a range of continua of uses can be squared with the absolute split between two highly different varieties postulated is a potentially worrying issue.

19. In a popular work of 2009 (McWhorter 2009), McWhorter actually achieves the neat trick of attributing the changes in English's morphosyntactic nature to *both* Celtic and Norse influence. Although

the book contains a number of overstatements and inconsistencies, it none the less provides the basis for an argument not dissimilar to that being made here.
20. Even if the Basque community in the Middle Ages and Early Modern period was rather less insular than might be expected, with contact with fishing communities who used a different language being particularly common (and, indeed, a pidginised form of Basque being used around the north Atlantic in the early modern period: Holm 1989: 628–30). To his credit, Trudgill (2011) also considers situations where largely inward-looking communities with highly limited contact beyond the immediate vicinity appear to have actually simplified their language, as in the case of, for instance, the consonant inventory of Hawaiian in comparison with proto-Polynesian. He explains this as being symptomatic of the 'restricted code' which tight-knit communities develop through a strong sense of common knowledge. This sounds convincing; it is difficult to see how it can be brought into line with his book's central premise, however.
21. This set of observations does not even attempt to address the issue of why *Apartheid*, whether in shock quotation marks or not, is a highly inappropriate term for describing this type of social relationship. The pre-1994 rulers of South Africa invested a good part of that country's considerable national product in the maintenance of a police state at all levels of society to observe and control its population through the employment of new technology. Even then, the Apartheid system proved unworkable in a variety of ways. The polities which made up Anglo-Saxon England were so utterly unlike this – if we can even talk about *states* during the period, rather than centres of power – that it would be difficult to do this difference justice.
22. Trudgill does, to be fair, attempt to construct a typology of complexity and simplicity, particularly important when considering inflectional morphology. A nagging suspicion remains, however, that what language a scholar uses affects his or her views on what is naturally representative of simplicity or its (apparent) opposite.
23. Nichols (2009: 120) also provides arguments, on this occasion from a typological viewpoint, for the reasons why simplification cannot always be readily distinguished from complexification.
24. McWhorter (2009) expands this coexistence of the diglossic model into the later Middle English period, which seems even less likely than what is being discussed here.
25. Trudgill (2011: 55) suggests that '[i]n the Highland zone of Britain,

it was the pidginised form of Old English which came to dominate, and it is therefore not surprising that it is in the north of England that evidence of linguistic simplification first appeared in the historical record.' This is, of course, a considerable leap of faith, but it demonstrates that he is aware of the issue. See below for further discussion.

26. It should be noted that Myers-Scotton (2002: 19) points out that 'In these [code-switching] phenomena, we cannot argue that all the abstract structure is derived from the grammar of one of the participating languages; rather it is clear that more than one language is the source of structure.' With languages which are distant relatives, if at all, keeping the two grammars separate in situations other than these might be straightforward; with closely related varieties, however, this would be much more difficult, as scholars such as Schmid (2011) demonstrate.

27. In many ways, these processes resemble the linguistic performance of *semi-speakers* in work such as, most famously, Dorian (1981), concerned with the process of language shift. The differences between the two phenomena are, of course, that while semi-speakers present evidence for the cessation of a language's active presence as a language, here there is more a sense of rebirth of earlier varieties in a new form. The nature of the contact may explain these dissimilarities, although it is dubious whether it would always be possible for the distinction to be perceived during its earliest period.

28. If Myers-Scotton (2002: Chapter 5) is correct in seeing grammatical case as something likely to be maintained – and even transferred from language to language – in contact contexts, we need to suggest why this *did not* happen in English. Arguments for this have already been made; at their heart lies near-relative contact.

References

Adams, G. B. (1948), 'An introduction to the study of Ulster dialects', *Proceedings of the Royal Irish Academy*, 52, 1–26.
— (1958), 'The emergence of Ulster as a distinct dialect area', *Ulster Folklife*, 4, 61–73.
— (1986) 'Northern England as a source of Ulster dialects', *Ulster Folklife*, 13, 69–75.
Adams, James (1799), *The Pronunciation of the English Language Vindicated from Imputed Anomaly & Caprice: In Two Parts. An analytical process respecting elementary combinations and variations, chiefly confined to monosyllables. An investigation of prosody in all the multiplied forms of words, syllables, Greek and Latin analogy, &c. With an appendix, on the dialects of human speech in all countries, and an analytical discussion and vindication of the dialect of Scotland*, Edinburgh: Printed for the author by J. Moir.
Adamson, Sylvia, Vivian Law, Nigel Vincent and Susan Wright (eds) (1990), *Papers from the 5th International Conference on English Historical Linguistics*, Amsterdam: Benjamins.
Aitken, A. J. (1992), 'Scottish English'. In McArthur (1992), 903–5.
Allen, Cynthia L. (1997), 'Middle English case loss and the "creolization" hypothesis', *English Language and Linguistics*, 1, 63–89.
Amer, Faten H., Bilal A. Adaileh and Belal A. Rakhieh (2011), 'Arabic diglossia: a phonological study', *Argumentum*, 7, 19–36.
Ammon, U. (ed.) (1989), *Status and Function of Language and Language Varieties*, Berlin: Walter de Gruyter.
Amoamo, Maria (2013), 'Empire and erasure: a case study of Pitcairn Island', *Island Studies Journal*, 8, 233–54.
Anderson, John (ed.) (1982), *Language Form and Linguistic Variation: Papers Dedicated to Angus McIntosh*, Amsterdam: John Benjamins: 285–306.
Bailey, Charles J. and Karl Maroldt (1977), 'The French lineage of English'. In Meisel (1977), 21–53.
Bailey, Guy (1997), 'When did Southern American English begin?' In Schneider (1997), 255–76.
Ballantyne, John H. and Brian Smith (eds) (1994), *Shetland Documents 1580–1611*, Lerwick: Shetland Islands Council and the Shetland Times.

— (1999), *Shetland Documents 1195–1579*, Lerwick: Shetland Islands Council and the Shetland Times.
Barber, Charles (1993), *The English Language: A Historical Introduction*, Cambridge: Cambridge University Press.
Bardon, Jonathan (1992), *A History of Ulster*, Belfast: Blackstaff Press.
Barnes, Michael P. (1998), *The Norn Language of Shetland and Orkney*, Lerwick: Shetland Times.
Baron, Naomi S. (1971), 'A reanalysis of English grammatical gender', *Lingua*, 27, 113–40.
Barrie, W. D. (1994), *The European Peopling of Australasia: A Demographic History*, Canberra: Australian National University.
Barry, Michael V. (1981a), 'The southern boundaries of northern Hiberno-English speech'. In Barry (1981b), 52–95.
— (ed.) (1981b), *Aspects of English Dialects in Ireland*, Belfast: Institute of Irish Studies.
Beekes, Robert S. P. (2011), *Comparative Indo-European Linguistics: An Introduction*, 2nd edn, Amsterdam: John Benjamins.
Berg, Kristian (2014), 'Stability and convergence in case marking: Low and High German'. In Braunmüller, Höder and Kühl (2014), 63–75.
Blake, N. F. and Charles Jones (eds) (1984), *English Historical Linguistics: Studies in Development*, Sheffield: Centre for English Cultural Tradition and Language, University of Sheffield.
Braunmüller, Kurt, Steffen Höder and Karoline Kühl (eds) (2014), *Stability and Divergence in Language Contact: Factors and Mechanisms*, Amsterdam: John Benjamins.
Breivik, Leiv Egil and Ernst Håkon Jahr (eds) (1989), *Language Change: Contributions to the Study of its Causes*, Berlin and New York: Mouton de Gruyter.
Brenzinger, Matthias (ed.) (1992), *Language Death: Factual and Theoretical Explorations with Special Reference to East Africa*, Berlin and New York: Mouton de Gruyter.
Brink, Stefan and Neil Price (eds) (2008), *The Viking World*, London: Taylor & Francis.
Britton, Derek (1991), 'On Middle English *she/sho*: a Scots solution to an English problem', *NOWELE*, 17, 3–51.
Buchanan, James (1757), *Linguæ Britannicæ Vera Pronunciatio, or, A New English Dictionary: Containing I. An explanation of all English words used by the best writers; the various senses of each word being distinctly pointed out by figures 1, 2, 3, &c. II. The language from which each word is derived. III. The part of speech to which it belongs. IV. A supplement of upwards of 4000 proper names. … To the whole is prefixed a dissertation on the species of sounds, &c. with practical observations on the various powers and formations of the letters. A work intirely new, and designed for the use of schools, and of foreigners, as well as natives who would speak, read, and write English with propriety and accuracy*, London: Printed for A. Millar.
Bybee, Joan and Suzanne Fleischmann (eds) (1995), *Modality in Grammar and Discourse*, Amsterdam: John Benjamins.

Calder, Daniel G. and T. Craig Christy (eds) (1988), *Germania: Comparative Studies in the Old Germanic Languages and Literatures*, Wolfeboro, NH: D. S. Brewer.
Canny, Nicholas (2001), *Making Ireland British, 1580–1650*, Oxford: Oxford University Press.
Carvalho, Ana Maria (2006), 'Nominal number marking in a variety of Spanish in contact with Portuguese'. In Face and Klee (2006), 154–66.
Chambers, J. K., P. Trudgill and N. Schilling-Estes (eds) (2001), *The Handbook of Language Variation and Change*, Oxford: Blackwell.
Cheshire, Jenny, Paul Kerswill, Susan Fox and Eivind Torgersen (2011), 'Contact, the feature pool and the speech community: the emergence of Multicultural London English', *Journal of Sociolinguistics*, 15, 151–96.
Chibnall, Marjorie (2000), *The Normans*, Oxford: Oxford University Press.
Clarke, Sandra (2004), 'The legacy of British and Irish English in Newfoundland'. In Hickey (2004), 242–61.
Cole, Marcelle (2014), *Old Northumbrian Morphosyntax and the (Northern) Subject Rule*, Amsterdam: John Benjamins.
Coleman, Julie (1995), 'The chronology of French and Latin loan words in English', *Transactions of the Philological Society*, 93, 95–124.
Combrink, Johan (1978), 'Afrikaans: its origins and development'. In Dutton and Prinsloo (1978), 69–95.
Corbett, Greville (1991), *Gender*, Cambridge: Cambridge University Press.
Corrigan, Karen P. (2010), *Irish English. Volume 1 – Northern Ireland*, Edinburgh: Edinburgh University Press.
Crowley, Terry (1990), *Beach-la-Mar to Bislama: The Emergence of a National Language in Vanuatu*, Oxford: Clarendon Press.
Crowley, Tony (2005), *Wars of Words: The Politics of Language in Ireland 1537–2004*, Oxford: Oxford University Press.
Dahl, Östen (2004), *The Growth and Maintenance of Linguistic Complexity*, Amsterdam: John Benjamins.
Dahlberg, T. (1954/6), 'Das Niederdeutsche im skandinavischen Raum', *Wirkendes Wort*, 6, 193–9.
Damousi, Joy (2010), *Colonial Voices: A Cultural History of English in Australia 1840–1940*, Cambridge: Cambridge University Press.
Dawkins, Richard M. (1916), *Modern Greek in Asia Minor*, Cambridge: Cambridge University Press.
Denison, David (1993), *English Historical Syntax*, London: Longman.
Deumert, Ana (2001), 'Language variation and standardization at the Cape (1880–1922): a contribution to Afrikaans sociohistorical linguistics', *Journal of Germanic Linguistics*, 13, 301–52.
Devitt, A. J. (1989), *Standardizing Written English: Diffusion in the Case of Scotland*, Cambridge: Cambridge University Press.
Dixon, R. W. (1997), *The Rise and Fall of Languages*, Cambridge: Cambridge University Press.

Dominigue, Nicole Z. (1977), 'Middle English: another creole?', *Journal of Creole Studies*, 1, 89–100.
Donaldson, Gordon (1983), 'The Scots settlement in Shetland'. In Withrington (1983), 8–19.
Dorian, Nancy C. (1981), *Language Death: The Life Cycle of a Scottish Gaelic Dialect*, Philadelphia: University of Pennsylvania Press.
Dossena, Marina (2005), *Scotticisms in Grammar and Vocabulary*, Edinburgh: John Donald.
Dossena, Marina and Charles Jones (eds) (2003), *Insights into Late Modern English*, Bern: Peter Lang.
Dossena, Marina and Roger Lass (eds) (2009), *Studies in English and European Historical Dialectology*, Bern: Peter Lang.
Drolc, Uschi (1999), *Swahili among the Maasai: On the Interlanguage Swahili by Maa Speakers*, Munich: Lincom Europa.
Dutton, L. and K. Prinsloo (eds) (1978), *Language and Communication Studies in South Africa*, Oxford: Oxford University Press.
Ejerhed, E. and I. Henrysson (eds) (1980), *Tvåspråkighet. Föredrag från Tredje Nordiska Tvåspråkighetsymposiet 4–5 Juni 1980, Umeå Universitet* ['Bilingualism. Proceedings from the third Nordic Bilingualism Symposium 4–5 June 1980, Umeå University'], Umeå: Umeå University.
Eliason, N. E. and P. A. M. Clemoes (eds) (1966), *Ælfric's First Series of Catholic Homilies (British Museum Royal 7 C.XII, fols. 4–218)*, Early English Manuscripts in Facsimile 13, Copenhagen: Rosenkilde & Bagger.
Emonds, Joseph Embley (2011), 'English as a North Germanic language: from the Norman Conquest to the present'. In Trušník, Nemčoková and Bell (2011), 13–26.
Emonds, Joseph Embley and Jan Terje Faarlund (2014), *English: The Language of the Vikings*, Olomouc: Palacký University, <http://anglistika.upol.cz/vikings2014> (last accessed 2 March 2015).
Escure, Genevieve and Armin Schwegler (eds) (2004), *Creoles, Contact and Language Change: Linguistics and Social Implications*, Amsterdam: John Benjamins.
Face, Timothy I. and Carol I. Klee (eds) (2006), *Selected Proceedings of the 8th Hispanic Linguistics Symposium*, Somerville, MA: Cascadilla Proceedings Project.
Fenton, Alexander (1968–9), 'The Tabu language of the fishermen of Orkney and Shetland', *Ethnologia Europaea*, 2–3, 118–22.
— (1978), *The Northern Isles: Orkney and Shetland*, Edinburgh: Donald.
Filppula, Markku (1999), *The Grammar of Irish English: Language in Hibernian Style*, London: Routledge.
Filppula, Markku, Juhani Klemola and Heli Pitkänen (eds) (2002), *The Celtic Roots of English*, Joensuu: University of Joensuu Faculty of Humanities.
Fischer, Olga (2013), 'The role of contact in English syntactic change in the Old and Middle English periods'. In Schreier and Hundt (2013), 18–40.

Fishman, Joshua (1967), 'Bilingualism with and without diglossia; diglossia with and without bilingualism', *Journal of Social Issues*, 32, 29–38.
Fisiak, Jacek (ed.) (2002), *Studies in English Historical Linguistics and Philology: A Festschrift for Akio Oizumi*, Bern: Lang.
Flinn, Derek (comp.) (1989), *Travellers in a Bygone Shetland: An Anthology*, Edinburgh: Scottish Academic Press.
Foley, William A. (1988), 'Language birth: the process of pidginisation and creolization'. In Niemeyer (1988), 162–83.
Galenson, David W. (1984), 'The rise and fall of indentured servitude in the Americas: an economic analysis', *Journal of Economic History*, 1, 1–26.
George, Stig Kennet John (2013), 'The potential for the invocation of an Anglo-Brittonic contact origin for the regularisation and reduction that afflicted the case category marking system of Old English', Unpublished MLitt dissertation, University of Aberdeen.
Gillespie, Raymond (1985), *Colonial Ulster: The Settlement of East Ulster, 1600–1641*, Cork: Cork University Press.
Godden, Malcolm, Douglas Gray and Terry Hoad (eds) (1994), *From Anglo-Saxon to Early Middle English: Studies Presented to E. G. Stanley*, Oxford: Clarendon Press.
Goebl, Hans (ed.) (1995), *Kontaktlinguistik: Ein internationales Handbuch*, 2nd vol., Berlin: de Gruyter.
Gordon, Elizabeth, Lyle Campbell, Jennifer Hay, Margaret Maclagan, Andrea Sudbury and Peter Trudgill (2004), *New Zealand English: Its Origins and Evolution*, Cambridge: Cambridge University Press.
Görlach, Manfred (1986), 'Middle English – a creole?' In Kastovsky and Szwedek (1986), 327–44.
Graham, John J. (1993), *The Shetland Dictionary*, 3rd edn, Lerwick: Shetland Times.
Grant, William and David D. Murison (1929–76), *The Scottish National Dictionary*, Edinburgh: Scottish National Dictionary Association.
Gregg, Robert J. (1972), 'The Scotch–Irish dialect boundaries in Ulster'. In Wakelin (1972), 109–39.
— (1985), *The Scotch–Irish Dialect Boundaries of the Province of Ulster*, Port Credit, Ontario: Canadian Federation of the Humanities.
Häcker, Martina (2006), 'An Englishman's vindication of Scots: James Adams (1737–1802) – Jesuit, teacher and linguist', *Historiographia Linguistica*, 33, 85–107.
Harreld, Donald J. (ed.) (2015), *A Companion to the Hanseatic League*, Leiden: Brill.
Haugen, Einar (1950), 'The analysis of linguistic borrowing', *Language*, 26, 210–31.
— (1976), *The Scandinavian Languages: An Introduction*, London: Faber & Faber.
Heddle, Donna (2010), 'The Norse element in the Orkney dialect'. In Millar (2010d), 48–57.
Hegedűs, Irén and Alexandra Fodor (eds) (2012), *English Historical Linguistics*

2010: Selected Papers from the Sixteenth International Conference on English Historical Linguistics (ICEHL 16), Pécs, 23–27 August 2010, Amsterdam: John Benjamins.

Heine, Bernd and Tania Kuteva (2005), *Language Contact and Grammatical Change*, Cambridge: Cambridge.

— (2006), *The Changing Languages of Europe*, Oxford: Oxford University Press.

Henry, Alison, 1995, *Belfast English and Standard English: Dialect Variation and Parameter Setting*, Oxford: Oxford University Press.

Hickey, Raymond (2007), *Irish English: History and Present-day Forms*, Cambridge: Cambridge University Press.

Hickey, Raymond (ed.) (2004), *Legacies of Colonial English: Studies in Transported Dialects*, Cambridge: Cambridge University Press.

— (2013), *The Handbook of Language Contact*, Chichester: Wiley Blackwell.

Higham, Nicholas (ed.) (2007), *Britons in Anglo-Saxon England*, Woodbridge: Boydell & Brewer.

Hill, J. Michael (1993), 'The origins of the Scottish plantation in Ulster to 1625: a reinterpretation', *Journal of British Studies*, 32, 24–43.

Hines, John (1991), 'Scandinavian English: a creole in context'. In Ureland and Broderick (1991), 403–27.

Höder, Steffen (2014), 'Convergence vs divergence from a diasystematic perspective'. In Braunmüller, Höder and Kühl (2014), 39–60.

Holm, John (1989), *Pidgins and Creoles. Volume II: Reference Survey*, Cambridge: Cambridge University Press.

— (2004), *Languages in Contact: The Partial Restructuring of Vernaculars*, Cambridge: Cambridge University Press.

Holmes, Janet (1997), 'Maori and Pakeha English: some New Zealand social dialect data', *Language in Society*, 26, 65–101.

Holmes, Janet and Paul Kerswill (2008), 'Contact is not enough: a response to Trudgill', *Language in Society*, 37, 273–7.

Horrocks, Geoffrey C. (1997), *Greek: A History of the Language and its Speakers*, London: Longmans.

Hotta, Ryuichi (2009), *The Development of the Nominal Plural Forms in Early Middle English*, Tokyo: Hituzi Syobo Publishing.

Ingham, Richard (2012), *The Transmission of Anglo-Norman: Language History and Language Acquisition*, Amsterdam: John Benjamins.

Jackson, Kenneth (1953), *Language and History in Early Britain: A Chronological Survey of the Brittonic Languages First to Twelfth Century AD*, Edinburgh: Edinburgh University Press.

Jahr, Ernst Håkon (ed.) (1995), *Nordisk og Nedertysk. Språkkontakt og Språkutvikling i Norden i Seinmellomalderen*, Oslo: Novus Forlag.

Jakobsen, Jakob (1932), *An Etymological Dictionary of the Norn Language in Shetland*, 2 vols, London: David Nutt; Copenhagen: Vilhelm Prior.

Jernsletten, Nils (1997), 'Norwegian – Saami'. In Goebl (1995), 957–61.

Jernudd, B. H. and M. J. Shapiro (eds) (1989), *The Politics of Language Purism*, Berlin: Mouton de Gruyter.

Johnston, Paul (1997), 'Regional variation'. In Jones (1997b), 433–513.

Jones, Charles (1967a), 'The functional motivation of linguistic change', *English Studies*, 48, 97–111.
— (1967b), 'The grammatical category of gender in early Middle English', *English Studies*, 48, 289–305.
— (1983), 'Determiners and case-marking in Middle English: a localist approach', *Lingua*, 59, 331–43.
— (1987), *Grammatical Gender in English 950–1250*, London: Croom Helm.
— (1993), 'Scottish Standard English in the late eighteenth century', *Transactions of the Philological Society*, 91, 95–131.
— (1995), *A Language Suppressed: The Pronunciation of the Scots Language in the 18th Century*, Edinburgh: John Donald.
— (1997a), 'Phonology'. In Jones (1997b), 267–310.
Jones, Charles (ed.) (1997b), *The Edinburgh History of the Scots Language*, Edinburgh: Edinburgh University Press.
Kallen, Jeffrey (1999), 'Irish English and the Ulster Scots controversy', *Ulster Folklife*, 45, 70–85.
Kastovsky, Dieter and Aleksander Szwedek (eds) (1986), *Linguistics across Historical and Geographical Boundaries: In Honour of Jacek Fisiak on the Occasion of His Fiftieth Birthday*, Vol. 1: *Linguistic Theory and Historical Linguistics*, Berlin: Mouton de Gruyter.
Kay, Christian, Carole Hough and Irené Wotherspoon (eds) (2004), *New Perspectives on English Historical Linguistics*, Vol. II: *Lexis and Transmission*, Amsterdam: John Benjamin.
Keller, Rudi (1994), *On Language Change: The Invisible Hand in Language Change*, London: Routledge.
Kerr, George H. (2000), *Okinawa: The History of an Island People*, 2nd edn, Tokyo: Tuttle Publishing.
Kerswill, Paul (2001), 'Koineization and accommodation'. In Chambers, Trudgill and Schilling-Estes (2001), 669–702.
Kerswill, Paul and Ann Williams (2000), 'Creating a New Town koiné: children and language change in Milton Keynes', *Language in Society*, 29, 65–115.
Keynes, Simon (1997), 'The Vikings in England, c. 790–1016'. In Sawyer (1997b), 48–82.
Kingsmore, Rona (1995), *Ulster Scots Speech: A Sociolinguistic Study*, Tuscaloosa: University of Alabama Press.
Klemola, Juhani (1997), 'Some evidence for loss of genitive inflection in English', *English Language and Linguistics*, 1, 349–53.
Kloss, Heinz (1967), 'Abstand languages' and 'Ausbau languages', *Anthropological Linguistics*, 9, 29–41.
— (1978), *Die Entwicklung neuer germanischer Kultursprachen seit 1800*, 2nd edn, Düsseldorf: Schwann.
Knooihuizen, Remco (2006), 'The Norn to Scots language shift: another look at the evidence', *Northern Studies*, 39, 5–16.
— (2007), 'Fishing for words: the taboo language of Shetland fishermen and

REFERENCES

the dating of Norn language death', *Transactions of the Philological Society*, 106, 100–13.

— (2009), 'Shetland Scots as a new dialect: phonetic and phonological considerations', *English Language and Linguistics*, 13, 483–501.

Kuryłowicz, Jerzy (1949), 'La nature des procès dits "analogiques"', *Acta Linguistica*, 5, 15–37.

Kusters, Wouter (2003), *Linguistic Complexity: The Influence of Social Change on Verbal Inflection*, Utrecht: LOT.

Laing, Margaret (ed.), (1989), *Middle English Dialectology: Essays on Some Principles and Problems by Angus McIntosh, M L Samuels and Margaret Laing*, Aberdeen: Aberdeen University Press.

Lamb, Gregor (1988), *Orkney Wordbook: A Dictionary of the Dialect of Orkney*, Birsay: Byrgisey.

Lanehart, Sonja L. (ed.) (2001), *Sociocultural and Historical Contexts of African American English*, Amsterdam: John Benjamins.

Lanham, L. W. and C. A. Macdonald (1979), *The Standard in South African English and its Social History*, Varieties of English around the World 1, Heidelberg: Julius Groos Verlag.

Lass, Roger (1987), 'How reliable is Goldswain? On the credibility of an early South African English source', *African Studies*, 46, 155–62.

— (1990), 'Where do extraterritorial Englishes come from? Dialect input and recodification in transported Englishes'. In Adamson et al. (1990), 245–8.

— (1994), *Old English: A Historical Linguistic Companion*, Cambridge: Cambridge University Press.

— (1995), 'South African English'. In Mesthrie (1995), 89–106.

— (2004), 'South African English'. In Hickey (2004), 363–86.

Laycock, D. (1989), 'The status of Pitcairn–Norfolk: creole, dialect, or cant?' In Ammon (1989), 608–29.

Lindqvist, Christer (2015), *Norn im keltischen Kontext*, NOWELE Supplement Series 26, Amsterdam: John Benjamins.

Lipski, John M. (1994), *Latin American Spanish*, London: Longman.

— (2006), 'Too close for comfort? The genesis of "portuñol/portunhol"'. In Face and Klee (2006), 1–22.

— (2013), 'Spanish and Portuguese in contact'. In Hickey (2013), 550–81.

Ljosland, Ragnhild (2012/13), '"I'll cross dat brig whin I come til him": grammatical gender in the Orkney and Shetland dialects of Scots', *Scottish Language*, 31/2, 29–58.

Long, Daniel (2007), *English on the Bonin (Ogasawara) Islands*, Publications of the American Dialect Society 91, Durham, NC: Duke University Press.

Low, George (1879), *A Tour through the Islands of Orkney and Schetland, containing hints relative to their ancient modern and natural history collected in 1774*, Kirkwall: William Peace & Son.

Lutz, Angelika (2012), 'Norse influence on English in the light of general contact linguistics'. In Hegedűs and Fodor (2012), 15–42.

Macafee, Caroline I. (1983), *Glasgow*, Amsterdam: John Benjamins.

— (1992 and following), *Characteristics of Non-standard Grammar in Scotland*, <https://docs.google.com/file/d/0BzVAfXkKg9UlV2dwNERCbUwtSGc/edit?pli=1> (last accessed 19 November 2015).

— (1994), *Traditional Dialect in the Modern World: A Glasgow Case Study*, Frankfurt am Main: Lang.

— (2002), 'A history of Scots to 1700'. In *A Dictionary of the Older Scottish Tongue*, 12, xxi–clvi, Oxford: Oxford University Press.

McArthur, T. (ed.) (1992), *The Oxford Companion to the English Language*, Oxford: Oxford University Press.

McCafferty, Kevin (2001), *Ethnicity and Language Change: English in (London) Derry, Northern Ireland*, Amsterdam and Philadelphia: Benjamins.

McClure, J. Derrick (1985), 'The Pinkerton syndrome', *Chapman*, 41: 2–8.

McIntosh, Angus and Michael Samuels (1968), 'Prolegomena to a study of medieval Anglo-Irish', *Medium Ævum*, 37, 1–11.

McMahon, April and Robert McMahon (2006), *Language Classification by Numbers*, Oxford: Oxford University Press.

McWhorter, John H. (2007), *Language Interrupted: Signs of Non-Native Acquisition in Standard Language Grammars*, Oxford: Oxford University Press.

— (2009), *Our Magnificent Bastard Tongue: The Untold History of English*, New York: Gotham Books.

Malkiel, Yakov (1981), 'Drift, slope and slant: background of, and variations upon, a Sapirian theme', *Language*, 57, 535–70.

Marwick, Hugh (1929 [1995]), *The Orkney Norn*, reprinted edition, Livingston: Brinnoven.

Mather, J. Y. and H. H. Speitel (eds) (1985), *The Linguistic Atlas of Scotland: Scots Section Volume 1*, London: Croom Helm.

Meisel, J. (ed.) (1977), *Langues en contact – pidgins – creoles*, Tübingen: Narr.

Melchers, Gunnel (1980), 'The Norn element in Shetland dialect today – a case of "never accepted" language death'. In Ejerhed and Henrysson (1980), 254–61.

Menteith, Robert (1711 [1845]), *Description of the Islands of Orkney and Zetland*, Edinburgh: Thomas G. Stevenson.

Mesthrie, Rajend (1991), *Language in Indenture: A Sociolinguistic History of Bhojpuri–Hindi in South Africa*, London and New York: Routledge.

— (2004a), 'Language change, survival, decline: Indian languages in South Africa'. In Mesthrie (2004b), 161–78.

Mesthrie, Rajend (ed.) (1995), *Language and Social History: Studies in South African Sociolinguistics*, Claremont, South Africa: David Philip Publishers.

— (2004b), *Language in South Africa*, Cambridge: Cambridge University Press.

Meurman-Solin, Anneli (1993), *Variation and Change in Early Scottish Prose: Studies Based on the Helsinki Corpus of Older Scots*, Helsinki: Suomalainen Tiedeakatemia.

Millar, Robert McColl (1996), 'Gaelic-influenced Scots in pre-revolutionary Maryland'. In Ureland and Clarkson (1996), 387–410.

— (1997), 'Some patterns in the non-historical demonstrative realisation of the *Peterborough Chronicle* annals 1070–1121', *Notes and Queries*, 242, 161–4.

— (1999), 'Some geographical and cultural patterns in the lexical/semantic structure of Scots', *Northern Scotland*, 18, 55–65.

— (2000), *System Collapse, System Rebirth: The Demonstrative Systems of English 900–1350 and the Birth of the Definite Article*, Bern and Oxford: Lang.

— (2002), 'After Jones: some thoughts on the final collapse of the grammatical gender system in English'. In Fisiak (2002), 293–306.

— (2003), '"Blind attachment to inveterate custom": language use, language attitude and the rhetoric of improvement in the first *Statistical Account*'. In Dossena and Jones (2003), 311–30.

— (2004), 'Kailyard, conservatism and Scots in the *Statistical Account of Scotland*'. In Kay, Hough and Wotherspoon (2004), 163–76.

— (2005), *Language, Nation and Power*, Basingstoke: Palgrave Macmillan.

— (2007), *Northern and Insular Scots*, Edinburgh: Edinburgh University Press.

— (2009), 'The origins of the northern Scots dialects'. In Dossena and Lass (2009), 191–208.

— (2010a), 'Linguistic marginality in Scotland: Scots and the Celtic languages'. In Millar (2010b), 5–17.

— (2010b), *Authority and Identity: A Sociolinguistic History of Europe before the Modern Age*, Basingstoke: Palgrave Macmillan.

— (2012), *English Historical Sociolinguistics*, Edinburgh: Edinburgh University Press.

— (2015), *Trask's Historical Linguistics*, 3rd edn, London: Routledge.

Millar, Robert McColl (ed.) (2010c), *Marginal Dialects: Scotland, Ireland and Beyond*, Aberdeen: Forum for Research on the Languages of Scotland and Ireland.

— (2010d), *Northern Lights, Northern Words: Selected Papers from the FRLSU Conference, Kirkwall 2009*, Aberdeen: Forum for Research on the Languages of Scotland and Ireland.

Millar, Robert McColl and Alex Nicholls (1997), 'Ælfric's *De Initio Creaturae* and London, BL Cotton Vespasian A.xxii: omission, addition, retention, and innovation'. In Szarmach and Rosenthal (1997), 431–63.

Milroy, Lesley (1980), *Language and Social Networks*, Oxford: Blackwell.

Mitchell, Bruce (1994), 'The Englishness of Old English'. In Godden, Gray and Hoad (1994), 163–81.

Momma, Haruko and Michael Matto (eds) (2008), *A Companion to the History of the English Language*, Chichester: Wiley–Blackwell.

Montgomery, Michael (1992), 'The anglicization of Scots in early seventeenth century Ulster', *Studies in Scottish Literature*, 26, 50–64.

— (2006), 'The morphology and syntax of Ulster Scots', *English World-wide*, 27, 295–329.

Montgomery, Michael (ed.) (1994), *The Crucible of Carolina: Essays in the Development of Gullah Language and Culture*, Athens: University of Georgia Press.

Mougeon, Raymond and Édouard Beniak (eds) (1994), *Les Origines du français québécois*, Sainte-Foy: Les Presses de l'Université Laval.
Moulton, William G. (1988), 'Mutual intelligibility among speakers of early Germanic dialects'. In Calder and Christy (1988), 9–28.
Mufwene, Salikoko S. (1997), 'Jargons, pidgins, creoles, and koines: what are they?' In Spears and Winford (1997), 35–70.
— (2001), *The Ecology of Language Evolution*, Cambridge: Cambridge University Press.
— (2008), 'Colonization, population and the emergence of new language varieties: a response to Peter Trudgill', *Language in Society*, 37, 254–8.
— (2013), 'Driving forces in English contact linguistics'. In Schreier and Hundt (2013), 204–21.
Mufwene, Salikoko S. (ed.) (2014), *Iberian Imperialism and Language Evolution in Latin America*, Chicago: University of Chicago Press.
Mühlhäusler, Peter (2007), 'The Pitkern-Norf'k language and education', *English World-Wide*, 28, 215–47.
Mühlhäusler, Peter, Thomas E. Dutton and Suzanne Romaine (2003), *Tok Pisin Texts: From the Beginning to the Present*, Amsterdam: John Benjamins.
Mustanoja, Tauno F. (1960), *A Middle English Syntax. Part 1: Parts of Speech*, Helsinki: Société Néophilologique.
Myers-Scotton, Carol (2002), *Contact Linguistics: Bilingual Encounters and Grammatical Outcomes*, Oxford: Oxford University Press.
Nelde, Peter H., P. Sture Ureland and Iain Clarkson (eds) (1986), *Language Contact in Europe. Proceedings of the Working Groups 12 and 13 at the XIIIth International Congress of Linguists, August 29–September 4, 1982, Tokyo*, Tübingen: Niemeyer.
Neustupný, J. V. (1989), 'Language purism as a type of language correction'. In Jernudd and Shapiro (1989), 211–23.
New Statistical Account (1841), *The New Statistical Account of Scotland, by the ministers of the respective parishes*, Edinburgh: no publisher given.
Nichols, Johanna (2009), 'Linguistic complexity: a comprehensive definition and survey'. In Sampson, Gil and Trudgill (2009), 110–25.
Niemeyer, Frederick J. (ed.) (1988), *Linguistics: The Cambridge Survey. Vol. 4: The Socio-Cultural Context*, Cambridge: Cambridge University Press.
O'Brian O'Keeffe, Katherine (1987), 'Orality and the developing text of Caedmon's hymn', *Speculum*, 62, 1–20.
O'Neil, Wayne (1982), 'Simplifying the grammar of English'. In Anderson (1982), 285–306.
Pavlenko, Alexander (1997), 'The origin of the *be* perfect with transitives in the Shetland dialect', *Scottish Language*, 16, 88–96.
Pereitsvaig, Asya (2014), 'Is it English or Engelsk?', <Languagesoftheworld. info> (last accessed 2 March 2015).
Peters, Pam (2008), 'Australian and New Zealand English'. In Momma and Matto (2008), 389–99.

Pintzuk, Susan (1999), *Phrase Structures in Competition: Variation and Change in Old English Word Order*, London: Garland.
Poplack, Shana and Sali A. Tagliamonte (2001), *African American English in the Diaspora*, Oxford: Blackwell.
Poussa, Patricia (1982), 'The evolution of early Standard English: the creolization hypothesis', *Studia Anglica Posnaniensia*, 14, 69–85.
Przedlacka, Joanna (2002), *Estuary English? A Sociophonetic Study of Teenage Speech in the Home Counties*, Bern: Peter Lang.
Przeździak, Agnieszka (2015), 'Germanisms in Polish as result of long-term language contact', Unpublished MA dissertation, University of Aberdeen.
Rendboe, Laurits (1984), 'How "worn out" or "corrupted" was Shetland Norn in its final stage?', *NOWELE*, 3, 53–88.
— (1987), *Det gamle shetlandske Sprog: George Low's Ordliste fra 1774*, NOWELE Supplement Volume 3, Odense: Odense Iniversitetsforlag.
Ringe, Don and Ann Taylor (2014), *The Development of Old English*, Oxford: Oxford University Press.
Rippley, La Vern J. (1984), *The German–Americans*, Lanham, MD: University Press of America.
Roberge, Paul T. (2004), 'Afrikaans: considering origins'. In Mesthrie (2004b), 79–103.
Roberts, Jane (1970), 'Traces of unhistorical gender congruence in a late Old English manuscript', *English Studies*, 51, 30–7.
Robinson, Philip (1984), *The Plantation of Ulster: British Settlements in an Irish Landscape 1600–1670*, Belfast: Ulster Historical Foundation.
Romaine, Suzanne (1995), 'The grammaticalization of irrealis in Tok Pisin'. In Bybee and Fleischmann (1995), 1–39.
— (1999), 'The grammaticalization of the proximative in Tok Pisin', *Language*, 75, 322–46.
Rot, Sandor (1984), 'Inherent variability and linguistic interference of Anglo-Old Scandinavian and Anglo-Norman French language contacts in the formation of grammatical innovations in late Old English and Middle English'. In Blake and Jones (1984), 67–86.
Sampson, Geoffrey, David Gil and Peter Trudgill (eds) (2009), *Language Complexity as an Evolving Variable*, Oxford: Oxford University Press.
Samuels, M. L. (1989a), 'Some applications of Middle English dialectology'. In Laing (1989), 64–80.
— (1989b), 'The Great Scandinavian Belt'. In Laing (1989), 106–15.
Sandve, B. H. (1976), 'Om talemålet i industristatene Odda og Tyssedal. Generasjonsskilnad of tilnærmind mellom de to målføra' ['On the spoken language in the industrial towns Odda and Tyssedal. Generational differences and convergence between the two dialects'], Unpublished Cand. philol. dissertation, University of Bergen.
Sankoff, Gillian (1990), 'The grammaticalization of tense and aspect in Tok Pisin and Sranan', *Language Variation and Change*, 2, 295–312.
Sapir, Edward (1921), *Language*, New York: Harcourt, Brace & World.

Sasse, Hans-Jürgen (1992), 'Theory of language death'. In Brenzinger (1992), 7–30.
Sawyer, Peter (1997a), 'The age of the Vikings and before'. In Sawyer (1997b), 1–18.
Sawyer, Peter (ed.) (1997b), *The Oxford Illustrated History of the Vikings*, Oxford: Oxford University Press.
Schmid, Monica S. (2011), *Language Attrition*, Cambridge: Cambridge University Press.
Schneider, Edgar W. (2007), *Postcolonial English: Varieties Around the World*, Cambridge: Cambridge University Press.
— (2008), 'Accommodation versus identity? A response to Trudgill', *Language in Society*, 37, 262–6.
Schneider, Edgar (ed.) (1997), *Englishes Around the World: Studies in Honour of Manfred Görlach*, Amsterdam: John Benjamins.
Schreier, Daniel (2003), *Isolation and Language Change: Contemporary and Sociohistorical Evidence from Tristan da Cunha English*, Basingstoke: Palgrave Macmillan.
— (2008), *St Helenian English: Origins, Evolution and Variation*, Amsterdam: John Benjamins.
Schreier, Daniel and Marianne Hundt (eds) (2013), *English as a Contact Language*, Cambridge: Cambridge University Press.
Schrijver, Peter (2002), 'The rise and fall of British Latin: evidence from English and Brittonic'. In Filppula, Klemola and Pitkänen (2002), 87–110.
— (2007), 'What Britons spoke around 400 AD'. In Higham (2007), 165–71.
— (2009), 'Celtic influence on Old English and phonetic evidence', *English Language and Linguistics*, 13, 193–211.
— (2014), *Language Contact and the Origins of the Germanic Languages*, London: Routledge.
Scott, Sir Walter (1822 [2001]), *The Pirate*, edited by Mark Weinstein and Alison Lumsden, Edinburgh: Edinburgh University Press.
Shuken, Cynthia (1984), 'Highland and Island English'. In Trudgill (1984), 152–66.
Siegel, Jeff (1985), 'Koinés and koinéisation', *Language in Society*, 14, 357–78.
— (1987), *Language Contact in a Plantation Environment*, Cambridge: Cambridge University Press.
— (2001), 'Koine formation and creole genesis'. In Smith (2001), 175–97.
Simpson, W. Douglas (ed.) (1954), *The Viking Congress Lerwick, July 1950*, Edinburgh: Oliver & Boyd.
Sinclair, Sir John (ed.) (1978), *The Statistical Account of Scotland*, Wakefield: EP Publishing.
Sinclair, Keith (ed.) (1996), *The Oxford Illustrated History of New Zealand*, 2nd edn, Auckland: Oxford University Press.
Smith, Norval (ed.) (2001), *Creolization and Contact*, Amsterdam: John Benjamins.
Sobin, Nicholas (1997), 'Default rules, and grammatical viruses', *Linguistic Inquiry*, 28, 318–43.

Spears, Arthur K. and Donald Winford (eds) (1997), *The Structure and Status of Pidgins and Creoles*, Amsterdam: John Benjamins.
Stenbrenden, Gjertrud F. (2013), 'Er engelsk et skandinavisk språk? – Neppe' ['Is English a Scandinavian language? – Nope'], *Apollon*, <http://www.apollon.uio.no/artikler/2013/1_engelsk-skandinavisk-motsvar.html> (last accessed 2 March 2015).
Sudbury, Andrea (2001), 'Falkland Islands English: a southern hemisphere variety?', *English World-wide*, 22, 55–80.
— (2004), 'English on the Falklands'. In Hickey (2004), 402–17.
Swan, Mary and Elaine M. Treharne (eds) (2000), *Rewriting Old English in the Twelfth Century*, Cambridge: Cambridge University Press.
Szarmach, Paul E. and Joel T. Rosenthal (eds) (1997), *The Preservation and Transmission of Anglo-Saxon Culture*, Studies in Medieval Culture XL, Kalamazoo: Western Michigan University.
Thomason, Sarah Grey (1997a), 'Mednyj Aleut'. In Thomason (1997b), 449–68.
— (2001), *Language Contact: An Introduction*, Edinburgh: Edinburgh University Press.
— (2012), 'English or Engelsk?', *Language Log*, <http://languagelog.ldc.upenn.edu/nll/?p=4351> (last accessed 2 March 2015).
Thomason, Sarah Grey (ed.) (1997b), *Contact Languages: A Wider Perspective*, Amsterdam: John Benjamins.
Thomason, Sarah Grey and Terrence Kaufman (1988), *Language Contact, Creolization, and Genetic Linguistics*, Berkeley: University of California Press.
Thomson, William P. L. (2001), *The New History of Orkney*, Edinburgh: Mercat Press.
Þórhallur Eyþórsson (2002), 'Hvaða mál talaði Egill Skalla-Grímsson á Englandi?' ['What language did Egill Skalla-Grimsson speak in England?'], *Málfríður*, 18, 21–6.
Thorsen, Per (1954), 'The third Norn dialect – that of Caithness'. In Simpson (1954), 230–54.
Townend, Matthew (2002), *Language and History in Viking Age England: Linguistic Relations between Speakers of Old Norse and Old English*, Turnhout: Brepols Publishers.
Trask, R. L. (1997), *The History of Basque*, London: Routledge.
Treharne, Elaine (2012), *Living Through Conquest*, Oxford: Oxford University Press.
Trudgill, Peter (1983), *On Dialect: Social and Geographical Perspectives*, Oxford: Blackwell.
— (1986), *Dialects in Contact*, Oxford: Blackwell.
— (1988), 'Norwich revisited: recent changes in an English urban dialect', *English World-wide*, 9, 33–49.
— (2002), *Sociolinguistic Variation and Change*, Edinburgh: Edinburgh University Press.
— (2004), *New-Dialect Formation: The Inevitability of Colonial Englishes*, Edinburgh: Edinburgh University Press.

— (2008), 'Colonial dialect contact is the history of European languages: on the irrelevance of identity to new-dialect formation', *Language in Society*, 37, 241–50.

— (2010), *Investigations in Sociohistorical Linguistics: Stories of Colonisation and Contact*, Cambridge: Cambridge University Press.

— (2011), *Sociolinguistic Typology: Social Determinants of Linguistic Complexity*, Oxford: Oxford University Press.

Trudgill, Peter (ed.) (1984), *Language in the British Isles*, Cambridge: Cambridge University Press.

Trušník, Roman, Katarína Nemčoková and Gregory Jason Bell (eds) (2011), *Theories and Practice: Proceedings of the Second International Conference on English and American Studies, September 7–8, 2010, Tomas Bata University in Zlín, Czech Republic*, Zlín: Universita Tomáše Bati ve Zlíně.

Tudor, John R. (1883), *The Orkneys and Shetland; Their Past and Present State*, London: Edward Stanford.

Tulloch, Graham (1980), *The Language of Walter Scott: A Study of his Scottish and Period Language*, London: André Deutsch.

Tuten, Donald N. (2008), 'Identity formation and accommodation: sequential and simultaneous relations', *Language in Society*, 37, 259–62.

Ureland, P. Sture (1986), 'Some contact-linguistic structures in Scandinavian languages'. In Nelde, Ureland and Clarkson (1986), 31–79.

— (1989), 'Some contact structures in Scandinavian, Dutch and Raeto-Romansch: inner-linguistic and/or contact causes of language change'. In Breivik and Jahr (1989), 239–76.

Ureland, P. Sture and George Broderick (eds) (1991), *Language Contact in the British Isles: Proceedings of the Eighth International Symposium on Language Contact in Europe, Douglas, Isle of Man, 1988*, Tübingen: Max Niemeyer Verlag.

Ureland, P. Sture and Iain Clarkson (eds) (1996), *Language Contact across the North Atlantic*, Tübingen: Niemeyer.

van Gelderen, Elly (2011), *The Linguistic Cycle: Language Change and the Language Family*, Oxford: Oxford University Press.

van Kemenade, Ans (1987), *Syntactic Case and Morphological Case in the History of English*, Dordrecht: Foris.

van Leyden, Klaske (2004), *Prosodic Characteristics of Orkney and Shetland Dialects: An Experimental Approach*, Utrecht: Lot.

Vennemann, Theo, gen. Nierfeld (2003), *Europa Vasconica, Europa Semitica*, Berlin: Mouton de Gruyter.

Wakelin, Martyn F. (ed.) (1972 [1977]), *Patterns in the Folk Speech of the British Isles*, London: Athlone Press.

Wallace, James (1700), *An Account of the Islands of Orkney*, London: Jakob Tonson.

Watts, Richard J. (2011), *Language Myths and the History of English*, Oxford: Oxford University Press.

Weinreich, Uriel (1953), *Languages in Contact, Findings and Problems*, New York: Linguistic Circle of New York.

Withrington, Donald J. (ed.) (1983), *Shetland and the Outside World 1469–1969*, Oxford: Oxford University Press.

Woolf, Alex (2007), 'Apartheid and economics in Anglo-Saxon England'. In Higham (2007), 115–29.

Wührer, K. (1954), 'Der Einfluss des Deutschen auf die skandinavischen Sprachen', *Muttersprache: Zeitschrift zur Pflege und Erforschung der deutschen Sprache*, 1, 448–59.

Yerastov, Yuri (2010), '*Done, finished*, and *started* as reflexes of the Scottish transitive *be* perfect in North America: their synchrony, diachrony, and current marginalisation'. In Millar (2010c), 19–52.

Index

Abstand, 10–13, 173
accommodation, 20–1, 29–30
acrolect, 109
adstratum, 3, 4–5
Ælfric, 125
Afrikaans, 25, 39, 110, 113–14, 115, 139, 140, 142, 153–4, 182n
Afro-Asiatic languages, 4
Albanian, 14
Aleut, Copper Island, 2, 9
Algonquin languages, 19
Anatolian languages, 14
Ancrene Riwle, 151
Anglo-Saxon Chronicle, 124, 125, 144
Aquitanian, 3
Arabic, 1, 4, 164–5
Armenian, 8, 14
Ausbau, 10–13
Austronesian languages, 114
Avadhi, 122

Baltic–Slavonic languages, 14
Bantu languages, 114
basilect, 109
Basque, 3–4, 10–11, 160, 184n, 188n
Bede, 144, 162
Beowulf, 147
Bernicia, 157, 165, 176
Bhojpuri, 122
  South African, 183n
borrowing, 9
Braje, 122
Breton, 145
British language, 145–6

Brut, Laʒamon's, 151
Bulgarian, 1, 130

Cædmon, 162
Celtic languages, 4, 14, 147
  influence on Old English, 144–6, 158–70, 174–6, 184n, 187–8n
  P-Celtic, 185n
  Q-Celtic, 185n, 187n
Chinese, 1, 12, 155
'Cockney' see English, London
Cocoliche, 13, 118
code-switching, 1
complexification, 160–1, 163–4, 174–5
conservative radicalism, 157
convergence, 13, 31–2, 116–19
Cornish, 145
Cree, 2
creolisation, 35, 41–2, 107–9, 110, 111, 112–13, 128, 152, 153, 174, 181n, 182n
  abrupt, 154
creoloid, 109–16, 153–6
Cushitic languages, 8
Czech, 11–12

Danish, 12, 87, 140, 148
De Initio Creaturae, 125–6
determinism, 28–34, 42, 47, 55, 172–3
Dhivehi, 121
divergence, 13
Dorian, Nancy, 189
Dravidian languages, 8, 114, 121
drift, 131–43, 155, 156, 157, 158, 169–70, 174, 184n

INDEX

Dutch, 11, 18, 60, 71, 86, 87, 92, 110, 113–14, 117, 140, 142–3, 150, 154, 182n, 184n
  Indonesia, 16
  'Lord's Prayer', 138–9

Emonds, Joseph Embley, 157–8, 186–7n
English, 140
  African American Vernacular, 35–7, 71
  American, 6, 20, 21, 22, 23, 111, 173, 180n
  Australian, 16, 22, 23, 24–5, 33, 40, 42, 112
  Bonin Islands, 110–11, 181
  British, 11
  Canadian, 44
  Caribbean, 16, 111
  Celtic influence on, 158–70
  creoloid, 113
  early contact with Norse, 146–7
  East Anglian, 26, 30, 148, 148, 155
  East Midlands, 158, 186n
  'Estuary', 49
  Falkland Islands, 20, 33–4, 42–4, 69–70, 112
  Highland, 7, 43, 45, 93
  Irish, 14, 30, 44, 45, 47–8, 56, 57, 80, 97–105, 180n
  Jamaican patois, 108
  London, 23, 24, 25, 30, 39, 48, 127–8
  'Lord's Prayer': contemporary, 131–2; modern, 137
  Lumbee, 75
  Māori, 21
  middle, 78–9, 81, 99, 100, 122, 124–70, 183n, 187n
  Midlands of England, 104
  Milton Keynes, 48, 173
  Newfoundland, 44–5
  New Zealand, 16, 25–8, 29, 30–4, 38, 39, 40, 42, 70, 112, 168–9, 172–3, 175, 176
  Norfolk Island, 111–13, 153
  Norse influence, 146–8, 152–3
  'Norsified', 154–6
  North American, 16, 23–4, 44
  North Midlands of England, 102, 155
  Northern England, 30, 47, 127, 170
  Northumbrian, Old, 135
  Old, 5, 12, 122, 119, 124–70, 183n
    'Lord's Prayer', 134–5
  Pitcairn Island, 111–13, 153
  'Received Pronunciation', 24, 42
  St Helenian, 41–2
  Scotticisms, 50–1, 53
  Scottish, 30, 180n; *see also* English, Scottish Standard; Scots
  Scottish Standard, 1, 26, 45, 49–54, 83
  South African, 25, 40, 42, 179–80n
  South-East England, 17, 26, 30, 38, 39, 41, 43–4, 48, 155
  Southern Hemisphere, 25, 33–4, 42
  Southern United States, 96
  South-West England, 43, 44, 99
  Standard, 23, 51–2, 60, 77, 82, 87, 93, 113, 128
  'transition period', 124–70, 174–6
  Tristan da Cunha, 40–2, 43, 70, 173, 181n
  Ulster, 101–4
  West Saxon, 134, 135, 148, 151, 186n
  white southern vernacular, 36–7

Faarlund, Jan Terje, 157–8, 186–7n
Faeroese, 116, 132
Finnic, 187n
Finnish, 163
Flemish, 99; see also Dutch
focusing, 31
founder principle, 34–8, 42, 43, 44, 47, 48, 54, 96–7, 104, 170, 171–2, 172–3
Frankish *see* German
French, 2, 5, 16, 35, 81, 114, 126, 143, 160, 164–5, 184n
  Canadian, 70
  Caribbean, 16, 35, 108
  contact with English, 149–52
  Indochina, 16
  Norman, 4, 7, 78–9, 97, 115, 149–52, 185–6n, 187n

French (cont.)
  Polynesia, 16
  Sub-Saharan, 16
  Fronterizo, 117–18

Gaelic, Scottish, 5, 7, 26, 43, 45, 76, 87, 90, 93, 94, 98, 99, 101, 181n
German, 1, 2, 11, 35, 129, 131, 133, 139, 140, 142–3, 150, 155, 186n
  Frankish, 5
  'Lord's Prayer': Modern, 137–8; Old High, 133–4
  Low, 92, 114–17, 118–19, 153–4, 155, 173, 176, 182n
  Old High, 136
  Standard, 118–19, 182n
Germanic languages, 14, 92, 130, 131–43, 155, 156, 166, 174, 184n
  East, 132–3
  North, 74, 75, 76, 81, 113–6, 119, 136–7, 141, 142–3, 146–8, 150, 153–4, 173, 176, 186–7n
  North-West, 152, 183n
  West, 115, 147, 186–7n
Gothic, 134, 136, 183n
  'Lord's Prayer', 132–3
'Great Scandinavian Belt', 148, 155, 157–8
Greek, 14, 130, 183n
  Asia Minor, 9
  Attic, 119
  Koine, 119–20, 156
  Tsakonian, 119
Gullah, 36

Haitian creole, 35, 108
Hawaiian, 188
Hickey, Raymond, 97–103, 180n
Hildina ballad, 77
Hindi
  Fiji, 116–19, 120–3, 156, 174, 182–3n
  Standard, 182–3n

Icelandic, 116, 140, 142–3
  'Lord's Prayer', 136

identity, 34
Indic languages, 8, 14, 114, 121
Indo-European languages, 8, 9, 13, 14, 121, 126, 131
  proto-, 130
inevitability see determinism
interdialect development, 31, 54, 93–4
interference, 9, 154
'invisible hand', 72
Iranian languages, 14
Irish, 45, 98–9, 100, 104
Italian, 13
Italic languages, 14

Jackson, Kenneth, 146
Jakobsen, Jakob, 77, 79, 85, 92
Japanese, 110–11
Jones, Charles, 127, 156–7, 167

Kerswill, Paul, 48
Khoe languages, 114
Kildare Poems, 180n
Kiswahili, 181n
Kloss, Heinz, 10–3
koineisation, 12, 18–19, 31, 34, 43, 93–4, 98, 100, 116, 119–23, 166, 168, 173–6, 177, 182
koineoid, 156–8

Latin, 3, 4, 10–11, 41, 81, 143, 183n, 184n, 185n
lexifier language, 108–9, 181n
lingua franca, 108
Lithuanian, 121
Long, Daniel, 110–11
Luxembourgish, 184

McClure, J. Derrick, 52
Macedonian, 130
McMahon, April and Robert McMahon, 167–8
McWhorter, John H., 160, 187–8n
Māori, 16, 22
marking, 30
Marwick, Hugh, 74, 83–4, 85
Melchers, Gunnel, 77
mesolect, 109

Michif, 1–2, 9
Montenegrin, 166
Motu, Police, 107
Mufwene, Salikoko S., 34–8, 43, 44, 71, 120, 170, 171–2
Myers-Scotton, Carol, 169, 189n

Neogrammarian hypothesis, 2
Nepali, 121
Norf'k *see* English, Norfolk Island
Norn, 57, 60, 63, 66, 73–85, 92, 93, 93–5, 96–7, 173
   Orkney, 'Lord's Prayer', 81
   Shetland, 'Lord's Prayer', 78
Norse, Old, 83, 89, 97, 119, 132, 136, 143, 152–3, 153–8, 187–8n; see also 'Lord's Prayer', 78, 136
Norse, Viking, 5, 12, 158, 174, 176
   influence on English, 152–3
Norse, West, 60
Norwegian, 1, 12, 31–2, 32–3, 75, 76, 81, 82, 86, 87, 140, 184n
   'Lord's Prayer', 139–40

Okinawan, 116–7

Peterborough Chronicle, 124–5
Pictish, 63
pidginisation, 19, 35, 107–9, 182
Pinkerton syndrome, 52
Pirate, The, 88–90
Pitkern *see* English, Pitcairn Island
Polish, 1, 2, 9, 11
   Silesian, 2
Polynesian, 112–3, 188
Portuguese, 16, 20
   Brazil, 17, 117–8
   Portugal, 17
post-creole continuum, 35, 108–9, 181

reallocation, 31, 94, 95
Romance languages, 3–4, 10–11, 122, 130
   Alpine, 4
Romanian, 1
runes, 183n
Russian, 2, 9, 166

Sámi, 10
Samuels, Michael L., 127–8, 148, 155, 157–8
San languages, 114
Sanskrit, 130
Sapir, Edouard, 141–2, 155
Sasse, Hans-Jürgen, 77–8
Saxon, Old
   paraphrase of 'Lord's Prayer', 135–6
   see also German, Low
Schmid, Monica, 189
Schneider, Edgar W., 17–23, 54, 72, 73, 96, 179n
Schreier, Daniel, 40–2
Scots, 5, 26, 49–54, 70, 86, 93, 98, 101, 126
   Black Isle, 74
   Caithness, 64, 66, 69, 74
   central, 45–8, 64, 67, 68, 70, 71, 72, 74, 75, 76, 86, 96, 97, 102, 104–5
   Glasgow, 45–8, 173, 180n
   insular, 105, 109, 126, 173
   North-East, 67, 68, 71–2, 94, 166
   Northern, 64, 66–7, 72, 88, 96, 99, 126, 141
   Orkney, 55, 57–85, 92–7
   Shetland, 55, 57–97
   South-West, 64, 68, 72, 102, 104
   Southern, 66, 72
   traditional, 127
   Ulster, 14, 56, 57, 64, 68, 72, 97, 101–4, 181n
Scott, Sir Walter, 88–90
Seaboard, Eastern, 23
Semitic languages, 4
   Ethiopian, 8
Siegel, Jeff, 120–3
simplification, 9, 109, 116, 122, 154, 160–1, 163–4, 165, 168, 174–5
Slavonic languages, 130, 166
Slovak, 11–2
Spanish, 1, 3–4, 16, 20, 43, 117
   Andalusian, 179n

Spanish (*cont.*)
  Canary Islands, 179n
  Caribbean, 16, 179n
  Cocoliche, 13, 118
  Fronterizo, 117–8
  Latin American, 16, 179n
  Philippines, 16
Sprachbund, 184n
substratum, 3–4
superstratum, 3, 148
swamping, 38–40, 42, 43, 47–8, 49, 55, 100, 104, 172–3, 179–80n
Swedish, 12, 140

tabula rasa, linguistic, 20, 69–73, 144, 173
Tahitian, 112–3

Thomason, Sarah Grey, 6–9, 107, 108, 176
Tocharian, 14
Tok Pisin, 107–8, 112, 181n
'transition period', 124–70, 174–6
Trudgill, Peter, 28–34, 38, 39, 42, 44, 47, 48, 54, 55, 72, 92, 93–4, 95, 96, 104, 110–1, 113–6, 153, 154, 158–70, 172–3, 188–9n
Turkish, 8, 9

Vulgate, Latin, 183n

Welsh, 97, 145

Yiddish, 6, 7, 9
'Yinglish', 6

EU representative:
Easy Access System Europe
Mustamäe tee 50, 10621 Tallinn, Estonia
Gpsr.requests@easproject.com

www.ingramcontent.com/pod-product-compliance
Lightning Source LLC
Chambersburg PA
CBHW051058230426
43667CB00013B/2345